The Wadsworth College Success Program *and*
Your College Experience: Strategies for Success,
CONCISE FIFTH MEDIA EDITION

By **John N. Gardner** *and* A. Jerome Jewler

We want to be your partners as you help students succeed in college.

For over twenty years, Wadsworth College Success has provided materials and training to help institutions and their students achieve the goals set forth in first-year seminars. Our team of authors, advisors, and facilitators has developed textbooks and training workshops that show instructors and administrators how to bring out the best in their teaching, their institutions, and their students. Because no two institutions, nor even two students, are exactly alike, we have found that there isn't one way that works for everyone. So we strive to assist both instructor and student with flexible, customizable programs that can fit a wide variety of needs using whatever medium (print, video, CD-ROM, Internet, etc.) that best accomplishes this endeavor.

To assist in your teaching and your students' learning, we offer outstanding enhancements to **John Gardner** and **Jerry Jewler's *Your College Experience: Strategies for Success,*** Concise Fifth Media Edition.

Instructor Resources

Custom Publishing Options *to meet your specific needs* (See page 7)

Instructor's Resource Suite: Manual and CD-ROM, *with all the help you may need to prepare your course* (See page 12)

ExamView® Computerized Test Bank *to create tests and track student progress* (See page 12)

CNN® Today: College Success Video Series, *with lecture-launching video clips* (See page 13)

Films for the Humanities College Success Video Series *to further educate students and stimulate class discussion* (See page 13)

Wadsworth Study Skills Videos *to help students take charge of improving their grades* (See page 13)

World of Diversity Videos *to address issues surrounding multiculturalism in the classroom* (See page 13)

Toll-Free Consultation Service *available to all instructors* (See page 13)

Wadsworth College Success Workshop Series *offered regionally on campuses nationwide and online* (See page 11)

Student Resources

Unbound Version of *Your College Experience*—*instructors can adopt this unbound version so students can instantly customize their own binders* (See page 8)

Student CD-ROM *with additional information not found in the text to add a new level of interactivity to the book* (See page 6)

 InfoTrac® College Edition *for instant access to a powerful online library* (See page 9)

WebTutor™ on WebCT and Blackboard *a Web-based teaching and learning application* (See page 9)

College Success Resource Center at http://success.wadsworth.com *with teaching downloads and relevant Web links* (See page 9)

College Success Agenda Planner *for success in time management* (See page 14)

College Success Factors Index Assessment Web Site *to help students identify their strengths and weaknesses in important areas* (See page 10)

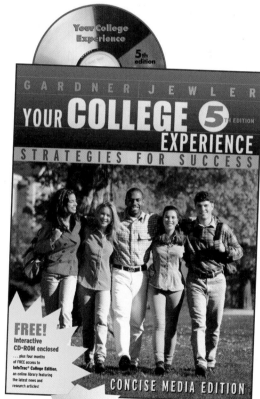

Amazing! In just 10 chapters you get Gardner/Jewler's philosophies about succeeding in college. Plus even more features on the accompanying CD-ROM!

THOMSON
WADSWORTH

Unmatched Expertise

John N. Gardner

A visionary educator, author, and lecturer, Professor Gardner has been instrumental in the founding and development of the National Resource Center for the First-Year Experience and Students in Transition at the University of South Carolina.

John Gardner served as the faculty director of University 101 1974–1999. This internationally acclaimed program has been an inspiration to hundreds of colleges and universities throughout the country. Gardner conducts First-Year Experience seminars and teleconferences throughout the world, assisting college educators in developing effective college orientation and retention programs.

Gardner, having retired after 32 years at the University of South Carolina, has founded the Policy Center on the First Year of College, funded by The Atlantic Philanthropies and The Pew Charitable Trusts. This new center's mission is to work with college and universities around the nation to develop and share a range of first-year assessment procedures and tools. These procedures and tools will be used to investigate student change during the first year as well as the effectiveness of first-year programs, policies, and structures. The Center provides a body of information on best practices in the first college year, and the findings are disseminated to other campuses that desire to increase student learning and success as measured by academic performance and retention.

A. Jerome Jewler

A best-selling author, educator, and lecturer, Professor Jewler has contributed his expertise and guidance to college success education and training since 1972.

A distinguished professor emeritus in the College of Mass Communications and Information Science at the University of South Carolina, Jewler served as the co-director for the school's University 101 program from 1983 to 1989 and was responsible for planning and conducting faculty development workshops focusing on teaching first-year students. More recently, in addition to teaching classes in advertising strategy, copywriting and the social effects of advertising, he has conducted two-day teaching workshops at many colleges, training participants to teach college experience courses.

He received the *Mortar Board* award for teaching excellence in 1993 and 1997 and, in 1996, was named the University of South Carolina's Faculty Advisor of the Year. In addition to *Your College Experience*, Jewler and co-author John N. Gardner have written *College Is Only the Beginning* (1985 and 1989), and *Step by Step to College Success* (1987). Jewler and colleague Bonnie Drewniany are authors of *Creative Strategy in Advertising* (1998). Jewler is a strong believer in active learning and its ability to encourage creative thinking and analysis.

"The text is written in a concise, lively, readable way which will appeal to first-year students. Unlike some texts, this one respects the intelligence of students and doesn't 'talk down' to them."
—DENISE RODE, Northern Illinois University

The Strategies That Lead to Success

Gardner and Jewler's research-proven *Strategies for Success* provide students with guidelines designed to help them realize their goals in college and in life. These *Strategies for Success* appear on the inside cover of the book, and at the beginning of each part of the book to reflect their importance. Now, the *Concise Fifth Media Edition* presents greater emphasis on time management, a newly redesigned CD-ROM, and coverage of both academic and personal skills. A new *Appendix* provides students with the opportunity to think critically and to reflect on the global issues affecting them as they begin college during these uncertain times. Additionally, a focus on values helps students see that success in college is based on more than just study skills.

Long-time users of this reliable text will appreciate the way the book continues to emphasize how planning ahead, becoming an active learner, honing skills, connecting with campus resources, and reflecting on one's own habits are essential to a meaningful college experience—while it introduces the latest research and information available.

An emphasis on writing, reflection, and experiential exercises

▶ Guides students to the best practices in studying and learning, including critical thinking and active learning

▶ Assists students in making personal choices that affect their success in college

▶ Synthesizes contributions of dozens of experts in a unified voice

▶ Concise but comprehensive coverage of both academic and personal skills

Your College Experience, Concise Fifth Media Edition offers a well-developed selection of activities including:

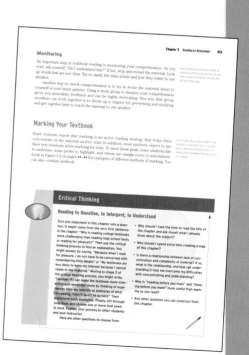

- **Writing** • **Journal Reflection** • **Critical Thinking** • **Resource Building**
- **Internet and Computer Technology** • **Self-Assessment** • **Presentation**
- **Goal Setting** • **Group Exercises** • **Class Discussion** • **Values**
- **Critical Thinking**

Ten succinct, to-the-point, dynamic chapters give students everything they need to master the skills they'll use in college—and in life.

Your College Experience: Strategies for Success,
Concise Fifth Media Edition

PART ONE: TAKE CHARGE OF LEARNING!

1. Time Management and 30 Strategies for College Success
2. Learning Styles: Discovering How You Learn Best

PART TWO: HONE YOUR SKILLS

3. Critical Thinking, Active Learning: Paths to True Understanding
4. Listening, Note Taking, and Participating: Getting the Most Out of Classes
5. Reading to Remember: Strategies for Understanding and Retaining Material
6. Taking Exams and Tests: Be Prepared, Confident, and Calm

PART THREE: KNOW YOURSELF

7. Developing Values: Choosing Unique Pathways
8. Careers and Courses: Making Sensible Choices
9. Creating Diverse Relationships: All Kinds of People, All Kinds of Ideas
10. Sex and Alcohol: Making Responsible Choices
APPENDIX: Beginning College in Uncertain Times: Perspectives on Terrorism, Prejudice, and Patriotism

Bonus Content on the CD-ROM:

▶ Managing Your Money: Your Checkbook to Success

▶ APPENDIX: Taking Online Courses: Succeeding through Web-Based Learning

Now more flexible and manageable for all courses

- *one-hour credit courses* ■ *quarter-length courses* ■ *two-semester courses*
- *customized courses—combine with your own materials!*

The most extensively revised and updated edition in the history of this popular textbook!

In addition to consistent and thorough updating—which has made this edition as current as possible—the authors have made these additional changes:

Ten dynamic chapters are presented in a new order that is more appropriate to the developmental timetable for new college students to be able to achieve academic success and adjustment. For instance:

▸ The authors now introduce *Time Management*—the foundation of success in college—in the first chapter, in order to help students learn to impose a critical level of self-management at the very beginning of their college experience.

▸ The ten-chapter structure is more flexible for instructors, more concise and streamlined, yet still presents first-time students with the tools they need to deal with transition issues and learn study skills.

Packaged FREE with every new copy of the book is a relevant and useful CD-ROM. Icons in every chapter of the text direct students to the CD-ROM so they can extend their learning through interactive exercises, readings, and unique content. The CD-ROM includes fascinating readings within the *Think Again!* sections, as well as additional text content, a new bonus chapter, an electronic journal, and more. This CD-ROM is truly in a class by itself. *See page 6 for additional information.*

An entire *Values* chapter defines values, helps students learn to evaluate their own thoughts and preferences, and helps them use their values to guide decision-making.

An updated chapter on *Careers and Courses*, with an expanded activities program, leads students to reflect on how their course choices relate to future career possibilities.

Every chapter includes a new *Speaking of Careers* feature that links chapter content to career decision making.

A *Critical Thinking* activity in every chapter illustrates how critical thinking skills can be applied in every area of a student's life.

An *Examining Values* activity in every chapter links this important topic to chapter content.

A new appendix titled **Beginning College in Uncertain Times: Perspectives on Terrorism, Prejudice, and Patriotism**, offers a series of readings and discussion questions that encourage students to think critically and reflect on the global issues that affect them.

A redesigned and updated CD-ROM . . . FREE with every NEW copy of the text!

This Concise Fifth Media Edition features a thoroughly updated CD-ROM—automatically packaged FREE with every new copy of the text. This valuable and dynamic CD-ROM has an engaging new design, additional content to the book, bonus readings, self-assessments, and more! **ISBN: 0-534-60761-6**

Designed to reinforce and extend the content of the text, the CD-ROM adds a new dimension as it leads students from the pages of the book to the vivid interactivity of multimedia!

Every chapter on the CD-ROM is designed to engage students and make them want to read further and study more. Thoroughly connected to the text, the CD-ROM includes:

▶ Self-assessments with personalized feedback

▶ *Think Again!* additional readings

▶ Bonus exercises for each topic in the book

▶ Electronic versions of book exercises

▶ A *Test Your Knowledge* interactive quiz for each topic covered in the book

▶ Internet activities

▶ *InfoTrac® College Edition* exercises

▶ An electronic journal for each chapter that encourages students to reflect on their progress and create their own set of campus-specific personal resources

▶ Franklin-Covey's popular **Mission Statement Builder** activity

The easy-to-use CD-ROM includes a **bonus chapter on Money Management** that includes a full program of exercises and self-assessments as well as an all-new appendix on *Taking Online Courses*.

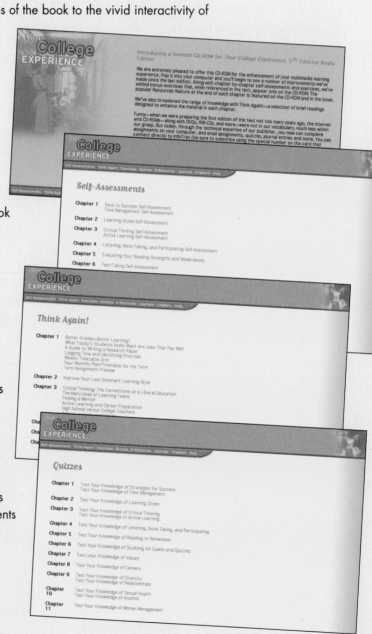

Your Course, Your Way . . .

Thomson Custom Publishing—*Creating the Perfect College Success Course*

Thomson Custom Publishing gives you the perfect opportunity to design your course exactly the way you want it. Order Gardner/Jewler's text fully customized to your course syllabus and teaching style—a text built to provide the best learning outcome for your students.

As the number one custom publisher for the college success market, Wadsworth delivers the personal touch that helps match materials to your course. Custom publishing may be the solution you are looking for if you would like to:

- ▶ Supplement your current Wadsworth text with handouts, including campus-specific information, such as drop/add forms, important phone numbers, schedules, a map of the school or information on financial aid. Combine materials from two or more Wadsworth books, and add articles about the latest current events.

- ▶ Add a custom cover to your book.

OR . . . *Instant Customization is just a click away!*

To make it even easier . . . **www.TextChoice.com**

In just minutes, **TextChoice** allows you to:

- ▶ Mix and match chapters from different books
- ▶ View chapters online as you create your custom book
- ▶ Preview your finished book and make changes as necessary.
- ▶ Add your own teaching material.

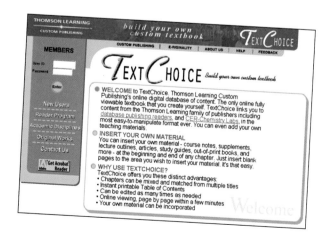

For more information contact your Thomson/Wadsworth representative or visit our Web site at:
http://success.wadsworth.com

For instant customization,
choose the unbound version!

The easiest way to customize **Your College Experience: Strategies for Success, Concise Media Fifth Edition** with your own campus-specific materials is to choose our three-hole punched version of the text.

Unbound, this version comes with a front and back cover and with all of the pages conveniently three-hole punched so students can create their own course-specific binders. This option gives students the ultimate freedom to create their own reference guide for the course, allowing them to add materials that appeal to them and collect articles for later reference. With their own binders that they create and maintain, they only need to carry the portions they choose!

As with the bound text, this unbound version comes packaged with the free student CD-ROM and *InfoTrac® College Edition*.
ISBN: 0-534-60763-2.

Today's technology for today's students . . . completely integrated!

The leading technologies that enhance *Your College Experience: Strategies for Success,* **Concise Media Fifth Edition** meet the challenges and expectations of today's students and instructors!

Web site for *Your College Experience: Strategies for Success,* **Concise Fifth Media Edition**

http://success.wadsworth.com

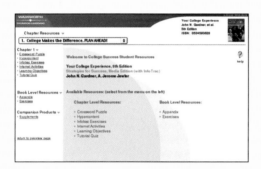

A robust resource with student learning tools, online quizzes, and updated Web links.

The Wadsworth College Success Resource Center

http://success.wadsworth.com

When you adopt Gardner/Jewler's text, you and your students have access to a rich array of teaching and learning resources that you won't find anywhere else. This outstanding site features everything from relevant journal to association links and downloadable teaching tools, forms and activities. It's the ideal way to make teaching and learning an interactive and exciting experience.

WebTutor™ . . . on WebCT and Blackboard

Online course management

"Out of the box" or customizable, this versatile online tool is filled with pre-loaded, text-specific content. For students, *WebTutor* offers access to a full array of study tools, including practice quizzes, and Web links. Instructors can use *WebTutor* to provide virtual office hours, post syllabi, set up threaded discussions, and track student progress with the quizzing material. Try **WebTutor** today at http://webtutor.thomsonlearning.com
WebCT ISBN: 0-534-60764-0
Blackboard ISBN: 0-534-60765-9.

FREE access to InfoTrac® College Edition

A four-month subscription to this extensive online library is FREE with every new copy of the book. **InfoTrac College Edition** includes articles from thousands of magazines, newsletters, and respected journals going back more than 20 years. These full-length articles (not just excerpts) are updated daily, expertly indexed, and ready to use—24 hours a day, seven days a week! Exercises on the student CD-ROM direct students to current articles online. *Available to college and university students only. Journals subject to change.*

College Success Factors Index Assessment Web Site

developed by Edmond Hallberg, Kaylene Hallberg, and Loren Sauer

Available exclusively on the Wadsworth College Success Web site—*password protected!*

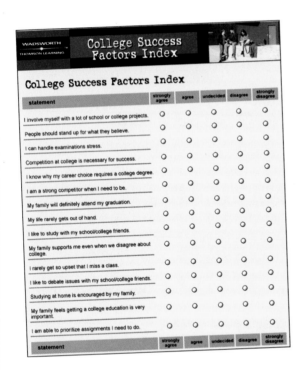

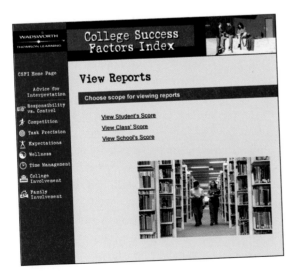

The perfect tool to help your students quickly assess their college success needs—and validate your college success program!

Does your College Success course make a difference in your students' academic success? Here's a survey that will give you the answers you're looking for! *The College Success Factors Index* survey (CSFI) is the perfect tool that allows you to track the progress of students in the course—and at the same time show students what they need to succeed.

Easy to take in or outside of class!

While many assessments take up valuable class time, the CSFI tool is conveniently housed on the Wadsworth Web site. Students can take the assessment on the Internet in a password-protected area either in a lab, in their home, or at their workplace. It is an 80-statement survey based on eight important areas that have been proven to correlate with college success:

- **Responsibility and Control** • **Competition**
- **Task Precision** • **Expectations** • **Wellness**
- **Time Management** • **College Involvement**
- **Family Involvement**

The results are correlated to **Your College Experience: Strategies for Success, Concise Fifth Media Edition,** so that students are pointed to the parts of the book that will most help them to succeed. Students can purchase passwords for the Assessment Tool with copies of **Your College Experience: Strategies for Success, Concise Fifth Media Edition.**

To see a demonstration or for more information on CSFI, visit the Wadsworth Web site
http:// success.wadsworth.com
or contact your local
Thomson/Wadsworth representative.

The Wadsworth College Success Workshop Series

We offer a variety of faculty development workshops regionally on campuses nationwide and online throughout the year. Visit our Web site for dates and places: **http://success.wadsworth.com**. Topics at these workshops include active learning strategies to engage first-year students, motivating students, using technology, working with peer leaders, and ways to promote critical thinking.

Let us help you get the most out of *Your College Experience*

When you adopt this text you may qualify to have one of our facilitators come to your campus to train your faculty on how to best use this learning-rich textbook for your college success program. Please call one of our consultants at 1-800-400-7609 for more details.

Wadsworth Regional Workshop Series— *join us at a location near you . . .*

The **College Success Regional Workshops** appear in locations throughout the U.S. focusing on the unique features of College Success programs, active learning exercises you can use to enhance your lectures, and technology tools designed to improve introductory courses. Our regional workshops serve as wonderful gathering centers for instructors and administrators of College Success programs to meet and exchange ideas. See the Wadsworth College Success Web site at **http://success.wadsworth.com** to learn more about the seminars we offer throughout the year, throughout the country.

Or you can run a workshop on your own campus with a little help from **Dr. Constance Staley** . . .

50 Ways to Leave Your Lectern

by Dr. Constance Staley, University of Colorado, Colorado Springs
This book is based on Staley's popular College Success workshop for instructors and her own experience designing and teaching the course. The book includes 50 classroom-tested activities and icebreakers that creatively address academic topics and personal decision-making in fun and engaging ways. **ISBN: 0-534-53866-5**

"Motivating, inspirational, and fun."
—Lenore Arlee, *University of Oklahoma*

"Constance Staley was very knowledgeable and passionate about student success."
—Denise Menchaca, *GateWay Community College*

"Dr. Staley knew the material. She explained things well and made me think how I can apply these ideas. The workshop was a wonderful investment in myself. Thanks!"
—Susann Deason, *Aiken Technical College*

An unparalleled array of teaching tools and additional resources

Instructor's Resource Suite: Manual and CD-ROM

Each chapter of this flexible and unique *Instructor's Manual* includes additional exercises, test questions, tips on teaching, a list of common concerns of first year students, and a case study relevant to the topics covered. The CD-ROM contains the entire *Instructor's Manual*, making it simple to customize and print material from the chapters that you teach and additional suggestions for activities. The CD-ROM also includes Microsoft® *PowerPoint®* slides and CNN® video clips. Additional activities to use in the classroom are also posted on the text-specific Web site. **ISBN: 0-534-60762-4**

ExamView® Computerized Test Bank

Enhance your range of assessment activities—and save yourself time in the process. With **ExamView** you can easily create and customize tests! **ExamView's** *Quick Test Wizard* guides you step-by-step through the process of creating and printing a test in minutes. You can build tests of up to 250 questions using up to 12 question types and enter an unlimited number of new questions or edit existing questions. Cross-platform **ISBN: 0-534-60766-7**

Plug in Your Course . . . FREE . . . with
MyCourse 2.0

http://mycourse.thomsonlearning.com
Whether you want only the easy-to-use tools to build it or the content to furnish it, *MyCourse 2.0* offers you the simple solution for a custom course Web site that allows you to assign, track, and report on student progress, load your syllabus, and more. Contact your Wadsworth/Thomson sales representative for details.

Wadsworth College Success Transparency Master Package

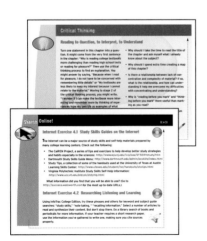

These 50 transparency masters cover a wide range of topics frequently referenced in first-year seminar courses. Subjects include *College Success Basics, Time Management, Money, Learning Styles, Study Skills, Critical Thinking, Technology, Test-Taking* and *Wellness*. You can download this fully customizable package in *PowerPoint®* on the College Success Web site,
http://success.wadsworth.com
ISBN: 0-534-57417-3

Video Presentation Tools

CNN® Today:
College Success Video Series

Launch your lectures with riveting footage from CNN, the world's leading 24-hour global news television network. The **CNN Today: College Success Video Series** is an exclusive series jointly created by Wadsworth and CNN. Each video in the series consists of approximately 45 minutes of footage originally broadcast on CNN within in the last several years and selected specifically to illustrate the relevance of course topics to students' everyday lives.
2004 Edition ISBN: 0-534-54142-9; 2002 Edition ISBN: 0-534-54140-2; 2003 Edition ISBN: 0-534-54141-0; 2001 Edition ISBN: 0-534-53799-5

College Success Films for the Humanities Series

A collection of topical videos chosen because of their relevance to subjects taught in first-year seminar courses. Includes videos on achieving academic success, communication, job hunting and careers, drugs and alcohol and making healthy choices. Videos are of varying length. Ask your College Success representative for details.

Wadsworth Study Skills Videos

Volume I: Improving Your Grades features students talking to students and involves viewers in the issues that contribute to their success. *Volume II: Lectures for Notetaking Practice* features a series of college lectures that provide students with the opportunity to practice their notetaking skills.
Volume I ISBN: 0-534-54983-7
Volume II ISBN: 0-534-54984-5

A World of Diversity Videos

This powerful two-video set addresses communication and conflict resolution between cultures. **Volume I ISBN: 0-534-23229-9**
Volume II ISBN: 0-534-23230-2

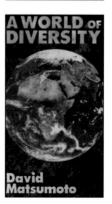

Toll-Free Consultation Service
available to all instructors at
1-800-400-7609

Package one of these resources with the text for added value

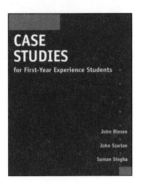

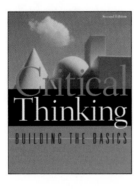

College Success Agenda Planner

Wadsworth offers inexpensive planners designed specifically for college students by experts in time management. These spiral-bound calendars are designed for first-year college students. Each planner features 18-month coverage, unique design, and plenty of room for students to record their academic and personal commitments and schedule. Ask your Thomson/Wadsworth representative for information on bundling the College Success Agenda Planner with your textbook at minimal charge.
ISBN: 0-534-55929-8

Case Studies for First-Year Experience Student

by **John Riesen, John Szarlan,** and **Suman Singha**   This collection of varied case studies present scenarios that first-year students of all ages and backgrounds are likely to face. Each case includes a set of individual and group discussion questions that challenge students to consider how they would react in similar situations. The case study approach is a proven technique that engages students in their own learning. Additional case studies are also available for custom publishing. **ISBN 0-534-26277-5.** To package with the text **ISBN: 0-534-06908-8**

The Successful Distance Learning Student

by **Carl Wahlstrom, Brian Williams,** and **Peter Shea**   This book is designed to teach students the skills they need to succeed in distance learning courses and to become better students in general. Regardless of the type of distance learning course—Internet-based, telecourse, prerecorded video, or interactive video—this book addresses a variety of student concerns in a quick and clear format.
ISBN 0-534-57712-1. To package with the text **ISBN: 0-534-06980-0**

Critical Thinking: Building the Basics, Second Edition

by **Tim Walter, Glenn M. Knudsvig,** and **Donald E.P. Smith**   This book includes over 100 pages of valuable guidance for improving learning through critical thinking. The authors advise students on how to apply critical thinking strategies to all of their textbooks and courses.
ISBN 0-534-59976-1. To package with the text **ISBN: 0-534-06962-2**

Chapter 1: Time Management and 30 Strategies for College Success

Ideas for Instruction and Instructor Training	Videos and CD-ROMs	Media Resources for Instructors	Media Resources for Students
Instructor's Manual Includes suggestions for teaching Chapter 1, lecture launchers, tips on integrating technology in the classroom, case studies, discussion questions, quiz questions, commentary about exercises in the book and student CD-ROM, and *PowerPoint*® slides. Also includes exercises and discussion questions to use along with CNN® video clips. **Additional Chapter Exercises:** • Suggestion for Exercises • Current Article Discussion • Strategies for Success Group Exercise • Interviewing Another Student • How to Use an Electronic Calendar **Test Bank Questions** Chapter 1: 10 Multiple-Choice, True/False and Essay Questions. Available in ***ExamView*®** *ExamView*® computerized test bank format.	**College Success** CNN. **CNN® Today Video Series: 2003 Edition** "Philanthropist Helps Makes College Dreams Come True" (2:05) "Corporate College Sponsorship" (1:59) **College Success** CNN. **CNN® Today Video Series: 2002 Edition** "Going to Canada for College" (2:15) **College Success** CNN. **CNN® Today Video Series: 2001 Edition** "Diversity Report Card" (2:40) "Perfectionism" (3:20) **College Success** CNN. **CNN® Today Video Series: 2000 Edition** "Student Day" (3:06) "Campus Politics" (2:06) **Films for the Humanities College Success Video Series** "Time Management" (18 minutes)	http://success.wadsworth.com *Resource Links* • Cornell Trainer Network • The Beloit College's Class of 2004 Mindset *General Resources* *Download on:* • Planning, Designing and Promoting the College Success Course • Syllabus Construction • Classroom Teaching **Microsoft® *PowerPoint*® Slides** • Take Charge of Learning! • Hone Your Skills! • Know Yourself! • First-Year Questions of Freedom and Commitment • Those Who Start and Those Who Finish • Education, Careers, and Income • Liberal Education and Quality of Life • Setting Goals for Success • Setting Priorities • Using a Daily Planner • Maintaining a "To Do" List • Guidelines for Scheduling Week By Week • Organizing Your Day • Making Your Time Management Plan Work • Time and Critical Thinking **Wadsworth College Success Transparency Masters** T 1-1 The Rewards of College T 1-2 Goals T 1-3 Setting Goals T 1-4 Habits of Highly Effective People T 1-5 Get Motivated **WebTutor™** Chapter 1 Course Management Tool for WebCT or Blackboard	http://success.wadsworth.com *Links to:* • An Online Student Survival Guide • Controlling Procrastination • How to Succeed as a Student • Academic Advising • Time Management Tips • Top Ten Tips for Surviving College **Media Edition CD-ROM** *Self-Assessment* *Think Again! Readings* • Better Grades=Better Learning • What Today's Students Really Want Are Jobs That Pay Well • A Guide to Writing a Research Paper • Logging Time and Identifying Priorities • Weekly Timetable Grid • Your Monthly Plan/Timetable for the Term *Test Your Knowledge* *InfoTrac® College Edition* *Journal* *E-Resources* *Exercises:* • Using the Digest of Education Statistics Online • Limiting Your Time Online • Researching the Value of Time and College • Procrastination Resources • Solving a Problem • Focusing on Your Concerns • Your Reasons for Attending College • The Many Reasons for College • The Ideal Class Schedule • Your Daily Plan • Goal-Setting for Courses **WebTutor™** webTUTOR Chapter 1 Text-specific online quizzes and Web links **InfoTrac® College Edition** *Keywords:* time management, liberal arts, procrastination, college success.

Chapter 2: Learning Styles: Discovering How You Learn Best

Ideas for Instruction and Instructor Training	Videos and CD-ROMs	Media Resources for Instructors	Media Resources for Students
Instructor's Manual Includes suggestions for teaching Chapter 2, lecture launchers, tips on integrating technology in the classroom, case studies, discussion questions, quiz questions, commentary about exercises in the book and student CD-ROM, and *PowerPoint®* slides. Also includes exercises and discussion questions to use along with CNN® video clips. **Additional Chapter Exercises:** • Suggestions for Peer Leaders • Working with Other Learning Styles • Assessing Your Courses and Instructors • Instructor's Learning Style • Strategies for Developing Other Learning Styles • Exams and Learning Styles **Test Bank Questions** Chapter 2: 10 Multiple-Choice, True/False and Essay Questions. Available in ***ExamView®*** ExamView® computerized test bank format.	**College Success** CNN **CNN® Today Video Series: 2003 Edition** "Hip Hop in the Classroom" (2:18) **College Success** CNN **CNN® Today Video Series: 2002 Edition** "Having a Learning Disability and Thriving" (2:19) **Films for the Humanities** **College Success Video Series** "Strategic Learning" (10 minutes) "Intelligence, Creativity, and Thinking Styles" (30 minutes) "Dyslexia: A Different Kind of Mind" (29 minutes) "Distance Learning: The Great Controversy" (57 minutes)	http://success.wadsworth.com *Resource Links* *Download on:* • Active Learning • Critical Thinking • Interactive Learning • Collaborative Learning **Microsoft® *PowerPoint®* Slides** *Discovering Your Own Learning Style* • Personality Preferences and Learning Style • Using Knowledge of Your Learning Styles • Dealing with Your Instructors' Teaching Styles **Wadsworth College Success Transparency Masters** T 4-1 Myers-Briggs Learning Styles T 4-2 Myers-Briggs Scales T 4-3 Different Lecture Styles **WebTutor™** WebTUTOR Chapter 2 Course Management Tool for WebCT or Blackboard	http://success.wadsworth.com *Links to:* • Online Learning Styles Inventory • Explanations of Myers-Briggs Types • Learning Style Evaluation • Multiple Intelligences and Technology • The Kiersey Temperament Sorter • The Personality Page **Media Edition CD-ROM** *Self-Assessment* *Think Again! Readings* • Improving Your Less Dominant Learning Styles *Test Your Knowledge* *InfoTrac® College Edition* *Journal* *E-Resources* *Exercises:* • Learning Style Inventory • Researching Learning Style Theory • Your Learning Style: A Quick Indication • Assessing Your Learning Style • Assessing Your Courses and Instructors **WebTutor™** WebTUTOR Chapter 2 Text-specific online quizzes and Web links **InfoTrac® College Edition** *Keywords:* learning style, Howard Gardner, Myers-Briggs, Kiersey, learning preference

Chapter 3: Critical Thinking, Active Learning: Paths to True Understanding

Ideas for Instruction and Instructor Training	Videos and CD-ROMs	Media Resources for Instructors	Media Resources for Students
Instructor's Manual Includes suggestions for teaching Chapter 3, lecture launchers, tips on integrating technology in the classroom, case studies, discussion questions, quiz questions, commentary about exercises in the book and student CD-ROM, and *PowerPoint®* slides. Also includes exercises and discussion questions to use along with CNN® video clips.	**College Success**  **CNN® Today Video Series: 2003 Edition** "New York Students Contemplate the Future After 9/11" (3:00) "Debate Over Affirmative Action on University Campuses" (1:33)	**http://success.** **wadsworth.com** *General Resources* Download on: • Critical Thinking • Active Learning • Interactive Learning • Collaborative Learning	**http://success.** **wadsworth.com** *Links to:* • Critical Thinking on the Web • How to Solve It • Critical Thinking Tutorial • The Center for Critical Thinking
Additional Chapter Exercises: • Participating in Classroom Thinking • Faculty Panel Discussion • Transition Issues • The Benefits and Pitfalls of Collaborative Learning • The One-Minute Paper • Charting Your Development • Describing Your Ideal Teacher • Describing Your Ideal Mentor	**Films for the** 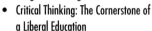 **Humanities College Success Video Series** "Intelligence, Creativity and Thinking Styles" (30 minutes) "Strategic Learning" (10 minutes).	**Microsoft® PowerPoint® Slides** • From Certainty to Healthy Uncertainty • A Higher-Order Thinking Process • A Skill to Carry You Through Life • Four Aspects of Critical Thinking • How College Encourages Critical Thinking • The Many Benefits of Active Learning • Why Active Learners Can Learn More Than Passive Learners • Becoming an Active Learner • The Value of Collaboration • Making Learning Teams Productive • Connecting with College Teachers • Academic Freedom in the Classroom • When Things Go Wrong Between You and a Teacher	**Media Edition CD-ROM** *Self-Assessment* *Think Again! Readings* • Critical Thinking: The Cornerstone of a Liberal Education • The Many Uses of Learning Teams • Finding a Mentor • Active Learning and Career Preparation • High School vs. College Teachers • Active Learning and Values *Test Your Knowledge* *InfoTrac® College Edition* *Journal* *E-Resources* *Exercises:* • Critical Thinking Resources • Your Teachers'- and Your Own- Responsibilities • Researching Critical Thinking and Active Learning • Reflection on Arguments • The Challenge of Classroom Thinking • Decision Making • Differences Between High School and College • Learning Actively • Forming Your Ideal Learning Team • To Collaborate or Not? • Interviewing a Teacher • A Teaching Experience
Test Bank Questions Chapter 3: 10 Multiple-Choice, True/False and Essay Questions. Available in **ExamView®** Computerized test bank format.		**Wadsworth College Success Transparency Masters** T 5-1 Stand Out as a Student T 5-2 Make the Most Out of Class T 7-1 The Uncritical Thinker T 7-2 The Critical Thinker T 7-3 Terms to Know T 7-4 Dealing with Claims T 7-5 Inductive vs. Deductive Reasoning T 7-6 The IDEAL Problem Solving Method	**WebTutor** Chapter 3 Text-specific online quizzes and Web links
		WebTutor™ Chapter 3 Course Management Tool for WebCT or Blackboard	**InfoTrac® College Edition** *Keywords:* critical thinking, creative thinking, abstract thinking

Resource Integration Guide—Make the Connection!

Chapter 4: Listening, Note Taking, and Participating: Getting the Most Out of Classes

Ideas for Instruction and Instructor Training	Videos and CD-ROMs	Media Resources for Instructors	Media Resources for Students
Instructor's Manual Includes suggestions for teaching Chapter 4, lecture launchers, tips on integrating technology in the classroom, case studies, discussion questions, quiz questions, commentary about exercises in the book and student CD-ROM, and *PowerPoint* slides. Also includes exercises and discussion questions to use along with CNN® video clips.	**College Success** CNN **CNN® Today Video Series: 2001 Edition** "College Students Buy Class Notes" (2:04)	http://success. wadsworth.com *Download on:* • Active Learning • Collaborative Learning	http://success. wadsworth.com *Links to:* • How to Study.com • Memory Theory and Techniques • Note-Taking Strategies • Online Guide for College Students with Learning Disabilities
Additional Chapter Exercises: • Testing Memory • Sample Lectures • Evaluating Student! Notetaking Strategies	**Wadsworth Study Skills Video, Volume 2: Lectures for Note-taking Practice** Have your students practice taking notes with a variety of lecture styles.	**Microsoft® *PowerPoint* Slides** • Memory: Listening and Forgetting • Using Your Senses in the Learning Process • Three Major Parts of Note-taking • Before Class: Prepare to Remember • During Class: Listen Critically • During Class: Listen Critically (2) • During Class: Take Effective Notes • Additional Note-taking Suggestions • After Class: Respond, Recite, Review • Participating in Class: Speak Up!	**Media Edition CD-ROM** *Self-Assessment* *Think Again! Readings* • Other Kinds of Notes *Test Your Knowledge* *InfoTrac® College Edition* *Journal* *E-Resources* *Exercises:* • Study Skills Guides on the Internet • Researching Listening and Learning • Listening and Memory • Comparing Notes • Memory: Using a Recall Column • Applying an Active Listening and Learning System • Looking Back on Your Notes
Test Bank Questions Chapter 4: 10 Multiple-Choice, True/False and Essay Questions. Available in *ExamView®* ExamView® computerized test bank format.	**Films for the Humanities College Success Video Series** "Strategic Learning" (10 minutes) "Note-taking" (9 minutes) "Listening" (15 minutes) "Reading Improvement" (12 minutes)	**Wadsworth College Success Transparency Masters** T 5-1 Stand Out as a Student T 5-2 Make the Most of Class T 5-3 Note-Taking Formats T 5-4 Note-Taking Tips	**WebTutor™** WebTUTOR Chapter 4 Text-specific online quizzes and Web links
		WebTutor™ WebTUTOR Chapter 4 Course Management Tool for WebCT or Blackboard	**InfoTrac® College Edition** *Keywords:* study skills, note-taking, recalling information, memory, active learning.

Chapter 5: Reading to Remember: Strategies for Understanding & Retaining Material

Ideas for Instruction and Instructor Training	Videos and CD-ROMs	Media Resources for Instructors	Media Resources for Students
Instructor's Manual Includes suggestions for teaching Chapter 5, lecture launchers, tips on integrating technology in the classroom, case studies, discussion questions, quiz questions, commentary about exercises in the book and student CD-ROM, and *PowerPoint* slides. Also includes exercises and discussion questions to use along with CNN® video clips. **Additional Chapter Exercises:** • Targeted Reading • Comparing Reading Strategies • Vocabulary Building **Test Bank Questions** Chapter 5: 10 Multiple-Choice, True/False and Essay Questions. Available in ***ExamView®*** **ExamView®** computerized test bank format.	**Films for the Humanities** **College Success Video Series** "Reading Improvement" (18 minutes)	**http://success. wadsworth.com** *Download on:* • Teaching Reading **Microsoft® *PowerPoint®* Slides** • 4-Step Reading Plan • Previewing • Some Tips for Previewing • Reading Your Textbook • Marking Your Textbook • Reviewing • Adjusting Your Reading Style • Developing Your Vocabulary **Wadsworth College Success Transparency Masters** T 6-1 The Keys to Successful Studying T 6-2 Understanding Your Memory T 6-3 Know the Difference T 6-4 Memorize to Learn T 6-5 Memory Boosters T 6-6 Levels of Reading **WebTutor™** WebTUTOR™ Chapter 5 Course Management Tool for WebCT or Blackboard	**http://success. wadsworth.com** *Links to:* • "Taking Notes and Reading" from College Study Skills • Assess Your Reading Habits • Checklist for an Informational Web Page • Evaluating World Wide Web Information • How to Read Essays You Must Analyze • How to Read Your Textbooks More Efficiently • Mark Your Books • Reading Tips for Adult Students • Six Reading Myths • SQ3R • Suggestions For Improving Reading Speed • Tips for Reading College Textbooks **Media Edition CD-ROM** *Self Assessment* *Think Again! Readings* • A Lifetime of Reading *InfoTrac® College Edition* *Journal* *E-Resources* *Exercises:* • Reading Web Pages Critically • Researching How to Read Texts • Previewing and Creating a Visual Map • Preparing to Read, Think, and Mark • How to Read Fifteen Pages of a Textbook in an Hour or Less • Expanding Your Vocabulary **WebTutor™** WebTUTOR™ Chapter 5 Text-specific online quizzes and Web links **InfoTrac® College Edition** *Keywords:* reading, college reading.

Chapter 6: Taking Exams and Tests: Be Prepared, Confident, and Calm

Ideas for Instruction and Instructor Training	Videos and CD-ROMs	Media Resources for Instructors	Media Resources for Students
Instructor's Manual Includes suggestions for teaching Chapter 6, lecture launchers, tips on integrating technology in the classroom, case studies, discussion questions, quiz questions, commentary about exercises in the book and student CD-ROM, and *PowerPoint* slides. Also includes exercises and discussion questions to use along with CNN® video clips. **Additional Chapter Exercises:** • Overcoming Test Anxiety • Discussing Cheating in College • Finding Out About a Test • Essay Tests • Multiple-Choice, True/False and Matching Exams **Test Bank Questions** Chapter 6: 10 Multiple-Choice, True/False and Essay Questions. Available in **ExamView®** ExamView® computerized test bank format.	**College Success** CNN **CNN® Today Video Series: 2000 Edition** "Drunken Memory" (1:42)	http://success. wadsworth.com *Download on:* • Student Assessment: Exams, Assignments, and Grades. **Microsoft® *PowerPoint*®** **Slides** • Academic Honesty • Academic Honesty (2) • Exams: The Long View • Planning Your Approach • Now It's Time to Study • Taking the Test • Types of Test Questions • Aids to Memory **Wadsworth College Success** **Transparency Masters** T 9-1 Avoid Cramming for Tests T 9-2 Tips for Taking Tests T 9-3 Tips for Multiple-Choice Tests T 9-4 Tips for Essay Tests T 9-5 Calculating Your GPA **WebTutor™** WebTUTOR™ Chapter 6 Course Management Tool for WebCT or Blackboard	http://success. wadsworth.com *Links to:* • Checklist for Essay Tests • Memory Improvement Techniques • Exam Preparation • Strategies for Beating Test- Taking Anxiety • Learning Center Model Test Study Schedule • Survival Strategies for Taking Tests • Test-Taking Skills • Test-Taking Tips • Test-Taking: How to Use Key Words in Essay Questions **Media Edition CD-ROM** *Self-Assessment* *Think Again! Readings* • Does Cheating Hurt Anyone? • Emergency? Your Instructors Need to Know • Writing Summaries—Another Way to Study • More Aids to Memory *InfoTrac® College Edition* *Journal* *E-Resources* *Exercises:* • Examining Institutional Values • More Memory Devices • Researching Good Study Habits • Designing an Exam Plan • Forming a Study Group • Writing a Summary **WebTutor™** WebTUTOR™ Chapter 6 Text-specific online quizzes and Web links **InfoTrac® College Edition** *Keywords:* mnemonics, memory, examinations, cheating in college, academic integrity, truth, honesty, public speaking.

Chapter 7: Developing Values: Choosing Unique Pathways

Ideas for Instruction and Instructor Training	Videos and CD-ROMs	Media Resources for Instructors	Media Resources for Students
Instructor's Manual Includes suggestions for teaching Chapter 7, lecture launchers, tips on integrating technology in the classroom, case studies, discussion questions, quiz questions, commentary about exercises in the book and student CD-ROM, and *PowerPoint®* slides. Also includes exercises and discussion questions to use along with CNN® video clips. **Additional Chapter Exercises:** • Critical Thinking • Value Dualisms • Take a Value Stand **Test Bank Questions** Chapter 7: 10 Multiple-Choice, True/False and Essay Questions. Available in **ExamView®** **ExamView®** computerized test bank format.	**College Success** CNN **CNN® Today Video Series: 2003 Edition** "Patriotism at Harvard University" (2:14) "Controversy Over Student Visas"(1:40) **College Success** CNN **CNN® Today Video Series: 2002 Edition** "Catching Plagiarized Papers" (2:10) **College Success** CNN **CNN® Today Video Series: 2001 Edition** "Students Experience Homelessness" (2:03)	http://success. wadsworth.com *Download on:* • Teaching Values **Microsoft® *PowerPoint®* Slides** • Challenges to Values in College • Defining Values • Another Way of Looking at Values • Types of Values • Societal Values in Conflict: Value Dualisms • Changing Society, Changing Values • Implementing Societal Values • Values and You **Wadsworth College Success Transparency Masters** T 10-1 Important Terms of Diversity T 10-2 Diversity Attitude Scale T 10-3 Keys to Successful Communication T 10-4 How Not to Communicate **WebTutor™** Chapter 7 Course Management Tool for WebCT or Blackboard	http://success. wadsworth.com *Links to:* • Center for Academic Integrity • Freedom of Speech and Academic Freedom **Media Edition CD-ROM** *Self Assessment* *Think Again! Readings* • Dictionary Definitions of Values • Seventeen Changes in American Society • Ends Values • Means Values • Changes in Values Over Four Years of College *Test Your Knowledge* *InfoTrac® College Edition* *Journal* *E-Resources* *Exercises:* • Obligations to Society • Researching Values • Friends and Values • Evidence of Values • Twenty Key Assumptions About American Life • Your Values and Your Families' Values • Values in Conflict • Shared Values? **WebTutor™** Chapter 7 Text-specific online quizzes and Web links **InfoTrac® College Edition** *Keywords:* values, core values, college students and values, values clarification, values and competition, values and age, values and gender, family values.

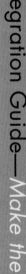

Chapter 8: Careers and Courses: Making Sensible Choices

Ideas for Instruction and Instructor Training	Videos and CD-ROMs	Media Resources for Instructors	Media Resources for Students
Instructor's Manual Includes suggestions for teaching Chapter 8, lecture launchers, tips on integrating technology in the classroom, case studies, discussion questions, quiz questions, commentary about exercises in the book and student CD-ROM, and *PowerPoint* slides. Also includes exercises and discussion questions to use along with CNN® video clips. **Additional Chapter Exercises:** • Choosing Courses • Effective Advisors • Student Speaker • Career Counselor/Center Visit **Test Bank Questions** Chapter 8: 10 Multiple-Choice, True/False and Essay Questions. Available in *ExamView®* computerized test bank format.	**College Success CNN® Today Video Series: 2003 Edition** "Working for Washington is Cool Again" (2:15) **College Success CNN® Today Video Series: 2002 Edition** "Employment Prospects After College" (1:43) "Emotional Intelligence and Career" (7:02) "Benefits of Community Service" (2:08) **College Success CNN® Today Video Series: 2001 Edition** "College Careers" (1:58) "Education for Jobs" (2:04) "Student Jobs" (2:21) "Summer Jobs" (2:23) "Americorps" (2:13) **Films for the Humanities College Success Video Series** "How to Find and Keep a Job" (30 minutes) "Interview Tips: What Employers Want" (30 minutes) "Jobs: Not What They Used to Be—The New Face of Work in America" (57 minutes)	http://success. wadsworth.com *Download on:* • Inviting Guest Speakers to the Classroom **Microsoft® *PowerPoint* Slides** • Careers and the New Economy • Finding a Major • Where to Go For Help • Surviving in a Fast Economy • Staring Your Career-Planning Program • Factors to Consider • Factors Affecting Career Choices • Exploring Your Interests • Getting Experience • Time for Action • Your Academic Advisor • Your College Catalog **Wadsworth College Success Transparencies** • Getting the Right Courses • Academic Advisors • Admissions Advisors • Current Resumé • Deal Resumé **WebTutor™** Chapter 8 Course Management Tool for WebCT or Blackboard	http://success. wadsworth.com *Links to:* • Career Profiles Index • "Choosing a College Major: How to Chart the Ideal Path" • What Can I Do with a Major in… • Career Exploration Links from UC Berkeley • Search the Occupational Outlook Handbook • The Catapult on JobWeb • Career Resource Center **Media Edition CD-ROM** *Self Assessment* *Think Again! Readings* • Careers and the New Economy • Liberal Arts Majors Are In • Mission and Vision *InfoTrac® College Edition* *Journal* *E-Resources* *Exercises:* • Mission and Vision • Internet Career Resources • Researching Careers and Courses • What Are Your Life Goals? • Personality Mosaic • The Holland Hexagon • Finding Your Interests • Writing a Resumé and Cover Letter • Your Academic Advisor/Counselor • Finding Your Catalog and Starting a File **WebTutor™** Chapter 8 Text-specific online quizzes and Web links **InfoTrac® College Edition** *Keywords:* career planning, careers, new economy, academic advisor, college majors, multi-national organizations.

Chapter 9: Creating Diverse Relationships: All Kinds of People, All Kinds of Ideas

Ideas for Instruction and Instructor Training	Videos and CD-ROMs	Media Resources for Instructors	Media Resources for Students
Instructor's Manual Includes suggestions for teaching Chapter 9, lecture launchers, tips on integrating technology in the classroom, case studies, discussion questions, quiz questions, commentary about exercises in the book and student CD-ROM, and *PowerPoint* slides. Also includes exercises and discussion questions to use along with CNN® video clips. **Additional Chapter Exercises:** • Dating Gripes • White Stereotypes • Creating a Shared Living Contract • Finding Common Ground • Diversity Exercises **Test Bank Questions** Chapter 9: 10 Multiple-Choice, True/False and Essay Questions. Available in ***ExamView*** ExamView® computerized test bank format.	**College Success** CNN **CNN® Today Video Series: 2003 Edition** "Diversity on Campus at Montana State University" (2:39) "Protesting Racial Intolerance at Penn State" (2:21) **College Success** CNN **CNN® Today Video Series: 2002 Edition** "In Response to Hate Crimes, A Gay Dorm" (1:43) "Women at Brown University Speak Out" (2:38) "Women on Welfare Go to College" (2:12) **College Success** CNN **CNN® Today Video Series: 2001 Edition** "Controversy Over Affirmative Admission" (2:23) **College Success** CNN **CNN® Today Video: 2000 Edition** "University Diversity" (2:32) **Films for the Humanities** 📼 **College Success Video Series** "Understanding Prejudice" (50 minutes) "Sexual Harassment: Crossing the Line" (58 minutes)	http://www.success. wadsworth.com *Download on:* • Diversity in the Classroom • Personal Relationships **Microsoft® *PowerPoint* Slides** • Race, Ethnic Groups and Culture • The Many Faces of Diversity • The Concept of Race on Campus • The Importance of Relationships • Dating and Mating • Married Life in College • You and Your Parents • Finding Diverse Friends • Expand Your View of Diversity • Long Distance Relationships • Electronic Relationships • Roommates • On-Campus Involvement • Off-Campus Involvement • Discrimination and Prejudice on College Campuses **Wadsworth College Success Transparency Masters** T 10-1 Important Terms of Diversity T 10-2 Diversity Attitude Scale T 10-3 Keys to Successful Communication T 10-4 How Not to Communicate **WebTutor™** Chapter 9 WebTUTOR Course Management Tool for WebCT or Blackboard	http://www.success. wadsworth.com *Links to:* • Diversity Web **Media Edition CD-ROM** *Self Assessment* *Think Again! Readings* • A Century of Change • The Changing U.S. Population • The Many Dimensions of Diversity • What Does the Future Hold for You, for Me, for Us? *InfoTrac® College Edition* *Journal* *E-Resources* *Exercises:* • Diversity on Campus • Looking for Love • Questions about Homosexuality • Researching Diversity • Sharing Your Background • Creating Common Ground • Diversity on Your Campus • Balancing Relationships and College • Student-Parent Gripes • Five Over 30 • Common Roommate Gripes • Roommate Roulette • Campus Organizations • Off-Campus Involvement • Combating Discrimination • Checking Your Understanding • Is Hate Speech Permitted on Your Campus? **WebTutor™** WebTUTOR Chapter 9 Text-specific online quizzes and Web links **InfoTrac® College Edition** *Keywords:* diversity and campus, ethnicity, hate crimes, disabilities and campus, sexual orientation.

Resource Integration Guide—*Make the Connection!*

Chapter 10: Sex and Alcohol: Making Responsible Choices

Ideas for Instruction and Instructor Training	Videos and CD-ROMs	Media Resources for Instructors	Media Resources for Students
Instructor's Manual Includes suggestions for teaching Chapter 10, lecture launchers, tips on integrating technology in the classroom, case studies, discussion questions, quiz questions, commentary about exercises in the book and student CD-ROM, and *PowerPoint* slides. Also includes exercises and discussion questions to use along with CNN® video clips. **Additional Chapter Exercises:** • Sexual Readiness • Role Playing • Individual Research Projects **Test Bank Questions** Chapter 10: 10 Multiple-Choice, True/False and Essay Questions. Available in ***ExamView*®** ExamView® Computerized test bank format.	**College Success** CNN **CNN® Today Video Series: 2003 Edition** "Date Rape on University Campuses" (2:17) "The Dangers of Taking Ecstasy" (1:54) "Federal Financial Aid and Drug Convictions" (2:24) **College Success** CNN **CNN® Today Video Series: 2002 Edition** "Binge Drinking Aftermath" (1:34) **College Success** CNN **CNN® Today Video Series: 2001 Edition** "Definition of Rape" (2:42) "AIDS 101" (1:46) "Binge Drinking" (2:06) "A Dorm Goes Drug Free" (2:39) "College Butts Out" (1:54) **Films for the** **Humanities College Success Video Series** "Date Rape: Behind Closed Doors" (45 minutes) "Portrait of Addiction" (57 minutes) "The Truth About Alcohol" (30 minutes) "Binge Drinking: The Right to Party?" (22 minutes)	http://success. wadsworth.com *Download on:* • Teaching About Drugs, Alcohol and Sexuality **Microsoft® *PowerPoint* Slides** • Sexual Decision Making • Birth Control • Sexually Transmitted Infections (STIs) • Options for Safer Sex • Unhealthy Relationships • Other Drugs • Three Reasons College Students Drink • Myths versus Realities of Student Drinking • Drinking and Blood Alcohol Content • Alcohol and Behavior • Heavy Drinking: The Danger Zone • Consequences for All • Long-Term Effects of Drinking • Making Decisions, Finding Help **Wadsworth College Success Transparency Masters** T 11-1 College Students and Alcohol T 11-2 College Lifestyles and Poor Health T 11-3 Facts About Smoking T 11-4 Cope with Stress **WebTutor™** Chapter 10 Course Management WebTUTOR Tool for WebCT or Blackboard	http://success. wadsworth.com • (Scary) Facts on Sexual Activity and Alcohol • What College Women Should Know about Sexual Assault • College Drinking Statistics • Binge Drinking on Campus: Results of a National Study **Media Edition CD-ROM** *Self Assessment* *Think Again! Readings* • Sexually Transmitted Infections • Avoiding Sexual Assault • What Is Alcohol? • Other Drugs • Examining Values: Sexuality • Sex in the Workplace • Student Drinking • High-Risk College Drinking *InfoTrac® College Edition* *Journal* *E-Resources* *Exercises:* • Confidential Information • Information about STIs • Core Alcohol and Drug Survey • Researching Alcohol and Other Drugs and Sexuality • Reflections on Sexuality • Which Birth Control Method? • What's Your Decision? • What's "Normal"? • Relationship Checkup • Sex and the Media • Survey of Alcohol Usage • A Safe Stress Antidote • Helping a Friend • Quality of Life • Lower the Drinking Age? **WebTutor™** WebTUTOR Chapter 10 Text-specific online quizzes and Web links **InfoTrac® College Edition** *Keywords:* sexual activity in college, alcohol abuse, date rape.

www.wadsworth.com

wadsworth.com is the World Wide Web site for Wadsworth and is your direct source to dozens of online resources.

At *wadsworth.com* you can find out about supplements, demonstration software, and student resources. You can also send email to many of our authors and preview new publications and exciting new technologies.

wadsworth.com
Changing the way the world learns®

The Wadsworth College Success Series

Clason and Beck, *On the Edge of Success* (2003). ISBN: 0-534-56973-0

Gordon and Minnick, *Foundations: A Reader for New College Students,* 2nd Ed. (2002). ISBN: 0-534-52431-1

Hallberg, Hallberg, and Rochieris, *Making the Dean's List: A Workbook to Accompany the College Success Factors Index* (2004). ISBN: 0-534-24862-4

Holkeboer and Walker, *Right from the Start: Taking Charge of Your College Success,* 4th Ed. (2004). ISBN: 0-534-59967-2

Petrie and Denson, *A Student Athlete's Guide to College Success: Peak Performance in Class and in Life,* 2nd Ed. (2003). ISBN: 0-534-57000-3

Santrock and Halonen, *Your Guide to College Success: Strategies for Achieving Your Goals,* Media Edition, 3rd Ed. (2004). ISBN: 0-534-60804-3

Steltenpohl, Shipton, and Villines, *Orientation to College: A Reader on Becoming an Educated Person,* 2nd Ed. (2004). ISBN: 0-534-59958-3

Van Blerkom, *Orientation to College Learning,* 4th Ed. (2004). ISBN: 0-534-60813-2

Wahlstrom and Williams, *Learning Success: Being Your Best at College & Life,* Media Edition, 3rd Ed. (2002). ISBN: 0-534-57314-2

The First-Year Experience™ Series

Gardner and Jewler, *Your College Experience: Strategies for Success,* Media Edition, 5th Ed. (2003). ISBN: 0-534-59382-8

Gardner and Jewler, *Your College Experience: Strategies for Success,* Concise Media Edition, 5th Ed. (2004). ISBN: 0-534-60759-4

Gardner and Jewler, *Your College Experience: Strategies for Success, Expanded Reader,* 5th Ed. (2003). ISBN: 0-534-59985-0

Study Skills/Critical Thinking

Longman and Atkinson, *CLASS: College Learning and Study Skills,* 6th Ed. (2002). ISBN: 0-534-56962-5

Longman and Atkinson, *SMART: Study Methods and Reading Techniques,* 2nd Ed. (1999). ISBN: 0-534-54981-0

Smith, Knudsvig, and Walter, *Critical Thinking: Building the Basics,* 2nd Ed. (2003). ISBN: 0-534-59976-1

Sotiriou, *Integrating College Study Skills: Reasoning in Reading, Listening, and Writing,* 6th Ed. (2002). ISBN: 0-534-57297-9

Van Blerkom, *College Study Skills: Becoming a Strategic Learner,* 4th Ed. (2003). ISBN: 0-534-57467-X

Watson, *Learning Skills for College and Life* (2001). ISBN: 0-534-56161-6

Student Assessment Tool

Hallberg, *College Success Factors Index,* http://success.wadsworth.com

Your College Experience

Strategies for Success

CONCISE MEDIA EDITION
FIFTH EDITION

JOHN N. GARDNER

Distinguished Professor Emeritus, Library and Information Science
Senior Fellow, National Resource Center for the First-Year Experience
   and Students in Transition
University of South Carolina, Columbia

A. JEROME JEWLER

Distinguished Professor Emeritus, College of Journalism and Mass Communication
University of South Carolina, Columbia

THOMSON

™

WADSWORTH

AUSTRALIA • CANADA • MEXICO • SINGAPORE • SPAIN • UNITED KINGDOM • UNITED STATES

THOMSON
WADSWORTH

Manager, College Success: Annie Mitchell
Assistant Editor: Kirsten Markson
Advertising Project Manager: Stacey Purviance
Project Manager, Editorial Production: Trudy Brown
Print/Media Buyer: Barbara Britton
Technology Project Manager: Barry Connolly
Permissions Editor: Bob Kauser
Production Service: The Cooper Company

Text Designer: Paul Uhl Associates
Photo Researcher: Terri Wright
Copy Editor: Jennifer Gordon
Cover Designer: Carole Lawson
Cover Image: Gary Buss, Getty Images
Compositor: New England Typographic Service
Printer: Transcontinental/Interglobe

Printed in Canada

1 2 3 4 5 6 7 07 06 05 04 03

For more information about our products, contact us at:
Thomson Learning Academic Resource Center
1-800-423-0563
For permission to use material from this text, contact us by:
Phone: 1-800-730-2214 **Fax:** 1-800-730-2215
Web: http://www.thomsonrights.com

Library of Congress Control Number: 2002113899

Student Edition with InfoTrac College Edition: ISBN 0-534-60759-4
Annotated Instructor's Edition: ISBN 0-534-60760-8
Loose-leaf Student Edition with InfoTrac College Edition: ISBN 0-534-60763-2

Wadsworth/Thomson Learning
10 Davis Drive
Belmont, CA 94002-3098
USA

Asia
Thomson Learning
5 Shenton Way #01-01
UIC Building
Singapore 068808

Australia/New Zealand
Thomson Learning
102 Dodds Street
Southbank, Victoria 3006
Australia

Canada
Nelson
1120 Birchmount Road
Toronto, Ontario M1K 5G4
Canada

Europe/Middle East/Africa
Thomson Learning
High Holborn House
50/51 Bedford Row
London WC1R 4LR
United Kingdom

Latin America
Thomson Learning
Seneca, 53
Colonia Polanco
11560 Mexico D.F.
Mexico

Spain/Portugal
Paraninfo
Calle/Magallanes, 25
28015 Madrid, Spain

Brief Contents

Part 1 Take Charge of Learning! 1

    1 Time Management and Thirty Strategies for College Success 3

    2 Learning Styles: Discovering How You Learn Best 27

Part 2 Hone Your Skills! 41

    3 Critical Thinking, Active Learning: Paths to True Understanding 43

    4 Listening, Note Taking, and Participating: Getting the Most Out of Classes 63

    5 Reading to Remember: Strategies for Understanding and Retaining Material 79

    6 Taking Exams and Tests: Be Prepared, Confident, and Calm 93

Part 3 Know Yourself! 111

    7 Developing Values: Choosing Unique Pathways 113

    8 Careers and Courses: Making Sensible Choices 129

    9 Creating Diverse Relationships: All Kinds of People, All Kinds of Ideas 149

    10 Sex and Alcohol: Making Responsible Choices 169

    Appendix Beginning College in Uncertain Times 201

On the CD-ROM:

    Taking Online Courses: Succeeding through Web-Based Learning

    Managing Your Money: Your Checkbook to Success

Contents

Part 1 Take Charge of Learning! 1

Chapter 1 Time Management and Thirty Strategies for College Success 3

SELF-ASSESSMENT: Time and Success 4

Take Charge of Learning! 5

Hone Your Skills! 6

Know Yourself! 7

First-Year Questions of Freedom and Commitment 8

Those Who Start and Those Who Finish 9

Education, Careers, and Income 9

CRITICAL THINKING: Successful Strategies 9

EXAMINING VALUES 10

Liberal Education and Quality of Life 11

SPEAKING OF CAREERS 11

Setting Goals for Success 12

Time Management: Foundation of Academic Success 12

Setting Priorities 13

Using a Daily Planner 14

Maintaining a "To Do" List 14

Guidelines for Scheduling Week by Week 14

Organizing Your Day 14

Making Your Time Management Plan Work 19

Reduce Distractions 19

SEARCH ONLINE! 19

Beat Procrastination 20

Exercises 20–22

SEARCH ONLINE! **Internet Exercise 1.1:** Using the *Digest of Education Statistics* Online; **Internet Exercise 1.2:** Researching the Value of College and Time Management; **Internet Exercise 1.3:** Limiting Your Time Online

ADDITIONAL EXERCISES **Exercise 1.1:** Solving a Problem; **Exercise 1.2:** Focusing on Your Concerns; **Exercise 1.3:** Your Reasons for Attending College

Your Personal Journal 23

Resources 24

Chapter 2 Learning Styles: Discovering How You Learn Best 27

SELF-ASSESSMENT: Learning Styles 28

Discovering Your Own Learning Style 29

Personality Preferences and Learning Style 29

CRITICAL THINKING: Stick with Your Own Types or Seek Out Other Types? 30

Strengths and Weaknesses 31

EXAMINING VALUES 32

Using Knowledge of Your Learning Style 32

Dealing with Your Instructors' Teaching Styles 32

Exam Preparation and Learning /Teaching Styles 32

Clues to Instructors' Teaching Styles 33

SPEAKING OF CAREERS 34

Exercises   35–38

    SEARCH ONLINE! **Internet Exercise 2.1:** Learning Style Inventory; **Internet Exercise 2.2:**
      Researching Learning Style Theory

    ADDITIONAL EXERCISES **Exercise 2.1:** Your Learning Style: A Quick Indication; **Exercise 2.2:**
      Assessing Your Learning Style

Your Personal Journal   39

Resources   40

Part 2   Hone Your Skills!   41

Chapter 3   Critical Thinking, Active Learning: Paths to True Understanding   43

    SELF-ASSESSMENT: Critical Thinking and Active Learning   44

Critical Thinking: The Search Beyond Right and Wrong   45

  From Certainty to Healthy Uncertainty   45

  A Higher-Order Thinking Process   46

  A Skill to Carry You Through Life   46

  EXAMINING VALUES   47

Four Aspects of Critical Thinking   47

  1. Abstract Thinking: Discovering Larger Ideas from Details   48

  2. Creative Thinking: Finding New Possibilities   48

  3. Systematic Thinking: Organizing the Possibilities   48

  4. Precise Communication of Your Ideas to Others   49

  How College Encourages Critical Thinking   49

  SPEAKING OF CAREERS   49

Active Learning   49

  The Many Benefits of Active Learning   50

  Why Active Learners Can Learn More Than Passive Learners   50

  Becoming an Active Learner   50

  The Value of Collaboration   52

  Making Learning Teams Productive   52

  Connecting with Your College Teachers   53

  Academic Freedom in the Classroom   54

  CRITICAL THINKING: What Do College Teachers Expect of Students?   54

  When Things Go Wrong Between You and a Teacher   55

    What If You Can't Tolerate a Particular Instructor?   55

    What If You're Not Satisfied with Your Grade?   55

    What If You're Dealing with Sexual Harassment or Sexism?   55

Exercises   56–57

    SEARCH ONLINE! **Internet Exercise 3.1:** Critical Thinking Resources; **Internet Exercise 3.2:**
      Your Teachers'–and Your Own–Responsibilities; **Internet Exercise 3.3:** Finding Faculty
      Email Addresses

    ADDITIONAL EXERCISES **Exercise 3.1:** Reflecting on Arguments; **Exercise 3.2:** The Challenge
      of Classroom Thinking; **Exercise 3.3:** Hard or Easy? **Exercise 3.4:** Gathering Information
      for Decision Making

Your Personal Journal   58

Resources   59

Chapter 4   Listening, Note Taking, and Participating: Getting the Most Out of Classes   63

    SELF-ASSESSMENT: Listening, Note Taking, and Participating   64

Short-Term Memory: Listening and Forgetting   65

Using Your Senses in the Learning Process   65

Before Class: Prepare to Remember   67

During Class: Listen Critically   68

During Class: Take Effective Notes   69

  EXAMINING VALUES   69

  Note Taking in Nonlecture Courses   70

  Comparing and Recopying Notes   71

The Value of Good Class Notes   71
Computer Notes in Class?   72
After Class: Respond, Recite, Review   72
Participating in Class: Speak Up!   74
CRITICAL THINKING   74
SPEAKING OF CAREERS   75
Exercises   75–76
SEARCH ONLINE! **Internet Exercise 4.1:** Study Skills Guides on the Internet; **Internet Exercise 4.2:** Researching Listening and Learning
ADDITIONAL EXERCISES **Exercise 4.1:** Listening and Memory; **Exercise 4.2:** Comparing Notes; **Exercise 4.3:** Memory: Using a Recall Column; **Exercise 4.4:** Applying an Active Listening and Learning System
Your Personal Journal   77
Resources   78

Chapter 5   Reading to Remember: Strategies for Understanding and Retaining Material   79
Previewing   80
SELF-ASSESSMENT: Evaluating Your Reading Strengths and Weaknesses   80
Mapping   81
Alternatives to Mapping   81
Reading Your Textbook   82
Monitoring   83
Marking Your Textbook   83
CRITICAL THINKING: Reading to Question, to Interpret, to Understand   83
Recycle Your Reading   86
Reviewing   86
EXAMINING VALUES   86
Adjusting Your Reading Style   87
SPEAKING OF CAREERS   87
Developing Your Vocabulary   88
Exercises   89–90
SEARCH ONLINE! **Internet Exercise 5.1:** Reading Web Pages Critically; **Internet Exercise 5.2:** Researching How to Read Texts
ADDITIONAL EXERCISES **Exercise 5.1:** Previewing and Creating a Visual Map; **Exercise 5.2:** Preparing to Read, Think, and Mark
Your Personal Journal   91
Resources   92

Chapter 6   Taking Exams and Tests: Be Prepared, Confident, and Calm   93
SELF-ASSESSMENT: Being Ready, Calm, and Confident   94
Academic Honesty   95
Types of Misconduct   95
Reducing the Likelihood of Problems   96
Exams: The Long View   97
EXAMINING VALUES   97
Planning Your Approach   98
Physical Preparation   98
Emotional Preparation   98
SPEAKING OF CAREERS   98
Find Out About the Test   99
Design an Exam Plan   99
Join a Study Group   99
Tutoring and Other Support   99
Now It's Time to Study   99
Review Sheets, Mind Maps, and Other Tools   99
Taking the Test   101
Essay Questions   102
CRITICAL THINKING   103

Multiple-Choice Questions 104
True/False Questions 104
Matching Questions 105
Aids to Memory 105
Remember How You Remember Best 106
Exercises 106–108
SEARCH ONLINE! **Internet Exercise 6.1:** Examining Institutional Values; **Internet Exercise 6.2:** More Memory Devices; **Internet Exercise 6.3:** Researching Good Study Habits
ADDITIONAL EXERCISE **Exercise 6.1:** Designing an Exam Plan
Your Personal Journal 109
Resources 110

Part 3   Know Yourself!   111

Chapter 7   Developing Values: Choosing Unique Pathways   113

SELF-ASSESSMENT: Values 114
Challenges to Personal Values in College 115
Defining Values 115
Another Way of Looking at Values 116
Types of Values 117
Moral Values 117
Aesthetic Values 118
Performance Values 118
Means Values Versus Ends Values 118
Societal Values in Conflict: Value Dualisms 118
Changing Society, Changing Values 120
EXAMINING VALUES 120
Implementing Societal Values 122
Values and the Family 122
Values and the Community 123
Values and Personal Responsibility 123
CRITICAL THINKING 123
Values and You 124
SPEAKING OF CAREERS 124
Exercises 125–126
SEARCH ONLINE! **Internet Exercise 7.1:** Obligations to Society; **Internet Exercise 7.2:** Researching Values
ADDITIONAL EXERCISES **Exercise 7.1:** Friends and Values; **Exercise 7.2:** Evidence of Values
Your Personal Journal 127
Resources 128

Chapter 8   Careers and Courses: Making Sensible Choices   129

SELF-ASSESSMENT: Careers and Majors 130
Careers and the New Economy 131
Finding a Major 131
Where to Go for Help 132
Surviving in a Fast Economy 132
CRITICAL THINKING: Facing Reality 133
Starting Your Career-Planning Program 134
Do's and Don'ts: Factors to Consider 134
Factors Affecting Career Choices 135
Exploring Your Interests 136
Getting Experience 138
SPEAKING OF CAREERS 138
Time for Action 139
Building a Résumé 139
Writing a Cover Letter 141

Your Academic Advisor   142
    Preparing for Your Meeting   143
    Is Your Advisor/Counselor Right for You?   143
Your College Catalog   144
    Publication Date and General Information   144
    General Academic Regulations   144
    Academic Programs   144
    EXAMINING VALUES   144
Exercises   145–146
    SEARCH ONLINE! **Internet Exercise 8.1:** Mission and Vision; **Internet Exercise 8.2:** Internet
        Career Resources; **Internet Exercise 8.3:** Researching Courses and Careers
    ADDITIONAL EXERCISE **Exercise 8.1:** What Are Your Life Goals?
Your Personal Journal   147
Resources   148

**Chapter 9   Creating Diverse Relationships: All Kinds of People, All Kinds
    of Ideas   149**

    SELF-ASSESSMENT: Relationships and Diversity   150
Race, Ethnic Groups, and Culture   151
    CRITICAL THINKING   151
    The Concept of Race on Campus   152
The Importance of Relationships   153
Dating and Mating   153
    Developing a Relationship   154
    Off Limits!   154
    Becoming Intimate   154
    Getting Serious   155
    Breaking Up   155
Married Life in College   156
You and Your Parents   156
Finding Diverse Friends   157
    Gays and Lesbians   157
    Returning Students   158
    Students with Disabilities   159
Finding Meaningful Relationships   159
    Long-Distance Relationships   159
    Electronic Relationships   159
    EXAMINING VALUES   160
Roommates   160
On-Campus Involvement   160
Off-Campus Involvement   161
    Co-op Programs   161
    Service Learning Opportunities   161
Discrimination and Prejudice on College Campuses   161
    SPEAKING OF CAREERS   162
Exercises   163–166
    SEARCH ONLINE! **Internet Exercise 9.1:** Diversity in the Population and on Campus; **Internet
        Exercise 9.2:** Questions about Homosexuality; **Internet Exercise 9.3:** Looking for Love;
        Internet Exercise 9.4: Researching Relationships and Diversity
    ADDITIONAL EXERCISES **Exercise 9.1:** Sharing Your Background; **Exercise 9.2:** Creating
        Common Ground; **Exercise 9.3:** Diversity on Your Campus; **Exercise 9.4:** Balancing
        Relationships and College; **Exercise 9.5:** Student-Parent Gripes
Your Personal Journal   167
Resources   168

Chapter 10   Sex and Alcohol: Making Responsible Choices   169

    SELF-ASSESSMENT: Evaluating Your Sexual Health and Your Use of Alcohol   170
Sexual Decision Making   171
Birth Control   171
    CRITICAL THINKING   175

Sexually Transmitted Infections (STIs)   175
    Chlamydia   175
    Human Papilloma Virus (HPV)   175
    Gonorrhea   176
    Herpes   176
    Hepatitis B   176
    Hepatitis C   177
    HIV/AIDS   177
Options for Safer Sex   178
    Celibacy   178
    Abstinence   178
    Masturbation   178
    Monogamy   178
    Condoms   178
    SELECTING A CONDOM   179
Unhealthy Relationships   179
    Intimate Partner Violence   179
        How to Tell If Your Relationship Is Abusive   180
        What to Do If Your Relationship Is Abusive   180
    Sexual Assault   180
    Relationships with Teachers   181
Using Alcohol and Other Drugs   181
Why College Students Drink   182
    Social Learning   182
        Parents   182
        Mass Media   182
        Peers   183
    Drinking to Feel Good or Not to Feel Bad   183
Myths Versus Realities of Student Drinking   183
    Why Students Overestimate Peer Drinking   184
    Consequences of Overestimating Peer Drinking   184
    EXAMINING VALUES: Alcohol and Other Drugs   185
Drinking and Blood Alcohol Content   185
Alcohol and Behavior   186
    Warning Signs, Saving Lives   187
    Death by Alcohol   187
Heavy Drinking: The Danger Zone   187
Consequences for All   189
Long-Term Effects of Drinking   190
    SPEAKING OF CAREERS   191
Making Decisions, Finding Help   192
Exercises   192–196
    SEARCH ONLINE! **Internet Exercise 10.1:** Getting Confidential Information; **Internet Exercise 10.2:** Gathering Accurate Information About STIs; **Internet Exercise 10.3:** The Core Alcohol and Drug Survey
    ADDITIONAL EXERCISES **Exercise 10.1:** Personal Reflections on Sexuality; **Exercise 10.2:** What's Your Decision?; **Exercise 10.3:** What's "Normal"?; **Exercise 10.7:** Survey of Alcohol Usage; **Exercise 10.8:** A Safe Stress Antidote. Exercises 10.4, 10.5, and 10.6 are on the CD-ROM.
Your Personal Journal   197
Resources   198

Appendix: Beginning College in Uncertain Times   201

Suggestions for Further Reading   215

Index/Glossary   221

On the CD-ROM

    Taking Online Courses: Succeeding Through Web-Based Learning
    Managing Your Money: Your Checkbook to Success

Preface to Students and Their Instructors

To Students: Best wishes on this journey, one of life's most important. You can and will achieve success—in college and in life— if you diligently practice the advice and skills within these covers. And when a task seems impossible, stop what you're doing, try to relax for a moment, and keep repeating, "If everyone else can do it, so can I." And we'll bet you can.
—John N. Gardner and A. Jerome Jewler

Just as first-year students are forever learning new ways to succeed, we as dedicated textbook authors are forever discovering new ways to help them. Each of us had shaky beginnings in college, yet by using common sense and relying on the advice of others, we made it. Not once during our college years did we realize what a powerful effect those college years would have on the rest of our lives—or on the lives of thousands of other students.

As founders and dedicated supporters of the First-Year Experience, we always have kept two ideas foremost in our minds:

- We believe that every student admitted to college possesses the ability to succeed if he or she has the will and the motivation to follow the advice in this book.
- As educators, we feel responsible for serving the unique needs of individual students by covering virtually every facet of first-year development in as many ways as possible.

This new concise media edition of *Your College Experience* continues to focus on these vital goals. We have received tremendous assistance in this major revision from the input of instructors who have used this text before, reviewers, our Wadsworth editorial staff, survey respondents who have shared their insights, new experts who assisted us in the preparation of many of these chapters, and of course, students.

Enhanced Strategies for Success

Research at the National Resource Center for the First-Year Experience and Students in Transition at the University of South Carolina, at the Policy Center for the First Year of college, and at other institutions continues to show that students are more likely to succeed if they follow the strategies in this text. These "Strategies for Success" touch all chapters. We introduce them in Chapter 1, in a summary chart for student reference on the inside front cover of this book, and in the accompanying CD-ROM. In this new edition, these 30 strategies are grouped into three categories to help clarify the major concepts of this book:

Take Charge of Learning! Among the most important things you must learn in college is how to manage time to avoid cramming for exams, getting too little sleep, or studying day and night with no fun breaks. Without planning, college can turn into a frightening maze of due dates that creep up too soon, missed classes, and sheer exhaustion. You will also be introduced to our 30 "Strategies for Success."

Hone Your Skills! You will discover more efficient and effective ways to read a text, take notes, study, and appreciate the value of study groups. We'll help you unleash your critical thinking skills that you may not have been aware of, and learn to communicate those thoughts in writing that is more concise and sharply focused.

Active participation is one of the key ingredients for taking charge of learning and of life. When you proudly speak up in class, learning is more exciting and productive for everyone—even your instructor!

Know Yourself! Uh … don't you already know yourself? But what about developing your potential? What about doing things to stay healthy? What about developing a set of personal values you can proudly share with others? What about those "hot" topics: sex and alcohol? These are part of this book, too. It is also critical in college to establish and maintain connections. You will discover the numerous benefits of participating in campus life, studying with a group, meeting with teachers outside of class, and choosing a good advisor or counselor.

Other New Features of This Edition

Unified Voice

In this major revision, we have consolidated the contributions of many experts from around the country into a single voice. One great strength of *Your College Experience* has always been its reliance on a multitude of experts whose knowledge comes from highly specialized studies in their particular fields. At the same time, the editors have worked diligently to ensure that this book is written for its intended audience.

Customized Learning with a CD-ROM Boost

The interactive CD-ROM accompanying this book represents a whole new generation in interactive learning. For the first time, the *Your College Experience* CD-ROM includes exercises and readings not found in your book. Follow the references in each chapter to access these CD-ROM features. The CD-ROM also includes tests for each chapter. Links to InfoTrac College Edition and additional Internet resources make this CD-ROM a priceless adjunct to this text.

New Material on Succeeding in Online Courses

Your CD-ROM also includes new appendixes on taking online courses and managing your money. The appendix on taking online courses may help you determine whether online education is the best choice for you.

Updated Material Throughout the Chapters

- **Critical Thinking and Active Learning.** An entire chapter that presents new information on these key topics.
- **Study Skills.** Revised chapters on time management, listening and learning, reading textbooks and making the grade.
- Extensively revised chapters on courses and careers, diversity, values, alcohol and sex, and managing money.

New Chapter Features

- **Self Assessment.** Students complete an inventory prior to reading each chapter, then are asked to return to the inventory when they finish the chapter to see if they would answer any items differently.
- **Examining Values.** We believe that the values that students bring to college and those they develop during college are the basis for lifetime behaviors. The chapter on values is enhanced throughout the text by a new chapter feature that gives students continuing challenges about how to approach both personal and academic decisions.
- **Critical Thinking.** Just as the "Examining Values" feature seeks to heighten awareness of values, so the new "Critical Thinking" feature in each chapter poses a situation related to the topic of the chapter and asks students to work toward a solution using critical thinking.
- **Speaking of Careers.** We know that most college students are concerned about how their education will prepare them for the world of work. In "Speaking of Careers" we suggest how the knowledge in each chapter will help them long after they have bid farewell to campus.

Collaborative Learning

Although individuals must be able to make it on their own, we know how essential it is to learn to work together. One sees collaboration in business as well as in colleges and universities. Studying with one other person or with a small group seems to benefit everyone who participates. Backed by the research of collaborative learning specialist Joseph Cuseo of Marymount College, this edition provides an ample supply of exercises and tips to encourage students to study and learn together.

Internet Connections

Each chapter contains Internet exercises, one of which uses the InfoTrac College Edition that may have come with this text.

Additional Exercises

At the conclusion of each chapter we've included exercises for individuals and teams. Many engage students in writing and critical thinking. And remember—more exercises are on the CD-ROM.

Teaching Aids for Instructors

Annotated Instructor's Edition of Your College Experience, Concise Media Edition, Fifth Edition

0534607608

Full textbook including annotations and suggestions for teaching written by the authors. Also features a Resource Integration Guide that correlates Wadsworth teaching resources and ancillary product offerings with individual chapter topics to simplify the process of using additional materials.

Instructor's Resource Suite: Manual and CD-ROM for Your College Experience: Strategies for Success, Concise Media Edition, Fifth Edition

0534607624

Each chapter of this flexible and unique Instructor's Manual includes additional exercises, test questions, tips on teaching, a list of common concerns of first-year students and a case study relevant to the topics covered. Also includes a variety of additional suggestions for activities and addresses the concerns of first-time First-Year Seminar instructors. Available in both print and CD-ROM format, the Instructor's Resource Manual Suite contains Microsoft PowerPoint slides and CNN video clips.

Your College Experience: Strategies for Success, Concise Media Edition, Fifth Edition Unbound Version

0534607632

Customize YOUR COLLEGE EXPERIENCE with your own campus-specific materials using this three-hole punch version of the text. This version is unbound and comes with a front and back cover with each page three-hole punched for easy customization.

Examview Computerized Test Bank for Your College Experience: Strategies for Success, Concise Media Edition, Fifth Edition

0534607667

Examview enhances the range or assessment and tutorial activities by providing a way to quickly create and customize tests and quizzes. The Examview test generator offers up to 250 questions made up of twelve different question types.

WebTutor on Web CT for Your College Experience: Strategies for Success, Concise Media Edition, Fifth Edition

0534607640

WebTutor on Blackboard for Your College Experience: Strategies for Success, Concise Media Edition, Fifth Edition

0534607659

A content-rich Web-based teaching and learning tool. Use WebTutor to post syllabi, set up threaded discussions, track student progress on quizzes and hold virtual office hours. WebTutor is easily customizable to specific course needs. In addition to course management capabilities, WebTutor contains an array of exercises, activities, electronic journal and additional resources.

CNN Today: College Success Video Series 2004 Edition

0534541429

CNN Today: College Success Video Series 2003 Edition

0534541410

CNN Today: College Success Video Series 2002 Edition

0534541402

CNN Today: College Success Video Series 2001 Edition

0534537995

Riveting clips from CNN on college success topics to launch lectures and stimulate discussion. Integrate the newsgathering and programming power of CNN into the classroom to show students the relevance of course topics to their lives. Organized by topics covered in a typical course, these videos are divided into short segment—perfect for introducing key concepts. Ask your Thomson/Wadsworth representative for more information.

College Success Films for the Humanities Series

A collection of topical videos chosen because of their relevance to topics taught in First-Year Seminar and College Success courses. Includes videos on achieving academic success, communication, careers, drugs and alcohol and making healthy choices. Ask your Thomson/Wadsworth representative for more information.

Wadsworth Study Skills Video, Volume 1: Improving Your Grades

0534549837

Features students talking to other students about issues and skills that contribute to their success.

Wadsworth Study Skills Video, Volume 2: Lectures for Note Taking Practice

0534549845

Features a series of college lectures that provide students with the opportunity to practice their note taking skills.

World of Diversity Videos

Volume I 0534549837, Volume 2 0534549845

This powerful two-video set addresses communication and conflict resolution between cultures. Ask your Thomson/Wadsworth representative for more information.

Wadsworth College Success Transparency Masters

0534574173

The Wadsworth College Success Transparency Master booklet is a collection of 50 transparency masters covering a wide range of topics frequently referenced in First-Year Seminar courses. Subjects covered include College Success Basics, Time Management, Money Management, Learning Styles, Study Skills, Critical Thinking, Technology, Test-Taking, and Wellness. This fully customizable package is also available as a PowerPoint download on the College Success Web site, www.success.wadsworth.com.

Critical Thinking: Building the Basics, Second Edition

0534599761

By Walter, Knudsvig, and Smith. Over one hundred pages of valuable guidance for improving learning through critical thinking. Advises students on how to apply critical thinking strategies to all of their textbooks and courses.

Case Studies for First-Year Experience Students

0534262775

By John Riesen, John Szarlan, and Suman Singha. A collection of varied case studies that present scenarios that first-year students of all ages and backgrounds are likely to face. Each case includes a set of individual and group discussion questions that challenge students to consider how they would react in similar situations. The case study approach is a proven technique that engages students in their own learning. Additional case studies are also available for custom publishing.

Fifty Ways to Leave Your Lectern

0534262783

By Constance Staley. This book is based on Staley's popular College Success workshop for instructors and her own experience designing and teaching the First-Year Seminar. Includes fifty classroom tested activities and icebreakers that creatively address academic topics and personal decision-making in fun and engaging ways.

Teaching College Success

0534536409

By Constance Staley. An all-inclusive package that contains everything you need to create your own tailored training program for college success instructors. Provides both information on the history and practice of teaching college success seminars and experiential activities to try with students. Contains an extensive array of print resources and dynamic PowerPoint presentations.

Student Resources

Interactive CD-ROM to accompany Your College Experience: Strategies for Success, Concise Media Edition, Fifth Edition

0534607616

Automatically packaged with every copy of the book. The interactive CD-ROM is newly designed, easy to use, and free with every copy of the book. This updated resource contains additional text, two bonus chapters on Money Management and Taking Online Courses, self assessments, electronic versions of exercises and additional exercises, and a Test Your Knowledge interactive quiz for each topic covered in the book. Also contains an E-resources section and an electronic journal for each chapter that encourage students to reflect on their progress and create their own set of campus-specific personal resources. The CD-ROM also features the popular Franklin-Covey Mission Statement Builder activity.

College Success Factors Index

Hosted on the Wadsworth College Success home page, this exclusive student assessment tool measures eight indices that can affect student adjustment to college life. An excellent pre- and post-test for incoming first-year students, this online assessment provides a way for individual instructors to tailor their course topics to the needs of the students. The data collected can also be applied to longitudinal studies of College Success and First-Year Seminars on a campus-wide level. Go to www.success.wadsworth.com for a link to the College Success Factors Index Web site. Also, ask your Thomson/Wadsworth representative for information on bundling the College Success Factors Index with your textbook at minimal charge.

College Success Agenda Planner

A spiral-bound calendar designed for first-year college students. Features 18-month coverage, unique design, and plenty of room for students to record their academic and personal commitments and schedule. A great way to encourage time management skills, this planner can be offered as a bundle with your textbook. Ask your Thomson/Wadsworth representative for information on bundling the College Success Agenda Planner with your textbook at minimal charge.

Acknowledgments

Although this text speaks through the voices of its two editors, it represents major contributions from many others. We gratefully acknowledge those contributions and thank these individuals whose special expertise has made it possible to introduce new college students to "their college experience" through the holistic approach we deeply believe in.

We would like to thank Joseph Cuseo for his thoughts on collaborative learning, Daniel J. Kurland for useful and imaginative Internet exercises, and Vincent Tinto, Syracuse University, for his pioneering research on leaving college.

Special thanks also to reviewers whose wisdom and suggestions guided the creation of this text: Marie Carrese, York College; Dot Clark, Montgomery County Community College; Greg Clary, Clarion University; Cheryl Evans, Northwest Oklahoma State; Charles R. Frederick, Jr., Indiana University, Bloomington; Laura Goppold, Central Piedmont Community College; Patty Hattaway, Florida State University; Hollace R. Hubbard, Lander University; Bryan Jack, St. Louis Community College, Meramec; Karen Kane, Hawaii Community College; Jane Kavanaugh, Vincennes University; Kelly Lock, Missouri Western State College; Frederick H. Lorensen, Duquesne University; Barbara Markley, University of Alaska, Anchorage; Jean Martin, Northwestern State University; Maritza Martinez, University at Albany, SUNY; Mary McNerney, Cottey College; Glenn Ricci, Lake Sumter Community College; Charlie Riley, University of Pittsburgh; Denise Rode, Northern Illinois University; Mary Scott, North Carolina Central University; Rita Sheldon, Palm Beach Community College; Karen A. Siska, Columbia State Community College; Kim Smokowski, Bergen Community College; Harvey Solganick, LeTourneau University; Brent Stewart, The Citadel; Michelle Teasley, Columbus State Community College; Mary Walz-Chojnacki, University of Wisconsin, Milwaukee; and Donald Williams, Grand Valley State University.

Finally, all this could not have happened without the Wadsworth team that supported our text, guided us through the writing and production, and worked at least as hard as we did to make *Your College Experience* one of the most popular texts in its field. We thank Kirsten Markson, developmental editor on this project, for her insight and enthusiasm. Our special thanks to Susan Badger, President; Sean Wakely, Senior Vice President and Editorial Director; Annie Mitchell, Manager, College Success; Elana Dolberg, Director of Marketing; Kirsten Markson, Assistant Editor for College Success; Trudy Brown, Senior Project Manager, Editorial Production; Stephen Rapley, Creative Director; Preston Thomas, Art Director; Cecile Joyner/The Cooper Company, Production; Paul Uhl and Delgado Design, Designers; Jennifer Gordon, Copy Editor; Barbara Britton, Senior Print/Media Buyer; and Bob Kauser, Permissions Manager.

We also want to thank Cynthia Sanner, Director of Technology Product Development; Barry Connolly, Technology Project Manager; Becky Stovall, Executive Producer; Carolyn Kuhn/Software Mart, Inc.; Tom Thackrey/Willow Glen Productions; Deborah Thackrey/Willow Glen Productions; Margaret Parks, Executive Director, Advertising and MarCom; Stacey Purviance, Advertising Project Manager; Jean Thompson/Two Chicks Marketing; Constance Staley, Workshop Facilitator; and Ilana Sims, Workshop Coordinator and College Success Consultant.

John N. Gardner   A. Jerome Jewler

Foreword to the Instructor

By Vincent Tinto
DISTINGUISHED UNIVERSITY PROFESSOR
SYRACUSE UNIVERSITY

I have been involved as a researcher and consultant in studies of student retention and retention programs for over 30 years. In that time, I have come to learn four important lessons about the character of successful retention strategies.

First, retention is the result of successful education. Students who learn, stay.

Second, becoming a successful learner takes time and skills, both academic and social. It is not easy, but it is doable.

Third, environment matters. Students who are involved, both academically and socially, are not only more likely to stay, but are more likely to learn while staying.

Fourth, the first year of college is a critical period for student learning and persistence. It is a period of transition and adjustment, both academically and socially, during which students acquire important skills that furnish the foundation for subsequent learning. It is a period when involvement matters most, and when learning is most readily shaped by educational programs designed to provide students with learning experiences that are motivating, challenging, and involving.

In this regard, I have also discovered that few individuals are more qualified to speak to the needs of new students and the first-year experience than Professors John Gardner and Jerry Jewler. They have been working with new students and with faculty who teach those students for more than 30 years. In that time, they have acquired knowledge that few can match of what works and what doesn't.

That knowledge is contained within the pages of this book and in the programs their work has inspired. The first section, **Take Charge of Learning!,** introduces students to the goal-setting process and the value of a liberal education, and provides them with a set of "strategies for success" that are developed subsequently throughout the book. It then focuses on time management, one of the most critical skills for college success, and discusses various learning styles and how to become familiar with how you learn best.

In the next section, **Hone Your Skills!,** you'll discover how to bring your study skills up to college level. Critical thinking, writing, taking notes, reading textbooks, preparing for exams, team learning, and conducting research are all covered within the chapters of this section.

Next, **Know Yourself!** looks at the more personal side of college success. You'll explore courses and careers, academic advisors or counselors, relationships with friends and family, and the value of getting involved on campus. You'll also learn how becoming actively involved with students of diverse backgrounds can be an education in itself. Finally, you'll read about sexuality and alcohol and other drugs.

Each chapter opens with a self-assessment tool and includes values, critical thinking, and careers features. At the end of each chapter are Internet exercises (Search Online!), including one calling for the use of InfoTrac® College Edition, plus additional exercises based on active and collaborative learning strategies that instructors may assign at will. Annotations in the Annotated Instructor's Edition suggest other activities for classroom use and the Instructor's Resource Manual provides additional ideas for teaching each chapter of the book.

I can't imagine a more comprehensive, yet concise, introduction to the college experience. So, as I would recommend to students, let me also recommend that you take Gardner and Jewler's advice seriously and use it as a guide to your own thinking about the education of new students on your campus. As I have found in my own institution, where I teach our version of the first-year seminar, their advice works.

Take Charge of Learning!

Strategies for Success

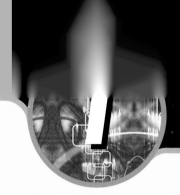

TAKE CHARGE OF LEARNING!

- Show up for class
- Have work done on time
- Set up a daily schedule
- If full-time student, limit work week to 15 hours; work on campus if possible
- If stressed, enroll part-time
- Assess how you learn best

HONE YOUR SKILLS!

- Improve your reading, note taking, and study habits
- Improve your writing
- Develop critical thinking skills
- Participate in class
- Practice giving presentations
- Learn how to remember more from every class
- Learn from criticism
- Choose instructors who favor active learning
- Study with a group
- Take workshops on how to study
- Get to know your campus library and other information sources
- Embrace new technologies

KNOW YOURSELF!

- Get to know at least one person on campus who cares about you
- Get involved in campus activities
- Learn about campus helping resources
- Meet with your instructors
- Find a great academic advisor or counselor
- Visit your campus career center
- Take advantage of minority support services
- Enlist support of your spouse, partner, or family
- Take your health seriously
- Have realistic expectations
- Learn how to be assertive, yet tactful
- Be proud of your heritage

Chapter 1

Time Management

and Thirty Strategies for College Success

PhotoDisc

IN THIS CHAPTER, YOU WILL LEARN

- Thirty valuable strategies for college success
- Why some students graduate and others don't
- The impact of college on your future earnings
- The advantages of a liberal education
- How to set your own goals for success
- How to prioritize your use of time
- How to use a daily planner
- How to organize your day, your week, your school term

The section on time management was written with the expert assistance of Jeanne L. Higbee, University of Minnesota

find your way

*A*t last I'm in college! Standing in line for 2 hours, spending more than a hundred dollars for two books. Wondering who'll tell me what to do and when to do it. Wondering how I'm going to keep track of my life!"

Welcome to college! And congratulations. The fact that you're here means you have met the admission standards for your campus and should have no trouble passing your classes and earning your degree. Yet so many entering students drop out or flunk out, and the highest dropout rate occurs during the first year.

Usually, dropping out has little to do with how smart you are. What then? One student was so intimidated by the social activities the school arranged for new students that she left before the first day of classes. Another student wanted to meet other students so much that he went out every night and never cracked a book. And the guy who maxed out his credit card the first week of the term had no money for food. Then there are those who lack clear goals for college or can't manage their time or never learned how to study for an exam or research a topic.

This book is a game plan for avoiding such pitfalls. A package of strategies that, if followed, can help you achieve your academic goals. And since you're going to be exercising your memory constantly in college, especially around exam time, begin now by memorizing the following three key strategies. One way to do this is to focus on the key words "charge," "skills," and "yourself." Try it. Read the list three times, close the book, and recite the three main strategies:

SELF-ASSESSMENT: TIME AND SUCCESS

Place a check mark in front of every strategy on the next few pages that will be challenging for you. Later in this course, as you master each strategy, come back and convert the check marks to Xs. By the time you complete this book, you will have learned how to master these strategies. Now, take a few moments to reflect on yourself and your past experiences with time. Then write a few paragraphs on how you use time, using these questions as guidelines:

- What are my personal views on time?

- How conscious am I of time passing? Do I always wear a watch?

- How have my views on time been influenced by my family, culture, lifestyle, gender, age, and other factors?

- Am I punctual or do I procrastinate? Can I concentrate or am I easily distracted? Do I try to control time or does it seem to control me?

- Am I early, prompt, or late to class, appointments, or meetings? Do I often skip class or miss appointments?

- How do I feel when someone wastes my time? How about when I am the one wasting time?

- Do I complete my assignments early, on time, or late?

Less Todd/Photo courtesy of Duke University

Take Charge of Learning!

Hone Your Skills!

Know Yourself!

In a moment, you will encounter a number of specific suggestions for each of these major strategies. Research has confirmed that, the more of them you master, the greater the chance you'll excel in college.

Later in the chapter we'll take you through what may be the most important strategy of all: managing your time wisely. Everything in life depends on time. Waking in time to get to class or work. Going to sleep on time so you'll wake on time. Being in class on time. Keeping an appointment on time. Never forgetting where you're supposed to be at a certain time. And so forth.

Take Charge of Learning!

1. **Show up for class.** Be there daily. When you're not there, you're missing something. You're also sending your instructor a message that you don't care. If you know you are going to miss class because of an appointment, sickness, or an emergency, contact your instructor as soon as possible and certainly before the next class meeting.

2. **Have work done on time.** Not only may you face a grade penalty if you don't, you will most certainly irritate your teachers if you are perpetually late with assignments. Some instructors have a policy of not accepting late work or penalizing you for it. Ask to be certain. If your work is late because of illness or an emergency, let your instructor know. It may help.

We highly recommend some get-acquainted activities the first day of class to lay the foundation for interaction and active learning. For example, ask students to find someone they don't know, pair up with them, and interview them for 5–8 minutes (their name, hometown, college major, career thoughts, etc.). Then have groups introduce one another to the whole class. At the close of the first class, ask for written anonymous feedback about the class. Ask them to include what they would like to learn from the class, too.

Ask students how many of these strategies they practiced in high school and how many represent new ways of behaving in college. Have them write down the strategies that are most important to them and explain why. Later, share what the class as a whole has chosen.

3. **Set up a daily schedule.** And stick to it. Learning how to manage your time can make the difference between success and frustration. Get a portable appointment calendar from your campus bookstore this week and always keep it handy.

4. **If you are a full-time student, limit your work week to 15 hours.** Most students begin a downhill slide after that. Need more money? Consult a financial aid officer. If you must work, look for a job on campus. Students who do and who work less than 15 hours have a higher graduation rate than those who work off campus and/or more than 15 hours.

5. **If stressed, enroll part-time.** Adjust the number of courses you're taking to reduce your stress. You're likely to do better in all classes.

6. **Assess how you learn best.** Explore learning style theory (Chapter 2), which suggests that we are all individuals with differing approaches to the world around us, the information we receive, the decisions we make, and the way we choose to live and to learn. Perhaps you'll understand why you hate math and love English, while your best friend is just the opposite.

Hone Your Skills!

Underscore the importance of planning by insisting that each student create a "week at a glance" calendar or a personal organizer and keep it current. Check periodically to see if students are tracking their deadlines, appointments, and so forth.

7. **Improve your reading, note taking, and study habits.** Starting with a time management plan, make every minute of every day count. Master the most effective methods for reading textbooks, listening, and taking notes in class, studying for exams, and using information sources on campus. If your campus has an academic skills center, visit it whenever you need help.

8. **Improve your writing.** Instructors—and employers—want people who can think *and* write. Learn to rehearse your thoughts, put them on paper, and revise them till they are clear, concise, and coherent. The more you write, the better you'll write—and the more you'll want to write.

9. **Develop critical thinking skills.** Ask why. Seek dependable information to prove your point. Look for unusual solutions to ordinary problems. Never believe things are either right or wrong, and never accept something as fact simply because you found it on the Internet or someone tells you it's true. And don't be swayed by your emotions when your logical thinking powers are at work.

10. **Participate in class.** Research indicates that students who involve themselves in class discussions usually remember more about the discussion than students who do not. As a result, they usually enjoy the class more and earn higher grades.

11. **Practice giving presentations.** This is another way to stay active in class and a skill most of you will be using for the rest of your lives. There *is* a way to overcome stage fright! Some actors do it before every performance.

12. **Learn how to remember more from every class.** Effective listening not only results in better notes but also helps you improve memory techniques, which is important as exams approach.

13. **Learn from criticism.** Criticism can be healthy. And helpful. It's how we all learn. If you get a low grade, ask to meet with your instructor to discuss what you should do to improve your work.

14. **Choose instructors who favor active learning.** The more you're asked to participate in class and to work in groups, the more you'll enjoy learning and the better you'll learn. Ask upper-class students who these instructors are.

15. **Study with a group.** Research shows that students who collaborate in study groups often earn the highest grades and survive college with fewer academic problems.

16. **Take workshops on how to study,** especially if you've been out of school for a while. Even after reviewing the study skills in this book, you may decide to

take a comprehensive study skills course. You also may need to review basic math or writing skills. Fortunately, relearning something is much easier than learning new material.

17. **Get to know your campus library and other information sources.** That means not only knowing how to do a conventional library search but getting comfortable with databases and the World Wide Web.

18. **Embrace new technologies.** If you don't already know, ask how to use word processors, databases, and spreadsheets; do a computerized library search; access journals online; and send and receive email. The computer skills you develop in college will prove valuable when you are employed.

Know Yourself!

19. **Get to know at least one person on campus who cares about you.** It might be the teacher of this course, some other instructor, your academic advisor, someone at the counseling or career center, an advisor to a student organization, or an older student. You may have to take the initiative to establish this relationship, but it will be worth it.

20. **Get involved in campus activities.** Check out the opportunities at the student activities office. Work for the campus newspaper or radio station. Join a club or support group. Play intramural sports. Most campus organizations crave newcomers—you're their lifeblood.

21. **Learn about campus helping resources.** Find out where they are. Academic and personal support services are usually free and confidential. Successful students use them.

22. **Meet with your instructors.** Students who do this tend to stay in college longer. Your instructors are required to have office hours, and they expect you to visit.

23. **Find a great academic advisor or counselor.** Be sure he or she is someone you can turn to for both academic and personal guidance and support.

24. **Visit your campus career center.** A career counselor can help you learn more about your academic major or find another major that suits you better. If you can't decide on a major immediately, remember that many first-year students are in the same boat. Discuss your options.

25. **Take advantage of minority support services.** If you are a minority student, find out if your campus has centers for minority students. Pay a visit and introduce yourself. Take advantage of mentoring programs such a center might offer.

26. **Enlist the support of your spouse, partner, or family.** If you are a returning student, you may need to adjust household routines and duties. Let others know when you need extra time to study. A supportive partner is a great ally, but a nonsupportive partner can threaten your success in college. If your partner feels threatened and tries to undermine what you are doing, sit down and talk it over, or seek counseling.

27. **Take your health seriously.** How much sleep you get, what you eat, whether you exercise, how stressed you are, and what decisions you make about drugs, alcohol, and sex all affect your well-being and how well you will do in classes. Your counseling center can help.

28. **Have realistic expectations.** At first you may be disappointed in the grades you make, but remember that college is a new experience, and things can, and probably will, improve. Thousands of other students have faced the same uncertainties you may be facing. Hang onto that positive attitude. It makes a difference.

These strategies are the heart and soul of this book. Ask students if they can define active learning, critical thinking, and learning style. Have them evaluate their writing and study skills for you.

These skills take a concerted effort on the part of the student since, generally, they won't be taught in most classes. Ask students to choose one or two skills they are most interested in honing and have them state how and when they plan to do so.

29. **Learn how to be assertive, yet tactful**. If you don't, others may walk all over you. If it's difficult for you to stand up for yourself, take assertiveness training. Your counseling center probably offers workshops that can teach you to stand up for your rights in a way that respects the rights of others.

30. **Be proud of your heritage**. No matter what your heritage, you may hear ugly remarks and witness or be the target of bigotry caused by ignorance or fear. Stand tall. Be proud. Refuse to tolerate disrespect. And remember that most of the college population embraces tolerance.

If you memorized the three major strategies, challenge yourself now to learn all of the strategies listed. Here's how: Take one of the three groups and learn it well, using the key-word idea suggested earlier. Then proceed to the next group and do the same. When you know that one, repeat the first and the second. Then go on to the third and continue the process. You may be amazed at how easy it is to remember information!

First-Year Questions of Freedom and Commitment

Of those who leave college during their first year, the majority are in good academic standing.

What is it, then, that causes so many new students to drop out of college? For those fresh out of high school, the overriding problem involves newfound freedom. No more will teachers tell you exactly what, how, or when to study. If you live on campus, your parents can't wake you in the morning, see that you eat properly and get enough sleep, monitor whether or how well you do your homework, or remind you to allow enough time to get to school. In almost every aspect of your life, it suddenly all depends on you.

For returning students, the opposite is true: a daunting lack of freedom. Working, caring for a family, and meeting other adult commitments and responsibilities compete for the time and attention it takes to do your best or even simply to persist in college. And the easiest thing to do is quit.

Whichever problem you are facing, what will motivate you to persist? And what about the enormous investment of time and money that getting a college degree requires? Will it all be worth it?

At most campuses offering courses such as the one you're taking, the first-year dropout rate has fallen, perhaps in part because students have found an outlet for expressing their concerns to others:

- This is the first time someone has not been there to tell me I had to do something. Will I be able to handle all this freedom?
- I've never been away from home before, and I don't know anybody. How am I going to make friends?
- I have responsibilities at home. Can I get through college and still manage to take care of my family?
- As a minority student on a primarily White campus, will I be in for some unpleasant surprises?
- Maybe college will be too difficult for me. I hear college teachers are more demanding than high school teachers.
- Not only do I miss being at home, but I hope I won't disappoint my family.
- Will I be tempted to cut corners, maybe even cheat?
- Will I like my roommate? What if he/she is from a different culture?
- I wouldn't want my family to sacrifice this much and then see me fail.
- Maybe I'm the only one who's feeling like this. Maybe everyone else is just smarter than I am.

Discuss helping resources in the context of the larger topic of assistance-seeking behavior—something many high school students have avoided, especially males. Remind them that (a) in college, the most able students are often the ones who seek help; (b) most of these services are at no additional cost and represent a healthy savings compared to outside providers; (c) all services are confidential; and (d) seeking help is not a form of weakness.

**SEE EXERCISE 1.1
SOLVING A PROBLEM**

Remind students that it all boils down to how they take care of their physical and emotional health, how good they feel about themselves, how realistically they set goals for the future.

Ask students to call out the different freedoms they face in college. Then divide them into small groups and have them reach consensus on which freedoms may pose the greatest challenges for college students. Make sure students understand the difference between achieving consensus by allowing all members to resolve their differences versus a simple majority vote, which often tends to ignore the concerns of the minority.

- Looking around class makes me feel so old! Will I be able to keep up at my age?
- Will some teachers be biased against students of my culture?

This book will help you find many of the answers to such questions. Each chapter will take you one step closer to your goal of making it through college. Why did you choose to go to college in the first place? Was it because everyone else was going? Was it to make enough money to support a family or to start a new midlife career? No matter your reason, it resulted from your own life experiences and your personal values system, a system that may be about to undergo major changes.

SEE "BETTER GRADES = BETTER LEARNING?"

Those Who Start and Those Who Finish

In 1900 fewer than 2 percent of Americans of traditional college age attended college. In the 21st century, new technologies and the information explosion are changing the workplace so drastically that few people can support themselves and their families adequately without some education beyond high school.

Today approximately 70 percent of high school graduates go on to college, with more than 4000 colleges serving more than 14.8 million students. About one-third of those enrolling in college right after high school begin in two-year institutions. Adult students are also enrolling in record numbers, with more than 37 percent of college students over age 25.

Half a century ago, most college students were White males. Today, women outnumber men, "minorities" are making steady gains in numbers (and in some colleges are now the majority), and college has become financially possible for nearly everyone, regardless of income.

That's the bright side. The not-so-good side is that 40 percent of students who start in four-year programs never finish their degrees. In two-year colleges, half or more of the entering class will drop out by the end of the first year.

SEE INTERNET EXERCISE 1.1 USING THE *DIGEST OF EDUCATION STATISTICS* ONLINE

Education, Careers, and Income

Facing a job market that places a high premium on education and technology, men and women with only a high school education will make less than their contemporaries who earn college degrees.

The gap in earnings from high school to college is widening. In 1996, men with college degrees were earning an average of one-and-a-half times the salary of high school graduates; in 1970, the difference was only one-and-a-quarter times as much. In 1999–2000 women with college degrees were earning nearly twice as much as women with high school diplomas ($32,145 versus. $16,770). One probable reason for the growing disparity is the sudden spurt of jobs in technology and information.

SEE EXERCISE 1.2 FOCUSING ON YOUR CONCERNS

Tell your students when and why your campus started its college success course. In so doing, you have an opportunity to explain the partnership between faculty and student services and how each helps new students succeed in college. If you did not take such a course, tell them why and what resulted.

Critical Thinking

Successful Strategies

Go back over the list of strategies and choose up to eight of them that you can identify with. In an essay, explain what influences or events in your life caused these strategies to be important to you, and how far along you believe you are in mastering each strategy.

Examining Values

First-year students are often startled at the diversity of personal moralities found on campus. For instance, you may have been taught that it is wrong to drink alcohol, yet you find that friends you respect and care about see nothing wrong with drinking, often to great excess. Students from more liberal backgrounds may be astonished to discover themselves forming friendships with classmates whose personal values are very conservative. So far, how has college life made you think about what you value strongly as compared with the values of others?

Whatever the reason, it becomes more evident each year that a college education is worth its cost.

A high school graduate working full-time can expect to earn about $1.2 million between ages 25 and 64, according to a recent survey by the Census Bureau, while a college education translates into much higher lifetime earnings: an estimated $4.4 million for doctors, lawyers, and others with professional degrees; $2.5 million for those with a master's degree; and $2.1 million for college graduates.

In the past several decades, college-educated women's wages have increased more quickly than the wages of college-educated men. However, much of that gain has come from working longer hours. Regrettably, college-educated men still earn substantially more than college-educated women. But these are averages, of course, and many women with college degrees have earnings equal to or higher than those of many men.

In addition to higher earnings, according to the Carnegie Commission on Higher Education, as a college graduate you will have a less erratic job history, will earn more promotions, and will probably be happier with your work. You will be less likely than a nongraduate to become unemployed. As the saying goes, "If you think education is expensive, try ignorance." As the statistics in Table 1.1 indicate, it pays to go to college in more ways than one. Not only does income go up, as a rule, with each degree earned, but the unemployment rate goes down. You not only earn more with a college degree, you also find it easier to get a job and hold on to it.

Have students study this table carefully. Ask whether this means to them that all people should strive for a doctorate or professional degree if they wish to be successful in life. Is there a trade-off between earnings and stress? Should people pursue a career for money or for satisfaction? Or both?

SEE "WHAT TODAY'S STUDENTS REALLY WANT ARE JOBS THAT PAY WELL"

TABLE 1.1   MEDIAN EARNINGS FOR YEAR-ROUND, FULL-TIME WORKERS AGES 25 AND OLDER, BY EDUCATIONAL ATTAINMENT

DEGREE	EARNINGS
Professional	$80,200
Doctorate	70,500
Master's	55,300
Bachelor's	46,300
Associate	35,400
Some college, no degree	32,400
High school diploma including GED	28,800
Some high school, no diploma	21,400

SOURCE: Bureau of Labor Statistics, 2002

Liberal Education and Quality of Life

Of course, college will affect you in other ways. No matter what your major, you will emerge from college with a liberal education. Liberal, as in "liberate" or "free," signifies that a well-rounded college education will expand life's possibilities for you by steeping you in the richness of how our world, our nation, our society, and its people came to be. Liberal education is about learning to learn, discovering how to think for yourself, on your own and in collaboration with others. The result is that you will understand how to accumulate knowledge and will learn more about how to appreciate the cultural, artistic, and spiritual dimensions of life. You will be more likely to seek appropriate information before making a decision. Also, such information will help you realize how our lives are shaped by global as well as local political, social, psychological, economic, environmental, and physical forces. You will grow intellectually through interaction with cultures, languages, ethnic groups, religions, nationalities, and social classes other than your own.

The evidence from many studies suggests that as a liberally educated college graduate, you will

- Know more, have more intellectual interests, be more tolerant of others, and continue to learn throughout life.
- Have greater self-esteem and self-confidence, which helps you realize how you might make a difference in the world.
- Be more flexible in your views, more future oriented, more willing to appreciate differences of opinion, more interested in political and public affairs, and less prone to criminal activity.
- Tend to delay getting married and having children, have fewer children, share child-care and household responsibilities with your partner, and devote more energy to child rearing.
- Have a slightly lower divorce rate than those who did not graduate from college.
- Have children with greater learning abilities who will achieve more in life.
- Be a more efficient consumer, save more money, make better investments, and spend more on home, intellectual, and cultural interests as well as on your children.
- Be better able to deal with bureaucracies, the legal system, tax laws, and advertising claims.
- Spend less time and money on television and movies for leisure and more on continuing education, hobbies, community and civic affairs, and vacations.

Note that, although the last few paragraphs emphasize the practical value of college, the following section does just the opposite. What's more important—education for its own sake or education for earning more money? Might be a lively debate.

SEE EXERCISE 1.3
YOUR REASONS FOR
ATTENDING COLLEGE

SEE EXERCISE 1.4
THE MANY REASONS FOR
COLLEGE

This list is but a starting point for other questions many have but few will ask. To keep things confidential, ask students to take 10 minutes to write down their thoughts at this moment about college. Tell them you will shuffle the papers and have each student read another's paper. Ask for no names on papers.

It may surprise students to learn that the benefits of a college education go far beyond being able to earn more money. Ask them to brainstorm the positive benefits of college. Then have them read the list of benefits here. Ask them which benefits were expected, which were unexpected, and which correlate most closely with their initial reasons for coming to college. See the discussion of critical thinking in Chapter 3.

Speaking of Careers

Several decades ago, the majority of students attending college claimed they were there, first and foremost, to gain an education for life. Today, most students will tell you their reasons for choosing college have more to do with finding careers that allow them to live comfortably. Bearing this in mind, think of college as an *investment in a fuller life*. By "investment," we mean the years of hard work as well as the cost. And by "a fuller life," we mean not only your future career, but the other parts of your life as well. College prepares you to be a more interesting person. Think about it. Isn't a "fuller life" what everyone ultimately wants?

- Be more concerned with wellness and preventive health care and consequently—through diet, exercise, stress management, a positive attitude, and other factors—live longer and suffer fewer disabilities.

Setting Goals for Success

Now that you've read the strategies for success, what should you be doing to accomplish them? One method is to set specific goals for yourself, beginning now, that will help you maximize your potential in college.

We know from years of working with new college students that many hold a number of negative self-fulfilling prophecies. A self-fulfilling prophecy is something you predict is going to happen, and by thinking that's how things will turn out, you greatly increase the chances that they will. This book is designed to help you rid yourself of your negative prophecies, replace them with positive ones, and learn how to fulfill them. Look back at the list of comments and questions on pages 8–9. If some of these sound familiar, take comfort: Most other entering students share the same fears.

College is an ideal time to begin setting and fulfilling short- and long-term goals. A short-term goal might be to set aside 3 hours this week to study chemistry, whereas a long-term goal might be to devise a strategy for passing chemistry with an A. It's okay if you don't yet know what you want to do with the rest of your life, or what your college major should be. More than 60 percent of college students change majors at least once. Using the strategies for success as a guide, practice the following process by setting some short-term goals now.[1]

1. **Select a goal.** State it in measurable terms. Be specific about what you want to achieve and when (for example, not "improve my study skills" but "master and use the recall column system of note taking by the end of October").
2. **Be sure that the goal is achievable.** Have you allowed enough time to pursue it? Do you have the necessary skills, strengths, and resources? If not, modify the goal to make it achievable.
3. **Be certain you genuinely want to achieve the goal.** Don't set out to work toward something only because you feel you should or because others tell you it's the thing to do. Be sure your goal will not have a negative impact on yourself or others and that it is consistent with your most important values.
4. **Know why the goal matters.** Be sure it has the potential to give you a sense of accomplishment.
5. **Identify and plan for difficulties you might encounter.** Find ways to overcome them.
6. **Devise strategies for achieving the goal.** How will you begin? What comes next? What should you avoid? Create steps for achieving your goal and set a time line for the steps.

SEE INTERNET
EXERCISE 1.2
RESEARCHING THE
VALUE OF COLLEGE AND
TIME MANAGEMENT

Time Management: Foundation of Academic Success

How do you approach time? Because people have different personalities and come from different cultures, they may also view time in different ways. Some of these differences may have to do with your preferred style of learning.

[1]Adapted from *Human Potential Seminars* by James D. McHolland and Roy W. Trueblood, Evanston, Illinois, 1972. Used by permission of the authors.

Time management is a lifelong skill. The better the job you have after college the more likely that you'll be managing your own and possibly other people's time.

Setting Priorities

Time management involves

- Knowing what your goals are
- Deciding where your priorities lie
- Anticipating future needs and possible changes
- Placing yourself in control of your time
- Making a commitment to being punctual
- Carrying out your plans

To make optimum use of your time, it's important to prioritize. In college, as in your future professional life, work often comes before pleasure. So begin with your priorities: attending classes, studying, working. Then think about the necessities of life: sleeping, eating, bathing, exercising, and relaxing. Leave time for fun things (talking with friends, watching TV, going out for the evening, and so forth); you deserve them. But finish what *needs* to be done before you move from work to pleasure. And, depending on your personality, you may need more or less time to be alone.

Setting priorities is an important first step. Besides attending classes, doing homework, and studying, you may also have a job, family responsibilities, extracurricular activities, athletic practices, social obligations, and other commitments. You are the only one who can decide what comes first.

What about classes? Do you prefer spreading your classes over all five days, or would you like to go to class just two or three days a week? Your decision may be influenced by your attention span as well as by your other commitments. Before you register, think about how you can create a schedule that allows you to use your time more efficiently.

These are important choices, and each student will need to make his or her own decisions regarding them. Advise them against bending to someone else's schedule just because they want to study together. Seek a compromise. If there is none, find another study partner or study alone.

**SEE EXERCISE 1.5
THE IDEAL CLASS
SCHEDULE**

Suggest that students print out the planner on the CD-ROM and make enough copies to cover the term.

**SEE "TERM ASSIGNMENT
PREVIEW"**

In groups of three to six, have students compare differences between high school and college with respect to the need for a better time management plan. Then have each group share its lists with another group by rotating clockwise and merging with an adjacent team, resulting in a "master list" that includes the important items generated by each team.

Students may question the value of spending so much time to save time. Ask that they be patient while assuring them that research indicates that college students who know how to plan their time can produce good work and have fun as well.

**SEE EXERCISE 1.6
YOUR DAILY PLAN**

Ask students to compare their "to do" lists in class. Have them explain how they set aside time for the "A" items on their list, whether they have been able to stick to their priorities, and how keeping a list has made a difference in how they approach things to do.

Have students pair off and exchange their week-by-week schedules. Ask them to offer suggestions to each other for making even more efficient use of their time. Then ask each pair to report to the class what they suggested.

SEE "WEEKLY TIMETABLE"

Using a Daily Planner

Use the term assignment preview on the CD-ROM to give yourself an idea of what's in store for you. You should complete your term assignment preview by the first week of classes. Then purchase a "week at a glance" organizer for the current year. Your campus bookstore may sell one designed just for your school, with important dates and deadlines already provided.

Enter the notes from your preview sheets, and continue to enter all due dates as soon as you know them. Write in meeting times and locations, events (jot down phone numbers, too, in case something comes up and you need to cancel), study time for each class you're taking, and so forth. Carry your planner with you from now on.

Check your notes daily for the current week and the coming week. Choose a specific time of day to do this, perhaps just before you begin studying in the evening. It takes just a moment to be certain you aren't forgetting something important and helps relieve stress.

Maintaining a "To Do" List

Keeping a "to do" list can also help you avoid feeling out of control. Some people start a new list every day or once a week. Use your "to do" list to keep track of all the tasks you need to remember, not just academics. Develop a system for prioritizing the items on your list—highlight, use colored ink, or mark with one, two, or three stars, or A, B, C. As you complete each task, cross it off your list. You will feel good knowing how much you have accomplished.

Guidelines for Scheduling Week by Week

- Examine your toughest weeks on your term assignment preview sheet (see Figure 1.1). If paper deadlines and test dates fall during the same week, find time to finish some assignments early to free up study time for tests.
- Break large assignments such as term papers into smaller steps (choosing a topic, doing research, writing an outline, writing a first draft, and so on). Add deadlines in your schedule for each portion.
- All assignments are not equal. Estimate how much time you'll need for each one, and begin early.
- Set aside time for research and other preparatory tasks. Most campuses offer tutoring, walk-in assistance, or workshops to assist you with computer functions at a learning center or computer center.
- Schedule at least three aerobic workouts per week. You need to maintain an elevated heart rate for 30 minutes, plus allow time for warming up, stretching, and cooling down.

Use Figure 1.2 to tentatively plan how you will spend your hours in a typical week.

Organizing Your Day

Being a good student does not necessarily mean grinding away at studies and doing little else. As you organize your day:

- Set realistic goals for your study time. Assess how long it takes to read a chapter in different types of texts and how long it takes you to review your notes from different instructors. Use Figure 1.3 to help you organize your day.
- Use waiting time (on the bus, before class, waiting for appointments) to review.

	Monday	Tuesday	Wednesday	Thursday	Friday
Week 1					
Week 2					
Week 3					
Week 4					

	Monday	Tuesday	Wednesday	Thursday	Friday
Week 5					
Week 6					
Week 7					
Week 8					

FIGURE 1.1 Term Assignment Preview
To see the big picture of your workload for this term, gather your syllabi and list all tests, reports, papers, and other projects.

	Monday	Tuesday	Wednesday	Thursday	Friday
Week 9					
Week 10					
Week 11					
Week 12					

	Monday	Tuesday	Wednesday	Thursday	Friday
Week 13					
Week 14					
Week 15					
Week 16					

FIGURE 1.1 Term Assignment Preview (continued)

	Sunday	Monday	Tuesday	Wednesday	Thursday	Friday	Saturday
6:00							
7:00							
8:00							
9:00							
10:00							
11:00							
12:00							
1:00							
2:00							
3:00							
4:00							
5:00							
6:00							
7:00							
8:00							
9:00							
10:00							
11:00							

FIGURE 1.2 Weekly Timetable
Using the suggestions in this chapter, create your perfect schedule for next term. Do you want your classes back-to-back or with breaks in between? How early in the morning are you willing to start classes? Are you willing to take evening classes? Are there times of day when you are more alert? Less alert? Do you want to attend classes two, three, five, or six days per week?

• Allow time for work, family responsibilities, and other obligations.
• Try to reserve 1 to 2 hours of daytime study for each class hour.
• Reserve time for exercise, meals, and free time.
• Try to plan a minimum of 1 hour additional study in evenings or on weekends for each class.

- Prevent forgetting by allowing time to review as soon as reasonable after class.
- Know your best time of day to study.
- Don't try to study on an empty or full stomach.
- Use the same study area regularly. Have everything you may need readily available, such as adequate lighting, a chair with sufficient back support, and enough desk space to spread out everything you need.
- Study difficult or boring subjects first, when you are fresh. (*Exception*: If you are having trouble making yourself get to work, it might be easier to get started with your favorite subject.)
- Divide study time into 50-minute blocks. Study for 50 minutes, then take a 10- or 15-minute break, then study for another 50-minute block. Try not to study for more than three 50-minute blocks in a row, or you may find that you are not accomplishing 50 minutes' worth of work.
- Break extended study sessions into a variety of activities, each with a specific objective.
- Restrict repetitive tasks (such as checking your email) to a certain time, not every hour.
- Be flexible! You cannot anticipate every disruption to your plans. Build extra time into your schedule so that unexpected interruptions do not prevent you from meeting your goals.
- Reward yourself! Develop a system of short- and long-term goals and reward yourself for meeting those goals.

If students think this text is suggesting that they can't concentrate for more than 50 minutes because they aren't smart, remind them that the whole world is more or less like this.

SEE INTERNET EXERCISE 1.3 LIMITING YOUR TIME ONLINE

DAILY PLANNER

DATE   MON   TUE   WED   THU   FRI   SAT   SUN

APPOINTMENTS

TIME

8
9
10
11
12
1
2
3
4
5
6
7
8

DAILY PLANNER

DATE   MON   TUE   WED   THU   FRI   SAT   SUN

✔   **TO DO**

PRIORITY   ESTIMATED TIME

FIGURE 1.3 Sample Daily Planner
(1) Circle the day of the week and list the day's appointments next to the appropriate times.
(2) On the opposite page, list your "to do" activities. Decide which are the most urgent and fill in the small priority boxes with an A for most important, B for less important, or C for least important.

Making Your Time Management Plan Work

If there's not enough time to carry your courseload and meet your commitments, drop some courses before the drop date. If you are on financial aid, keep in mind that you must be registered for a certain number of hours to be considered a full-time student. Learn to say no. Do not take on more than you can handle. Do not feel obligated to provide a reason; you have the right to decline requests that will prevent you from getting your own work done.

If you're a commuter student, or if you must work so that you can afford school, you may prefer block scheduling, which runs classes together without breaks. Although block scheduling allows you to cut travel time by attending school one or two days a week, there's little time to study between classes. If you become ill on a class day, you could fall behind in all of your classes. You may become fatigued sitting in class after class. Finally, you might become stressed when exams are held in several classes on the same day.

Have a discussion with the class about the advantages and problems of block scheduling versus spreading classes over more days in the week.

Reduce Distractions

Where should you study? Not at places associated with leisure, such as the kitchen table, the living room, or in front of the TV, because they lend themselves to interruptions by others. And your association with social activities in these locations can distract you even when others aren't there. Similarly, don't study on your bed. You may find yourself drifting off when you need to study, or you may learn to associate your bed with studying and not be able to sleep.

Try to stick to a routine as you study. Take advantage of large blocks of time that may be available on the weekend to review or catch up on major projects, such as

Search Online! ⟪ • ⟫

Welcome to InfoTrac College Edition! A Powerful Research Database

InfoTrac® College Edition is a powerful information database that includes numerous encyclopedias and other reference works as well as articles from many academic journals and magazines. You may find a comprehensive version of InfoTrac College Edition available on your campus.

Your Direct Access to InfoTrac College Edition

If your instructor arranged for your purchase of this textbook to include a subscription, you can also access InfoTrac College Edition on the Internet using your own computer. To set up your 4-month InfoTrac College Edition account, go to http://www.infotrac-college.com/wadsworth and submit the account number issued on the InfoTrac College Edition insert that accompanied this book. The program will lead you through the enrollment process.

InfoTrac College Edition includes more than 600 current magazines and journals and is growing. You'll find it easy to search for information using key words or by using the extensive subject guide. Many entries include the complete text of an article, which you can download to your computer. Each entry starts with an abstract to give you an idea of whether the article is likely to meet your needs.

In each chapter of this book, you'll find key-word and subject-guide phrases for the topic of that chapter. Make InfoTrac College Edition a regular part of your strategies for success. Use it to find information for writing papers and for broadening your learning in other courses, too.

term papers. Break down large tasks and take one thing at a time; then you'll make more progress toward your ultimate goal—high grades.

Here are some more tips to help you deal with distractions:

- Don't eat while you study. You want your body to be focused on thinking.
- Leave the TV, CD player, tape deck, and radio off, unless background noise or music helps you concentrate.
- Don't let personal concerns interfere with studying. If necessary, call a friend or write in a journal before you start to study and then put your worries away.
- Develop an agreement with the people you live with about "quiet" hours.

Beat Procrastination

Here are some ways:

- Say to yourself, "I need to do this now, because I will pay a price if I don't."
- Using your "to do" list, check off things as you get them done. Move the things that aren't getting done to the top of your next day's list.
- Break big jobs into smaller steps. Tackle easy-to-accomplish tasks first.
- Apply the goal-setting technique in this chapter to whatever you are putting off.
- Promise yourself a suitable reward (an apple, a phone call, a walk) whenever you finish something difficult.
- Take control of your study environment. Say no to friends who want your attention. Agree to meet them later. Let them be your reward for studying.
- Don't make or take phone calls during planned study sessions. Close your door.

SEE INTERNET EXERCISE 1.4 PROCRASTINATION RESOURCES

SEE EXERCISE 1.7 GOAL SETTING FOR COURSES

Search Online!   《●》

Internet Exercise 1.1 Using the *Digest of Education Statistics* Online

The Internet is particularly useful as a source of government statistics and information. The *Digest of Education Statistics* provides extensive data on postsecondary education in the United States. Figure 15 in Chapter 3 of the 1997 edition, the most recent version currently available on the Web (http://nces.ed.gov/pubs/digest97/d970003.html), presents a graph "Enrollment in institutions of higher education, by age: Fall 1978 to fall 2007." (*Note:* Go to http://success.wadsworth.com/book_resources/updated_links.html for the most up-to-date URLs.) Visit the Web site and answer the following questions:

Which age group has the highest percentage of individuals enrolled?   _____

Which age group has the smallest percentage of individuals enrolled?   _____

For the years 1970 to 1995, which age group increased the most?   _____

For the years 1970 to 1995, which age group increased the least?   _____

What do these trends say about how the profile of college students will change in the coming years?   _____

What explanation can you offer for these changes?   _____

A key-word search is not always the best way to find information on the Web. When searching for statistical data, you may have better luck starting from a resource menu such as the University of Michigan Documents Center (http://www.lib.umich.edu/libhome/Documents.center), a central reference and referral point for government information; Uncle Sam–Statistical Resources of the United States (http://www.lib.memphis.edu/gpo/statis1.htm); or Argus Clearinghouse, formerly known as the Clearinghouse for Subject-Oriented Internet Resource Guides (http://www.clearinghouse.net).

(continued)

Search Online!

Internet Exercise 1.2 Researching the Value of College and Time Management

Using InfoTrac College Edition, try key-word and subject-guide searches using these phrases: "college success," "liberal arts," "personal values," "goal setting," "college," "universities and colleges," "time management," "procrastination," and "goal setting." Then do a library search of books and periodicals for more information. Interview experts on the topic; a teacher, for example, might tell you how he or she copes with a busy schedule. If your instructor requires a short research paper, use the information you've gathered to write one, being sure you cite your sources properly.

Internet Exercise 1.3 Limiting Your Time Online

Anyone who has surfed the World Wide Web has realized its addictive nature. As with any addiction, the first step is to realize that you have a problem. Make a log of how you spend your time at each of the following activities in one week. Then create a target time for each area.

	Actual Time	Target Time
Reading and writing academic email	_____	_____
Reading and writing personal email	_____	_____
Surfing casually for academic topics	_____	_____
Surfing casually for personal interest	_____	_____
Searching rigorously for academic materials	_____	_____
Searching rigorously for personal information	_____	_____
Number of times a day you check your email	_____	_____

How might you limit the time you spend on each activity?

_____

_____

Additional Exercises

These exercises at the end of each chapter will help you sharpen what we believe are the critical skills for college success: writing, critical thinking, learning in groups, planning, reflecting, and taking action. Also check out the CD-ROM that came with your book—you will find more exercises as well as resources for this chapter.

Exercise 1.1 **Solving a Problem**

What has been your biggest unresolved problem to date in college? What steps have you taken in attempting to solve it? Write a letter or memo to your instructor about these two questions. Read your instructor's response and see if it's of any help to you. If you still have questions, ask to meet with your instructor or talk with a counselor if you prefer.

Exercise 1.2 **Focusing on Your Concerns**

Browse the table of contents of this book. Find one or more chapters that address your most important concerns. Take a brief look at each chapter you have chosen. If a chapter appears to be helpful, read it before your instructor assigns it and try to follow its advice.

Internet addiction is prevalent among college students. This exercise can help students compare how much time they spend "fun surfing" with how much time they use the Internet to gather specific information. For links to resources on Web addiction, see Online Addiction at http://www.cmhc.com/guide/iad.htm and Mike Wendland's article and resource listings at http://www.pcmike.com/Special%20Reports/netaddicts.html. (Go to http://success.wadsworth.com for the most up-to-date URLs.)

Exercise 1.3 Your Reasons for Attending College

List three reasons you chose to go to college:

1. _____

2. _____

3. _____

Which one of these was the most important? Why?

_____

_____

_____

Now list three reasons you chose this college:

1. _____

2. _____

3. _____

Which one of these was the most important? Why?

_____

_____

_____

_____

Your Personal Journal

Each chapter of this book will ask you to write your thoughts about the material you've just read. This is another way to remember the content of the chapter, so you might try it with your other classes as well. Choose one or more of the following questions. Or choose another topic related to this chapter and write about it.

1. Go back to the list of concerns on pages 8–9. Which of them are you feeling right now? How do you think you can begin overcoming them?
2. Of the three major strategies, which will give you the greatest challenge? Which will be easiest? Why?
3. Before you completed the exercises in this chapter, how successful were you at managing your time?
4. If you have completed the exercises, what difference—if any—have they made in the way you think about time?
5. How can you modify the ideas in this chapter to fit your own habits and biological clock?
6. What behaviors are you thinking about changing after reading this chapter? How will you go about changing them?
7. What else is on your mind this week? If you wish to share it with your instructor, add it to this journal entry.

Review the journal process carefully with students. Tell them that this activity provides an opportunity for additional writing practice, reflection, and two-way feedback between you and them. Remind them that many great artists, writers, thinkers, and leaders keep journals to record important thoughts for possible later use. Collect journals frequently—whether in class, by email, or through your class Internet page—and return them promptly with your comments. Clearly explain that the journal is confidential communication and that this confidence will not be violated except in cases that clearly fall under your campus' policy about privileged communication (e.g., when a student might express suicidal thoughts or threaten possible harm to others). Assure students that you will not be grading their journals but that they are both essential and required.

Resources

This book can be a continuing resource for you throughout your college career. Many of the activities and topics covered in this book will be important throughout your life. The resource pages at the end of each chapter are for you to fill with names, phone numbers, addresses, email addresses, and other helpful information. When you're done, you'll have a valuable personal resource file for college success. Keeping such a list handy can save you time.

Your Personal Information

Your name ....

School name ....

Local address ....

Permanent address ....

Social Security number ....   School ID number ....

Driver's license—state and number ....

(Marking or engraving your belongings with your driver's license number can help you recover them if they are stolen.)

Key Personal Resources

List several names, phone numbers, and addresses for the following. Choose people who are supportive of your college goals, good listeners when you need to talk, and fun to hang out with.

FAMILY

Name ....   Phone ....   Email ....

Name ....   Phone ....   Email ....

Name ....   Phone ....   Email ....

Name ....   Phone ....   Email ....

FRIENDS

Name ....   Phone ....   Email ....

Name ....   Phone ....   Email ....

Name ....   Phone ....   Email ....

Name ....   Phone ....   Email ....

FACULTY

Name ....   Phone ....   Email ....

Name ....   Phone ....   Email ....

Name ....   Phone ....   Email ....

Name ....   Phone ....   Email ....

EXTRACURRICULAR GROUPS

Name ....   Phone ....   Email ....

Name ....   Phone ....   Email ....

Name ....   Phone ....   Email ....

Name ....   Phone ....   Email ....

Academic advisor

Campus security/local police

Campus health center/hospital

Doctor/dentist

Campus counseling center

Career advising and placement office

Dean of students

Campus legal services

Child-care centers

Emergency road service/mechanic

Landlord (home and work)

Employer (home and work)

Tutorial/learning center

Commuter student service center

Neighbors

Taxi service

Campus and public libraries

Campus fax numbers

Learning About Campus Resources

Fill in the boxes provided below for the campus support services or resources you might be interested in using. Include not only serious support needs but also things that will help you relax and enjoy campus life to the fullest. Pool your list with the lists of others in your class. Use a campus map, student handbook, or other guide to find out which resources are available on your campus and how to find them.

Where to Go for Help

	Contact Person	Phone Number	Web Address
Academic Advisement Center			
Academic Skills Center			
Academic Computing Center			
Adult Re-Entry Center			
Career Planning and Placement			
Chaplains			
Commuter and Off-Campus Services			
Counseling Center			
Financial Aid and Scholarhip Office			
Health Center and Enrichment Services			
Housing Office			

	Contact Person	Phone Number	Web Address
Legal Services			
Math Center			
Physical Education Center			
Services for Students with Disabilities			
Writing Center			
Others:			

Learning Styles

Discovering How You Learn Best

IN THIS CHAPTER, YOU WILL LEARN

- How to determine your learning preferences
- How your learning style can affect your classroom behavior
- How a mix of learning styles can enhance study groups
- How to deal with your instructors' teaching styles

This chapter was written with the expert assistance of Steven Blume, Marietta College.

figure yourself out

"Bill has a ball when he's around people. I like some time to myself. Janine can remember every date in a history lecture. I don't remember any, but I do pick up on the big ideas better than she does. Fred argues about issues based on how he feels about them, not on the facts themselves. I do just the opposite. What makes my friends so different and why is it that, despite those differences, I like them all?"

In high school, perhaps you found history easier than mathematics or biology easier than English. Part of the explanation for this has to do with what is called your learning style—that is, the way you prefer to acquire knowledge.

Learning style affects not only how you absorb material as you study but how you draw conclusions from it. Some students learn more effectively through visual means, others by listening to lectures, and still others through class discussion, hands-on experience, memorization, or various combinations of these.

For example, visual learners have to "see it to believe it." They may have artistic ability (including a strong sense of color), may be irritated by some sounds, and may have trouble following lectures. They may do better if they use graphics as a learning aid, color-code their notes, and write out everything for quick and frequent visual review. They tend to remember notes by visualizing precisely where on their notebook page they wrote the information they seek.

SELF-ASSESSMENT: LEARNING STYLES

Check the items that apply to you. After you finish, review the checked items. What are you most comfortable with? Look at the unchecked items. What are you least comfortable with? What does this tell you about the way you prefer to learn?

_____ I like when people tell me I'm imaginative.

_____ I like when people tell me I get the facts straight.

_____ I enjoy spending some of my time alone with my thoughts.

_____ It's important for me to be with people as often as I can.

_____ I like to stick to tried and proven ways of getting things done.

_____ It's fun to experiment with new ways to get things done.

_____ I absolutely must set a schedule for myself and stick to it.

_____ I don't bother with schedules. Most times, things get done.

_____ I enjoy meeting new people—the more, the merrier.

_____ I value having just a few close friends—that's enough.

You will be asked to complete a more comprehensive learning style inventory later in this chapter.

Auditory learners remember what they hear. They may have difficulty following written directions and may find reading and writing laborious. They may do better if they use tapes for reading and for lecture notes, participate in discussions, and summarize on tape what they read.

Tactile learners tend to remember what they touch. They like hands-on learning, may have difficulty sitting still, and learn better through physical activity. They may do better if they are actively engaged in learning (as in lab work or role playing), take frequent study breaks, and use a computer.

Some people learn better by studying alone, and others prefer study groups. Although no one learning style is inherently better than another, you will need to learn to work comfortably no matter what style is required in a course. An awareness of your learning style can be helpful in emphasizing your strengths and helping you compensate for the learning styles you don't prefer. It also can help you understand and adjust to the teaching styles of faculty.

Discovering Your Own Learning Style

Think about three or four of your favorite courses from high school or college so far. What do they have in common? Did they tend to be hands-on courses or more abstract? Did they focus more on mastering facts or on broader interpretations? Was there a lot of discussion or did the teacher mainly lecture? Then think about your least favorite courses. How did they tend to differ from the courses you liked?

Being aware of your personal learning style preferences can help you exploit your strengths as you prepare for classes and exams. It can also help you understand why you're having difficulty with some of your courses and what you can do to improve.

Personality Preferences and Learning Style

One way to determine your preferred learning style is to explore the basic personality preferences that make people interested in different things and draw them to different fields and lifestyles. As an example, the Myers–Briggs Type Indicator, based on Carl Jung's theory of psychological types, uses four scales to define eight preferences:

- **E/I (Extroversion/Introversion)** Extroverted persons are attuned to the culture, people, and things around them. The extrovert is outgoing, socially free, interested in variety and in working with people. The extrovert may become impatient with long, slow tasks and does not mind being interrupted by people.

  Persons more introverted than extroverted tend to make decisions somewhat independently of culture, people, or things around them. They are quiet, diligent at working alone, and socially reserved. They may dislike being interrupted while working and may tend to forget names and faces.

  After reading this, would you call yourself more E or more I?

- **S/N (Sensing/Intuitive)** This scale describes how you prefer to acquire information. Sensers tend to take facts as they are and remember the details, whereas intuitors are more likely to absorb a number of facts, look for relationships among them, and emerge with broad concepts. The sensing type prefers the concrete, factual, tangible here and now, becoming impatient with theory and the abstract and mistrusting intuition. The sensing type thinks in detail, remembering real facts, but possibly missing the "big idea" they add up to.

  In contrast, the intuitive person prefers possibilities, theories, invention, and the new and becomes bored with nitty-gritty details and facts unrelated to

Few students have considered how they learn. It is important that they begin to understand now so they can take advantage of their strengths and learn to adapt to learning styles they are less comfortable with. An awareness that students have individual approaches to learning and that instructors have individual teaching styles offers students a logical means of analyzing classes and teachers, which may help them earn higher grades.

By a show of hands, find out whether students believe their learning style is more auditory or visual. Discuss how they can strengthen their less preferred learning style.

SEE INTERNET EXERCISE 2.1 LEARNING STYLE INVENTORY

E versus I.
Avoid stereotyping I's as loners. Explain that E's tend to draw energy from the external world of people, activities, and things whereas I's tend to draw energy from the inner world of ideas, emotions, and impressions. Remind students that most are a mix of the two extremes.

S versus N.
Explain that S types tend to pay attention to information perceived directly through the five senses and focus on what actually exists whereas N types tend to pay attention to information through a "sixth sense" and notice what might or could be, rather than what actually exists.

concepts. The intuitive person thinks and discusses in spontaneous leaps of intuition that may neglect details. Problem solving comes easily for this individual, although there may be a tendency to make errors of fact.

After reading this, would you call yourself more S or more N?

SEE EXERCISE 2.1
YOUR LEARNING STYLE:
A QUICK INDICATION

- **T/F (Thinking/Feeling)** This scale describes whether you make decisions by analyzing and weighing evidence or by analyzing and weighing feelings. The thinker makes judgments based on logic, analysis, and evidence, avoiding decisions based on feelings and values. As a result, the thinker is more interested in verifiable conclusions than in empathy or values. The thinker may step on others' needs, values, and feelings without realizing it.

T versus F.
Explain that T types tend to organize information logically and objectively as a basis for decision making whereas F types may organize information to decide in a personal, values-oriented way. To feelers, the latter remains a highly logical method of decision making.

The feeler makes judgments based on empathy, warmth, and personal values. As a consequence, feelers are more interested in people and feelings than in impersonal logic, analysis, and things, and in achieving harmony more than in being on top or achieving impersonal goals. The feeler gets along well with people in general. The feeler may bend the rules if he or she feels more good will come of it.

After reading this, would you call yourself more T or more F?

- **J/P (Judging/Perceiving)** This scale describes whether you relate to the outer world in a planned, orderly way or in a flexible, spontaneous way. The judger is decisive, firm, and sure, setting goals and sticking to them. The judger wants to make decisions and get on to the next project. When a project does not yet have closure, judgers will leave it behind and go on to new tasks.

J versus P.
Explain that J types are the "time managers" who prefer living a planned and organized life, whereas P types prefer living more spontaneously and flexibly.

The perceiver is a gatherer, always wanting to know more before deciding, holding off decisions and judgments. As a consequence, the perceiver is open, flexible, adaptive, nonjudgmental, able to see and appreciate all sides of issues, always welcoming new perspectives. However, perceivers may become involved in many tasks that do not reach closure, so that they become frustrated at times. Even when they finish tasks, perceivers will tend to look back at them and wonder whether they could have been done better.

After reading this, would you call yourself more J or more P?

SEE INTERNET
EXERCISE 2.2
RESEARCHING LEARNING
STYLE THEORY

SEE EXERCISE 2.2
ASSESSING YOUR
LEARNING STYLE

You will often feel most comfortable around people who share your preferences, and you will probably be most comfortable in a classroom where the instructor's preferences for perceiving and processing information are most like yours. But the Myers–Briggs instrument also emphasizes our ability to cultivate both processes on each scale.

Once students have completed the inventory in Exercise 2.2, pass around a sheet on which students can list their four-letter learning styles, along with their four scores. Share and discuss the class profile by revealing the number of I versus E types, and so on.

Just as no person's fingerprints are right or wrong, so no one's learning preferences are right or wrong. The purpose of this inventory is to give you a clue to your preferences. Keep in mind that those preferences have nothing to do with intelligence. All eight preferences are present to some degree in all people. It is the

Critical Thinking

Stick with Your Own Types or Seek Out Other Types?

If you feel most comfortable around friends and teachers who share your preferences, why bother making it a point to be around those with differing preferences? Can you think of any situations where it would be better to seek out a different learning type? Review your decisions, share them with another student, and get his or her feedback.

extremes that are described here. The strength of a preference is indicated by the score for that dimension on an inventory such as the one in Exercise 2.2.

Strengths and Weaknesses

Each person has strengths and weaknesses as a result of these preferences. Committees and organizations with a preponderance of one type will have the same strengths and weaknesses.

Stress that one style is not "better" than another. Instead, by knowing your learning style, you can build on your strengths and compensate for your weaknesses. The key word is "preference," not right/wrong, better/worse, good/bad. Although most of us can operate on either side of each scale, we tend to prefer one way over the other.

	POSSIBLE STRENGTHS	POSSIBLE WEAKNESSES
Extrovert (E)	Interacts well with others	Does not work well without other people
	Is open	Needs change, variety
	Acts, does	Is impulsive
	Is well understood	Is impatient with routine
Introvert (I)	Is independent	Avoids others
	Works alone	Is secretive
	Reflects	Loses opportunities to act
	Works with ideas	Is misunderstood by others
	Avoids generalizations	Dislikes being interrupted
	Is careful before acting	May miss deadlines
Senser (S)	Attends to detail	Does not see possibilities
	Is practical	Loses the overall in details
	Has memory for detail, fact	Mistrusts intuition
	Is patient	Is frustrated with the complicated
	Is systematic	Prefers not to imagine future
Intuitor (N)	Sees possibilities	Is inattentive to detail, precision
	Works out new ideas	Is inattentive to the actual and practical
	Works with the complicated	Is impatient with the tedious
	Solves novel problems	Loses sight of the here and now
	Has inspirations	Jumps to conclusions
Thinker (T)	Is logical, analytical	May not notice people's feelings
	Is objective	Misunderstands others' values
	Is organized	Is uninterested in conciliation
	Has critical ability	Does not show feelings
	Is just	Shows less compassion
	Stands firm	Will not budge
Feeler (F)	Considers others' feelings	Is not guided by logic
	Understands needs, values	Is not objective
	Is interested in conciliation	Is less organized
	Demonstrates feelings	Is overly accepting
Judger (J)	Decides	Is stubborn
	Plans	Is inflexible
	Orders	Decides with insufficient data
	Makes quick decisions	Is controlled by task or plans
	Remains with a task	Wishes not to interrupt work
Perceiver (P)	Compromises	Is indecisive
	Sees all sides of issues	Does not plan
	Is flexible	Does not control circumstances
	Decides based on all data	Is easily distracted from tasks
	Is not judgmental	Does not finish projects

Examining Values

Can learning preferences have an influence on your value system? Certainly those who value time and organization may do so because of their J learning preference. Conversely, those who value the freedom to be on "their own" schedules may do so as a result of their P learning prefer- ence. After you have completed Exercise 2.2, review the characteristics of your learning prefer- ences and write a paper in which you speculate on how those preferences may help deter- mine some of the things you value most and least.

**SEE EXERCISE 2.3
ASSESSING YOUR
COURSES AND
INSTRUCTORS**

As you reflect on the results of Exercise 2.2 at the end of this chapter, keep in mind that your score merely suggests your preferences; it does not judge, stereo- type, or pigeonhole you. Remember, too, that no one learning style is inherently preferable to another and that everyone knows and uses a range of styles. The fact that many of us exhibit behaviors that seem to contradict our preferences shows that each of us embraces a wide range of possibilities.

Using Knowledge of Your Learning Style

Discovering your stronger preferences empowers you to recognize what you already do well. Discovering your less dominant preferences is also useful, because it is to your advantage to cultivate these less dominant learning styles. Although certain disciplines and certain instructors may take approaches that favor certain styles, no course is going to be entirely sensing or entirely intuitive, entirely thinking or entirely feeling, just as you are not entirely one thing or another. You can also use your learning style data to determine how to study more effectively. Diagram? Study aloud? Annotate texts in margins? Focus on details or concepts?

Knowing your own learning style preferences can also help you to study more effectively with other students. When you form a study group, seek out students with some opposite learning preferences, but be sure that you also have some pref- erences in common. The best teamwork seems to come from people who differ on one or two preferences. If you prefer intuitive fact gathering, for example, you might benefit from the details brought forth by a sensing type.

Help students understand the value of studying with students whose learning preferences are different from their own by forming groups of students with different learning styles and asking them to share their study processes/ habits with one another.

Dealing with Your Instructors' Teaching Styles

Just as your learning style affects how you study, perform, and react to various courses and disciplines, so your instructors' learning styles affect what and how they teach.

Exam Preparation and Learning/Teaching Styles

Understanding learning styles can help you perceive more clearly the expectations of an instructor whose teaching style is incompatible with your learning style and thus allow you to prepare more effectively for his or her exams.

When Steven Blume, the main contributor to this chapter, was learning about the Myers–Briggs Type Indicator, he attended a workshop for college instructors. Those attending the workshop were divided into two groups—sensing and intuitive.

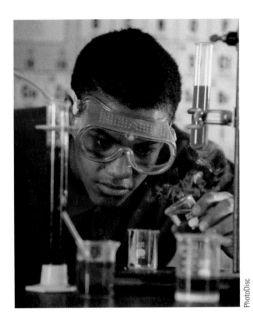 

One student's analytical style may thrive on the complexities of history. Another's satisfaction at mastering facts and understanding how they are related may lead him into science.

Each group was given a five-page essay about the effects of divorce on young children and asked to construct a short exam based on the reading. The sensing group was then asked to take the exam constructed by the intuitive group while the intuitive group was asked to take the exam constructed by the sensing group.

As soon as they read the questions, they could not believe that both groups had read and discussed the same essay. Those in the intuitive group had been asked to construct lists of details and respond to much factual data that they had regarded as less essential than the more analytical and conceptual themes of the essay. And those in the sensing group were taken aback by the very broad thematic questions the intuitive group had asked about the implications of divorce on the children and the larger questions about the children's future.

Clues to Instructors' Teaching Styles

The best clue to your instructor's teaching style is the language he or she uses. If your learning style is more visual, you can sense those clues from printed material, such as the syllabus and course handouts. If your learning style is more auditory, pay attention to the language your instructor uses when lecturing, asking discussion questions, or phrasing oral test questions.

For example, earlier we discussed two ways of receiving and processing information: (1) sensing (factual and informational) and (2) intuitive (analytical and conceptual). An instructor who uses words such as *define, diagram, label, list, outline,* and *summarize* will tend to have a more sensing teaching style and will want you to be extremely specific and provide primarily factual information. Words such as these ask for very restricted answers.

But an instructor whose syllabus or lecture is sprinkled with words such as *concept, theme, idea, theory,* and *interpretation* will tend to have a much more intuitive and analytical learning style and expect similar kinds of responses from students. On exams or on assignments, he or she may use terms such as *describe, compare, contrast, criticize, discuss, evaluate, explain, interpret, justify,* or *relate.* You may notice that, instead of asking you to provide factual data or information, these words ask you to use information in relation to other pieces of information, to evaluate it, or to examine it in terms of your own experience.

Share your learning style preferences with your students. Discuss why instructors need to use various teaching strategies (lecture, discussion, small-group work, writing on board, overheads, visual aids, etc.) to increase the chances of reaching most students. Share how your learning preferences helped and hindered you in college and what you did about the problematic ones.

Speaking of Careers

Most workers find that the best way to get the job done is through collaboration with others. After college, chances are you will be collaborating, too. But what if your learning style is strongly introverted? Obviously, you will have to make a special effort to work smoothly with others. Or you might find a way to complete part of the job on your own. What if you prefer feeling to thinking, and most of your colleagues are "thinkers"? You may want to rehearse expressing what you "feel" in a logical, organized fashion. Each of us will spend much of our life working hard to work with others. No matter what your learning preferences are, you can master some opposite skills, too, or learn how to use your strengths in harmony with the strengths of coworkers.

An instructor who uses these words has a much more intuitive teaching style and will expect you to see information in a new context rather than simply restate the facts as they have been given to you or as they appear in the textbook. Part of your grade may depend on how well you state your answers and how clearly you relate one piece of information to another.

If your instructor's teaching style is compatible with your learning style, you should be able to perform well simply by keeping up with your work. If your instructor's style is incompatible with yours, you might consider (as an I) mastering more factual material or (as an S) analyzing that material in order to be better prepared. In any case, a greater awareness of both your learning style and your instructor's teaching style can be of real benefit.

A variety of additional tests, generally available through your career or learning center, can help you understand more about your learning style. A guidance counselor will both administer the test and help you interpret the results. Ask about the following:

- The Myers–Briggs Type Indicator
- The complete Hogan/Champagne Personal Style Inventory
- The Kolb Learning Style Inventory

Above all, remember: There are no good or bad learning styles, only different ones. And isn't that fortunate? What a dull, predictable world this would be if each of us analyzed information in exactly the same manner!

How many students have discovered teachers with learning styles similar to their own? Somewhat similar (two or more dimensions)? Extremely different (three or more different dimensions)? Is there any correlation between a teacher's learning preference and how well a student might do in the class?

Search Online!

Internet Exercise 2.1 Learning Style Inventory

Which of the following best describes your most efficient learning style?

Visual learner—rely on visual cues, on things you see _____

Auditory learner—rely on auditory stimuli, on things you hear _____

Tactile learner—rely on touch, on working with your hands _____

Go to http://bsd-server.nc.edu/virtcol/ss/learn.html#styles and take the Learning Style Evaluation. (Go to http://success.wadsworth.com for the most up-to-date URLs.) Record your scores here:

Visual Preference Score _____

Auditory Preference Score _____

Tactile Preference Score _____

What do your scores suggest about your learning style? How might you adjust your study habits to optimize your learning?

Internet Exercise 2.2 Researching Learning Style Theory

Using InfoTrac College Edition, try these phrases and others for key-word and subject-guide searches: "learning style," "Howard Gardner," "Keirsey," "Myers-Briggs," "learning preference." Take notes and develop a short research paper, making sure you attribute sources properly.

Additional Exercises

These exercises at the end of each chapter will help you sharpen what we believe are vital skills for college success: writing, critical thinking, learning in groups, planning, reflecting, and taking action. Also check out the CD-ROM that came with your book— you will find more exercises as well as resources for this chapter.

Exercise 2.1 Your Learning Style: A Quick Indication

A List three or four of your favorite courses from high school or college:

1. _____

2. _____

3. _____

4. _____

What did these courses have in common? Did they tend to be hands-on courses? Lecture courses? Discussion courses? What were the exams like? Do you see a pattern from one course to the next? For example, did your favorite courses tend to use information-oriented tests such as multiple choice or true/false? Or did they often include broader essay exams? Did the tests cover small units of material or facts, or did they draw on larger chunks of material?

Now list your least favorite courses from high school or college:

1. _____

2. _____

3. _____

4. _____

What did these courses and their exams have in common? How did they tend to differ from the courses you liked?

 B After doing Part A, form a small group with two or three other members of the class. Brainstorm about what courses you are taking that seem to require factual learning styles, analytical learning styles, or a combination of both. Prepare an oral group presentation to the class about your conclusions and the reasons for them. What is the best way to prepare for an exam in these classes and why? (Read this entire chapter before you present.)

Assign as homework. Be certain students know how to score the inventory. Note that pairs are opposite one another.

Exercise 2.2 Assessing Your Learning Style

The following items are arranged in pairs (a and b), and each member of the pair represents a preference you may or may not hold. Rate your preference for each item by giving it a score of 0 to 5 (0 meaning you feel strongly negative about it or strongly positive about the other member of the pair, 5 meaning you strongly prefer it or do not prefer the other member of the pair). The scores for a and b must add up to 5 (0 and 5, 1 and 4, or 2 and 3). Do not use fractions.

I prefer:

_____ 1a. making decisions after finding out what others think.

_____ 1b. making decisions without consulting anyone.

_____ 2a. being called imaginative or intuitive.

_____ 2b. being called factual or accurate.

_____ 3a. making decisions about people based on available data and systematic analysis.

_____ 3b. making decisions about people based on empathy, feelings, and understanding of their needs and values.

_____ 4a. allowing commitments to occur if others want to make them.

_____ 4b. pushing for definite commitments to ensure they are made.

_____ 5a. quiet, thoughtful time alone.

_____ 5b. active, energetic time with people.

_____ 6a. using methods I know well that can get the job done.

_____ 6b. thinking of new ways to do tasks when confronted with them.

_____ 7a. drawing conclusions based on logic and careful analysis.

_____ 7b. drawing conclusions based on what I feel and believe about life and people from past experiences.

_____ 8a. avoiding making deadlines.

_____ 8b. setting a schedule and sticking to it.

_____ 9a. inner thoughts and feelings others cannot see.

_____ 9b. activities and occurrences in which others join.

_____ 10a. the abstract or theoretical.

_____ 10b. the concrete or real.

_____ 11a. helping others explore their feelings.

_____ 11b. helping others make logical decisions.

_____ 12a. communicating little of my inner thoughts and feelings.

_____ 12b. communicating freely my inner thoughts and feelings.

____ 13a. planning ahead based on projections.	____ 13b. planning as needs arise, just before carrying out the plans.
____ 14a. meeting new people.	____ 14b. being alone or with one person I know well.
____ 15a. ideas.	____ 15b. facts.
____ 16a. convictions.	____ 16b. verifiable conclusions.
____ 17a. keeping appointments and notes written down as much as possible.	____ 17b. using appointment and notebooks as little as possible (although I may use them).
____ 18a. carrying out carefully laid, detailed plans with precision.	____ 18b. designing plans and structures without necessarily carrying them out.
____ 19a. being free to do things on the spur of the moment.	____ 19b. knowing well in advance what I am expected to do.
____ 20a. experiencing emotional situations, discussions, movies.	____ 20b. using my ability to analyze situations.

Personal Style Inventory Scoring

Note:
I + E scores should = 25.
N + S scores should = 25.
T + F scores should = 25.
P + J scores should = 25.

Instructions: Transfer your scores for each item to the appropriate blanks. Be careful to check the a and b letters to be sure you are recording scores in the proper spaces.

I	E	N	S	T	F	P	J
1b.____	1a.____	2a.____	2b.____	3a.____	3b.____	4a.____	4b.____
5a.____	5b.____	6b.____	6a.____	7a.____	7b.____	8a.____	8b.____
9a.____	9b.____	10a.____	10b.____	11b.____	11a.____	13b.____	13a.____
12a.____	12b.____	15a.____	15b.____	16b.____	16a.____	17b.____	17a.____
14b.____	14a.____	18b.____	18a.____	20b.____	20a.____	19a.____	19b.____

TOTALS

I____   **E**____   **N**____   **S**____   **T**____   **F**____   **P**____   **J**____

Personal Style Inventory Interpretation

Letters on the score sheet stand for:

I—Introversion   E—Extroversion
N—iNtuition   S—Sensing
T—Thinking   F—Feeling
P—Perceiving   J—Judging

If your score is	**The likely interpretation is**
12–13	Balanced preference on this dimension, indicating you can "go with the flow"
14–15	Some preference in one direction over the other
16–19	Considerable preference in one direction
20–25	Strong, definite preference for one direction over the other

Your typology consists of those four dimensions for which you had scores of 14 or more, although the relative strengths of all dimensions actually constitute your typology. Scores of 12 or 13 show relative balance in a pair so that either member could be part of the typology.

Note: This exercise is an abridgment of the *Personal Style Inventory* by Dr. R. Craig Hogan and Dr. David W. Champagne, adapted and reproduced with permission from Organization Design and Development, Inc., 2002 Renaissance Blvd., Suite 100, King of Prussia, PA 19406. For information on using the complete instrument, please write to the above address.

Your Personal Journal

Here are several things to write about. Choose one or more, or choose another topic related to learning styles.

1. Understanding their learning styles helped the authors of this book in many ways. It improved their relationships with people. It made them feel better about some things that had bothered them before. It showed them how to cope with what had been difficult situations. How has knowledge of your learning style helped you?

2. Think of one or more of your teachers whose teaching methods make you uncomfortable. See if you can describe the four dimensions of his or her learning style. Explain how this might help you do better in this class.

3. Have a chat with one or two classmates about your learning style and theirs. Then write about the discussion.

4. What behaviors are you thinking about changing after reading this chapter? How will you go about changing them?

5. Anything else on your mind this week that you'd like to share with your instructor? If so, add it to your journal entry.

_____

_____

_____

_____

_____

_____

_____

_____

_____

_____

_____

_____

_____

_____

_____

_____

_____

_____

_____

_____

_____

_____

Resources

Read the following descriptions of the sixteen different Myers–Briggs types. Put your name in the box that best describes your type. Where do the other significant people in your life fit? Put their names in the boxes that best describe their type preferences.

	SENSING TYPES		INTUITIVES	
	WITH THINKING	WITH FEELING	WITH FEELING	WITH THINKING

ISTJ
Serious, quiet, earn success by concentration and thoroughness. Practical, orderly, matter-of-fact, logical, realistic and dependable. See it that everything is well organized. Take responsibility. Make up their own minds as to what should be accomplished and work toward it steadily, regardless of protests or distractions.

_____

_____

ISFJ
Quiet, friendly, responsible and conscientious. Work devotedly to meet their obligations and serve their friends and school. Thorough, painstaking, accurate. May need time to master technical subjects, as their interests are not often technical. Patient with detail and routine. Loyal, considerate, concerned with how other people feel.

_____

_____

INFJ
Succeed by perseverance, originality and desire to do whatever is needed or wanted. Put their best efforts into the work. Quietly forceful, conscientious, concerned for others. Respected for their firm principles. Likely to be honored and followed for their clear convictions as to how best to serve the common good.

_____

_____

INTJ
Have original minds and great drive which they use only for their own purposes. In fields that appeal to them they have a fine power to organize a job and carry it through with or without help. Skeptical, critical, independent, determined, often stubborn. Must learn to yield less important points in order to win the most important.

_____

_____

ISTP
Cool onlookers, quiet, reserved, observing and analyzing life with detached curiosity and unexpected flashes of original humor. Usually interested in impersonal principles, cause and effect, or how and why mechanical things work. Exert themselves no more than they think necessary, because any waste of energy would be inefficient.

_____

_____

ISFP
Retiring, quietly friendly, sensitive, modest about their abilities. Shun disagreements, do not force their opinions or values on others. Usually do not care to lead but are often loyal followers. May be rather relaxed about assignments or getting things done, because they enjoy the present moment and do not want to spoil it by undue haste or exertion.

_____

_____

INFP
Full of enthusiasms and loyalties, but seldom talk of these until they know you well. Care about learning ideas, language, and independent projects of their own. Apt to be on yearbook staff, perhaps as editor. Tend to undertake too much, then somehow get it done. Friendly, but often too absorbed in what they are doing to be sociable or notice much.

_____

_____

INTP
Quiet, reserved, brilliant in exams, especially in theoretical or scientific subjects. Logical to the point of hair-splitting. Interested mainly in ideas, with little liking for parties or small talk. Tend to have very sharply defined interests. Need to choose careers where some strong interest of theirs can be used and useful.

_____

_____

ESTP
Matter-of-fact, do not worry or hurry, enjoy whatever comes along. Tend to like mechanical things and sports, with friends on the side. May be a bit blunt or insensitive. Can do math or science when they see the need. Dislike long explanations. Are best with real things that can be worked, handled, taken apart or put back together.

_____

_____

ESFP
Outgoing, easygoing, acceptive, friendly, fond of a good time. Like sports and making things. Know what's going on and join in eagerly. Find remembering facts easier than mastering theories. Are best in situations that need sound common sense and practical ability with people as well as with things.

_____

_____

ENFP
Warmly enthusiastic, high-spirited, ingenious, imaginative. Able to do almost anything that interests them. Quick with a solution for any difficulty and ready to help anyone with a problem. Often rely on their ability to improvise instead of preparing in advance. Can always find compelling reasons for whatever they want.

_____

_____

ENTP
Quick, ingenious, good at many things. Stimulating company, alert and outspoken, argue for fun on either side of a question. Resourceful in solving new and challenging problems, but may neglect routine assignments. Turn to one new interest after another. Can always find logical reasons for whatever they want.

_____

_____

ESTJ
Practical realists, matter-of-fact, with a natural head for business or mechanics. Not interested in subjects they see no use for, but can apply themselves when necessary. Like to organize and run activities. Tend to run things well, especially if they remember to consider other people's feelings and points of view when making their decisions.

_____

_____

ESFJ
Warm-hearted, talkative, popular, conscientious, born cooperators, active committee members. Always doing something nice for someone. Work best with plenty of encouragement and praise. Little interest in abstract thinking or technical subjects. Main interest is in things that directly and visibly affect people's lives.

_____

_____

ENFJ
Responsive and responsible. Feel real concern for what others think and want, and try to handle things with due regard for other people's feelings. Can present a proposal or lead a group discussion with ease and tact. Sociable, popular, active in school affairs, but put time enough on their studies to do good work.

_____

_____

ENTJ
Hearty, frank, able in studies, leaders in activities. Usually good in anything that requires reasoning and intelligent talk, such as public speaking. Are well-informed and keep adding to their fund of knowledge. May sometimes be more positive and confident than their experience in an area warrants.

_____

_____

Left margin: INTROVERTS — JUDGING / PERCEPTIVE; EXTRAVERTS — PERCEPTIVE / JUDGING

Right margin: INTROVERTS — JUDGING / PERCEPTIVE; EXTRAVERTS — PERCEPTIVE / JUDGING

"Effects of the Combinations of All Four Preferences in Young People," pp. A-7, A-8, *People Types and Tiger Stripes: A Practical Guide to Learning Styles* by Gordon Lawrence, published by Center for the Application of Psychological Type, Inc. Gainesville, Florida, 1982.

Hone Your Skills!

Strategies for Success

TAKE CHARGE OF LEARNING!

- Show up for class
- Have work done on time
- Set up a daily schedule
- If full-time student, limit work week to 15 hours; work on campus if possible
- If stressed, enroll part-time
- Assess how you learn best

HONE YOUR SKILLS!

- Improve your reading, note taking, and study habits
- Improve your writing
- Develop critical thinking skills
- Participate in class
- Practice giving presentations
- Learn how to remember more from every class
- Learn from criticism
- Choose instructors who favor active learning
- Study with a group
- Take workshops on how to study
- Get to know your campus library and other information sources
- Embrace new technologies

KNOW YOURSELF!

- Get to know at least one person on campus who cares about you
- Get involved in campus activities
- Learn about campus helping resources
- Meet with your instructors
- Find a great academic advisor or counselor
- Visit your campus career center
- Take advantage of minority support services
- Enlist support of your spouse, partner, or family
- Take your health seriously
- Have realistic expectations
- Learn how to be assertive, yet tactful
- Be proud of your heritage

Critical Thinking, Active Learning

Paths to True Understanding

Stephen Frink/Index Stock Imagery/PictureQuest

go deep

**IN THIS CHAPTER,
YOU WILL LEARN**

- Why there are no right and wrong answers to many important questions

- Four aspects of critical thinking

- How critical arguments differ from emotional arguments

- The importance of critical thinking beyond college

- The big difference between high school and college

- Why most students learn better through active learning

- The value of collaboration

- How to choose the best teachers and be comfortable with them

- What to do if things go wrong between you and your teacher

"*On my history quiz I had to analyze the causes of the American Civil War and back them with evidence. And I worked on learning the dates of events, the places where major battles took place, and some quotes from generals on both sides. My college teachers aren't like my teachers in high school. They toss out ideas and then ask me and other students to explain them. Isn't that what they're being paid for? What am I supposed to be learning, anyway?*"

Go around the room and ask each student which type of question would be easier for them to answer and why. Pick up on any words (*analyze, challenge, concept,* etc.) that you can link to the idea of critical thinking and write them on the board. Then use those words and other comments from students to begin your discussion of critical thinking.

In college, one of the most important lessons has less to do with *what* you're learning and more to do with *how* you're learning. You can be a passive learner or an active learner, a memory hound or a critical thinker. Another way to say this is that you can simply memorize the facts and spit them back on an exam or you can provide new insights into those facts that demand true thinking. You can sit back and listen to your instructor and classmates, or you can ask questions, provide comments, agree or disagree.

Our position? We support the ideas of critical thinking and active learning. This chapter will explain.

SELF-ASSESSMENT: CRITICAL THINKING AND ACTIVE LEARNING

Check all items that apply to you.

_____ I never allow my emotions to get in the way of making the right decision.

_____ I can appreciate the achievements of a person, even if I find that person irritating.

_____ I hold on to all ideas that I come up with. As a result, I come up with a number of good ideas.

_____ While it's easy for me to memorize facts, I prefer quizzes that require me to explain things.

_____ A question can have any number of "right" answers.

_____ I'm usually comfortable asking a question or making a comment in class.

_____ Whether the class has 15 students or 150, it's okay to say something.

_____ I have participated in study teams.

_____ I go to the library with classmates so that we can collaborate on our research.

_____ I try to sit as close to the front as possible in every class.

_____ If I can't tolerate an instructor, I try to get out of that class as soon as possible.

NOTE: The more items you left blank, the more you need to read this chapter to learn how to incorporate these behaviors into your learning experience.

Critical Thinking:
The Search Beyond
Right and Wrong

Imagine your instructor saying on the first day of class:

> *I'm going to fill your minds with lots of important facts, and I expect you to take extensive notes and to know those facts in detail. The important thing in my class is how well you learn the material and how frequently you choose the right answers. And remember, there is only one answer that is correct.*

In another class, the instructor introduces the course quite differently:

> *Each time a new group of students begins this course, they bring their own values, ideas, and past knowledge with them. The important thing is that you use your heads. You certainly will need to read the assignments and take notes on the material in class. But that's only the beginning. What's most important is that you learn to analyze facts, decide which facts are supportable by evidence, and know how to convince others of your beliefs. And remember, while there are lots of wrong conclusions, there also may be more than one right conclusion.*

When you earn your college degree and land a job, chances are your employer is going to be more interested in how well you can think than in how well you can memorize. The second instructor seems to be moving in that direction. She admits that many possibilities may exist.

The first instructor will *tell you what you should know;* the second instructor wants you—through class discussion, small-group sessions, problem solving, research, and other methods—to *discover the truths yourself.* When you do, you will probably have more faith in your conclusions and remember the information much more easily.

From Certainty to Healthy Uncertainty

If you have just completed high school, you may be experiencing an awakening as you enter college. (Even if you're an older returning student, discovering that your instructor trusts you to find valid answers may be somewhat discomfiting.) In high school, you may have been conditioned to believe that things are either right or wrong. If your high school teacher asked, "What are the three branches of the U.S. government?" you had only one choice: "legislative, executive, and judicial." What you might have learned were the names of the three branches, but knowing names doesn't help you understand what the branches do, or how they do it—even though these three names suggest certain basic functions.

A college instructor might ask instead, "Under what circumstances might conflicts arise among the three branches of government, and what does this reveal about the democratic process?" Certainly, there is no simple—or single—answer. Most likely, your instructor is not attempting to embarrass you for giving a wrong answer but to engage you in critical thinking.

Critical thinking is one of the most important concepts of this book, and students will be asked to use their critical thinking skills in every chapter.

Because most students believe that college is primarily a path to a high-paying job, here's a golden opportunity to sell them on the merits of critical thinking. You might invite someone from your career center to address the critical thinking skills sought by employers who interview graduating seniors.

SEE "CRITICAL THINKING: A NECESSARY PART OF A LIBERAL EDUCATION"

Assign one-third of your class to read about the legislative branch, one-third to read about the judicial branch, and one-third to read about the executive branch. Ask these three groups to discuss what they learned above and beyond the names of the branches. Then ask them to appoint a speaker to summarize this to the other two-thirds of the class.

A Higher-Order Thinking Process

Critical thinking is a process of choosing alternatives, weighing them, and considering what they suggest. Critical thinking involves understanding why some people believe one thing rather than another—whether you agree with those reasons or not. Critical thinking is learning to ask pertinent questions and testing your assumptions against hard evidence.

If you lack critical thinking capabilities, you might exhibit behaviors similar to these:

Some of these behaviors may seem downright stupid to your students. Ask them why these situations demonstrate a lack of critical thinking and which situations are more believable than the others.

- You try to reach a classmate on the phone to ask a question about tomorrow's quiz. When you can't reach him, you become so anxious that you can't study or sleep.
- You are asked to read two news articles about the 2000 presidential election. One claims the electoral college system is outdated, the other defends that system. After reading them, you can't see how both sides can be right. You don't even know which one is wrong.
- On the day an important paper is due, a heavy snowstorm rolls in. You brave the cold to get to class. When you arrive, no one—including the teacher—is there. You take a seat and wait for class to begin.

Now let's transform you into a critical thinker:

- When you can't reach a classmate on the phone to ask a question about tomorrow's quiz, you review the material once more, then call one or more other classmates.
- Instead of deciding on one point of view for each important topic, you decide to keep in mind all of those you've discussed that make sense, leaving your final decision until you have the quiz in your hand.
- You compare the representation afforded by the electoral college system with the representation afforded by the popular vote, using InfoTrac College Edition to find at least three articles defending each side of the issue. You look further to see if any article supports the system as it now stands. Now you have a number of things to write about. You find there isn't a clear-cut answer. That's okay.
- On the day an important paper is due, a heavy snowstorm rolls in. You check the college Web site first thing that morning and discover that classes have been cancelled. You stay home.

A Skill to Carry You Through Life

Employers hiring college graduates often say they want an individual who can find information, analyze it, organize it, draw conclusions from it, and present it convincingly to others. One executive said she looked for superior communication skills "because they are in such short supply these days." These skills are the basic ingredients of critical thinking, which includes the ability to:

Ask students how they would define the terms "manage," "interpret," "examine," "argument," and "reliable evidence" as they apply to the critical thinking process.

- Manage and interpret information in a reliable way.
- Examine existing ideas and develop new ones.
- Pose logical arguments that further the absorption of knowledge. In college, the term *argument* refers not to an emotional confrontation but to reasons and information brought together in logical support of some idea.
- Recognize reliable evidence and form well-reasoned arguments.

When thinking about an argument, a good critical thinker considers questions like the following:

- Is the information given in support of the argument true? For example, could it be possible that both the electoral college system and the popular vote system might be equally representative?
- Does the information really support the conclusion? If you determine that each system has its merits (the electoral college gives more voting power to the less populated states, whereas the popular vote represents how the majority of voters feel), can you conclude that there may be a more judicious way to employ both systems in presidential elections?
- Do you need to withhold judgment until better evidence is available? Maybe it's time to set up a trial using a small sample.
- Is the argument really based on good reasoning, or does it appeal mainly to your emotions? You may think the electoral vote is a poor substitute for the popular majority vote, as evidenced in the 2000 presidential election. But you need to ask if your emotions are guiding you to this conclusion.
- Based on the available evidence, are other conclusions equally likely? Is there more than one right answer? Perhaps there is a third way to count the vote by replacing the electoral college concept with something else.
- You may need to do more reading about the election process and find some evidence that the system didn't work as planned in earlier presidential elections. Then you might try to find out how people felt about the voting system. Perhaps you should hold a forum with local voters to gain more views on the pros and cons of the electoral college system.

When communicating an argument or idea to others, a good critical thinker knows how to organize it in an understandable, convincing way in speech or in writing.

Ask what the next step should be when the assumptions do not support the conclusion reached. (Go back and review the assumptions; seek further evidence, etc. Never reach an unsupportable conclusion. Why?)

SEE EXERCISE 3.1
REFLECTING ON
ARGUMENTS

In this scenario, as in others, creative thinking and logical thinking seem opposed to one another. So how can creative and imaginative thinking help one solve a logical problem?

Four Aspects of Critical Thinking

Critical thinking cannot be learned overnight nor always accomplished in a neat set of steps. Yet as interpreted by William T. Daly, teacher of political science at The Richard Stockton College of New Jersey, the critical thinking process can be divided into four basic steps. Because these four aspects are so important, we've woven them into discussions and exercises throughout this book. Practicing these basic ideas can help you become a more effective thinker.

Suggest that students consider the merits of using critical thinking as they form relationships in college. For example, is love necessarily blind and/or should it be? What might be the negative consequences of that in college?

Examining Values

If critical thinking involves making informed decisions based on reliable evidence, what happens when you uncover evidence that conflicts with your values? For example, what if you value your independence so much that you have decided to take your time finding a long-term mate. Then you read a study that suggests that people who choose mates early in life tend to live longer and enjoy life more fully than singles and that the happiest couples make it a point to spend some time away from each other. How would you use critical thinking to come to some closure with these bits of information?

A good class becomes a critical thinking experience. As you listen to the teacher, try to predict where the lecture is heading and why. When other students raise issues, ask yourself whether they have enough information to justify what they have said. And when you raise *your* hand to participate, remember that asking a sensible question may be more important than trying to find the elusive right answer.

© Chuck Savage/Photo courtesy of Beloit College

Because first-year college students may find it difficult to deal with abstractions, ask them to name three inanimate objects they use frequently. Then have the class guess how each person in the room spends a great deal of his or her time. Next, ask them to abstract, from all the answers in the class, what first-year college students do with their time and what this suggests about what they value as a group.

**SEE EXERCISE 3.2
THE CHALLENGE OF
CLASSROOM THINKING**

Warn students not to rely solely on the Internet for information. Because any-one can publish on the Internet, some sources are questionable. Students must learn to analyze and critically evaluate sources and content of infor-mation when dealing with the glut of information literally at their fingertips. Also, though many publications have no site on the Internet, you will probably find them in the library.

Point out that this is creative thinking at its best—a way to brainstorm for new ideas, which, subsequently, must be proved.

**SEE INTERNET
EXERCISE 3.1
CRITICAL THINKING
RESOURCES**

**SEE EXERCISE 3.3
HARD OR EASY?**

Although the previous stage is a time for exploring all possibilities, this stage demands that one narrow the list of choices to those that make logical and practical sense. Ask if anyone has gone through a similar process to find the right idea.

1. Abstract Thinking: Discovering Larger Ideas from Details

From large amounts of facts, seek the bigger ideas or the abstractions behind the facts. Even fields like medicine, which involve countless facts, culminate in general ideas such as the principles of circulation or the basic pattern of cell biology. Ask yourself what larger concepts the details suggest. For example, you read an article that describes how many people are using the Internet now, how much consumer information it provides, what kinds of goods you can buy cheaply over the Internet, and also that many low-income families are still without computers. Thinking care-fully about these facts, how many different important generalizations might you arrive at?

2. Creative Thinking: Finding New Possibilities

Use the general idea you have found to see what further ideas it suggests. This phase can lead in many directions. It might involve searching for ways to make the Internet more available to low-income households. Or it might involve searching out more detailed information on how interested big companies really are in marketing various goods to low-income families. In essence, the creative thinking stage involves extending the general idea—finding new ways it might apply or further ideas it might suggest. The important thing at this stage is not to reject any ideas, but to explore wherever your general idea may take you.

3. Systematic Thinking: Organizing the Possibilities

Systematic thinking involves looking at the outcome of creative thinking in a more demanding, critical way. Which of your solutions seem promising? Which should you throw away? Do some conflict with others? Which ones can be achieved? If you have found new evidence to refine or further test your generalization, what does that new evidence show? Does your original generalization still hold up? Does it need to be modified? What further conclusions do good reasoning and evidence support? This is where you narrow that list from Step 2.

4. Precise Communication of Your Ideas to Others

Great conclusions aren't very useful if you cannot communicate them to others. Consider what your audience will need to know to follow your reasoning and be persuaded.

How College Encourages Critical Thinking

Critical thinking depends on your ability to evaluate different perspectives and to challenge assumptions made by you or others. In order to challenge how you think, a good college teacher may insist that *how* you solve a problem is as important as the solution.

Because critical thinking depends on discovering and testing connections among ideas, your instructor may ask open-ended questions that have no clear-cut answers, questions of "Why?" "How?" or "What if ?" For example: "In these essays we have two conflicting ideas about whether bilingual education is effective at helping children learn English. What now?" Your instructor may ask you to break a larger question into smaller ones: "Let's take the first point. What evidence does the author offer for his idea that language immersion programs get better results?"

She or he may insist that there is more than one valid point of view, or require you to explain concretely the reason for any point you reject. He or she may challenge the authority of experts: "Dr. Fleming's theory sounds impressive. But here are some facts he doesn't account for . . ." You may discover that often your instructor reinforces the legitimacy of your personal views and experiences, and you also will discover that you can change your mind.

It is natural for new college students to find this mode of thinking difficult and to discover that answers are seldom entirely wrong or right but more often somewhere in between. Yet the questions that lack simple answers usually are the ones most worthy of study.

SEE EXERCISE 3.4 GATHERING INFORMATION FOR DECISION MAKING

Give students a topic—such as drinking on campus, a healthy diet, time management, and so on—and ask them to write questions beginning with "Why?" "How?" or "What if?" Ask them to reflect on where such questions might lead them, as opposed to questions that ask "Who?" "What?" or "When?"

Remind students that they should never argue about an idea unless they are ready with their reasons for arguing.

Your students may disagree that the questions that lack simple answers are the most worthwhile to study. Once they have read "Four Aspects of Critical Thinking," have them complete steps 1 and 2 of the critical thinking process in small groups and steps 3 and 4 by writing a paper defending or refuting this statement.

Active Learning

Because most college teachers emphasize critical thinking, they offer you the chance to move from a pattern of being taught *passively* to one of *learning actively.*

Active learning is simply a method that involves students, or learners, in an active manner. It takes place whenever your teacher asks you a question in class, puts you in groups to solve a problem, requires you to make an oral presentation to the class, or does anything else that gives you and other students a voice in the learning process.

Speaking of Careers

Trying to name all the possible careers in which you'll use critical thinking may be impossible. The truth is, whether you're an auto mechanic trying to determine why an engine is running rough, a management executive reviewing sales data for a business meeting, or a theater director poring over the script of a play to determine how you want your actors to approach it, you will be using critical thinking skills.

**SEE EXERCISE 3.5
DIFFERENCES BETWEEN
HIGH SCHOOL AND
COLLEGE**

In the Hawaiian language, the words "teaching" and "learning" are one and the same. Ask students how they would explain this. How can one be "teaching" and "learning" at the same time? Why is it okay to collaborate with another student? What makes that different from cheating?

Take an informal survey of the class to find out how many of their instructors employ active learning techniques (discussion, hands-on projects, small-group work, etc.) as opposed to how many just lecture. Ask how many students prefer each style and why. Then ask if it's more important to memorize facts or to learn to question facts.

Some students may find the college classroom that stresses active learning a scary environment. This would be a good time to ask students whether your active learning approach is making them a bit uncomfortable and why. If they harbor misconceptions about why you're asking them to talk instead of lecturing to them, now is a good time to dispel as many myths as possible.

**SEE EXERCISE 3.6
LEARNING ACTIVELY**

The Many Benefits of Active Learning

In addition to placing you "in the center" of learning, active learning teaches you a variety of skills employers want most: thinking, writing, oral communication, goal setting, time management, relationship building, problem solving, ethical reasoning, and more.

A teacher who urges students to collaborate on an assignment is aware that two or more heads may be far more productive than one. Each student turns in an original piece of work, but is free to seek advice from another student. More than likely, this is how you'll be working after college. It makes sense to learn collaboration—not competition—now.

Students who embrace active learning not only learn better but enjoy their learning experiences more. Even if you have an instructor who lectures for an entire period and leaves little or no time for questions, you still can form a study group with three or four other students. Or you might ask the teacher for an appointment to discuss unanswered questions, thus turning a passive learning situation into an active one.

Active learners try new ideas and discover new knowledge by exploring the world around them instead of just memorizing facts. Here are some things you can do to practice learning actively:

- Ask other students which teachers will actively engage you in learning.
- Even in a class of 200, sit as close to the front as you can and raise your hand if you don't understand something. Chances are, the other 199 didn't understand it either.
- Study with other students. Talking about assignments and getting other points of view will help you learn the material faster and more thoroughly.
- Follow the suggestions in this book about managing your time, optimizing your learning style, taking class notes, reading texts, and studying for exams.
- Politely question your instructor. When you don't agree, explain why. Good teachers will listen and may still disagree, but they may think more of you for showing you can think and that you care enough to question them.
- Stay in touch with teachers, other students, and your academic advisor through email or voice mail.

Why Active Learners Can Learn More Than Passive Learners

Through active learning, you will learn not only the material in your notes and textbook, but also how to

- Work with others
- Improve your critical thinking, listening, writing, and speaking skills
- Function independently and teach yourself
- Manage your time
- Gain sensitivity to cultural differences

Becoming an Active Learner

Active learning requires preparation before and after every class. It may include browsing in the library, making appointments to talk to faculty members, making outlines from your class notes, attending cultural events, working on a committee, asking someone to read something you've written to see if it's clear, or having a serious discussion with students whose personal values are different from yours.

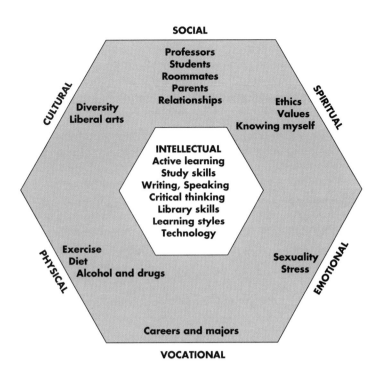

SOCIAL

Professors
Students
Roommates
Parents
Relationships

CULTURAL

Diversity
Liberal arts

SPIRITUAL

Ethics
Values
Knowing myself

INTELLECTUAL
Active learning
Study skills
Writing, Speaking
Critical thinking
Library skills
Learning styles
Technology

PHYSICAL

Exercise
Diet
Alcohol and drugs

EMOTIONAL

Sexuality
Stress

Careers and majors

VOCATIONAL

FIGURE 3.1
Aspects of
Student Development

Yet some students resist active learning out of fear of trying something new and challenging. One student described an active learning class as "scary" and a more traditional class as "safe" because the teacher did not make students sit in a semi-circle, and he used a textbook and lectures to explain ideas. In an active class, the process, the uncertainty, and the openness were scary.[1]

According to student development theory, an active approach to learning and living has the potential to produce individuals who are well rounded in all aspects of life. The hexagon in Figure 3.1 depicts seven aspects of personal development, with intellectual development at its center. Optimal personal development depends on each area's supporting every other area. Good active learning skills will help you feel more comfortable socially, gain a greater appreciation for diversity and the liberal arts, and be better able to clarify your major and future career. Staying physically active can reduce stress and keep your mind alert while you study. Developing a sense of values (see Chapter 7) can help you choose your friends more carefully and decide how to manage your time.

Instead of blending in with your peers—as many new students seem to do—ask the questions in class others probably want to ask but don't. Try to do something innovative with every paper and project. Sure, you'll make some mistakes, but your instructor probably will appreciate your inventiveness, reward you for it, and be more willing to help you improve your work.

Good teachers keep the lines of communication open. Some comments may provoke open discussion in and out of the classroom. In fact, some of the best learning may take place one-on-one in the instructor's office. Research shows that students who have frequent conferences with their teachers outside of class have a greater chance of returning to college for their second year.

One way to practice active learning and critical thinking daily is through a process called the "1-minute paper." During a study of teaching at Harvard

Ask each student to construct his or her own personal development grid using the hexagon in Figure 3.1. Under each of the six dimensions, have them write what they do best in that area. Then have them write what they want to improve in each area. In class, form small groups and ask students to share their strengths and perceived weaknesses and to try to find someone with opposing strengths who might help them. Try to have each student visit each group to mine as many resources as possible.

[1]Adapted from Russell A. Warren, "Engaging Students in Active Learning," *About Campus,* March–April 1997.

Ask students to write such a paper at the end of class. Ask them to include what they have learned today, how they have reacted to it, and how they can apply it. Give them the opportunity to tell you something they didn't under-stand, so you can clarify that point next time. This is one more way to let them know you care and are willing to listen. Share the results in the next class.

SEE EXERCISE 3.7 FORMING YOUR IDEAL LEARNING TEAM

One thing we know from research on college students is that the greatest influence on them is other students. With that in mind, (1) establish whether any students have had a positive expe-rience with collaborative learning in school and get them to share those thoughts with the class, and (2) bring successful juniors and seniors to class to talk about their positive experiences with collaborative learning.

SEE "THE MANY USES OF LEARNING TEAMS"

Chances are, many of your students have had more experience working in teams outside a formal school setting than inside it. Ask them to reflect upon some of those experiences, such as in athletics, part-time employment, and so on. Have them discuss what general principles they learned from those experiences that they could apply to working as part of an academic team. Remind them that another skill sought by most employers is the ability to work in groups. Suggest that the more they can document such experiences on their résumés, the more attractive they may be to future employers.

SEE EXERCISE 3.8 TO COLLABORATE OR NOT?

University, one of many suggestions for improving learning was this: At the end of each class, students were asked to write what they thought was the main issue of that class and what their unanswered questions were for the next class.

Even if your instructors don't require it, try writing your 1-minute paper each day at the end of class. Use it to think about the main issues discussed that day, and save it so that you can ask good questions at the next class meeting.

The Value of Collaboration

Collaborative learning occurs when groups of students work together for the good of all. How does collaboration improve learning? Joseph Cuseo of Marymount College points to these factors:

- Learners learn from one another as well as from the instructor.
- Collaborative learning is by its very nature active learning, and so tends to increase learning by involving you more actively.
- "Two heads are better than one." Collaboration can lead to more ideas, alterna-tive approaches, new perspectives, and better solutions.
- Learners who might not speak out in larger classes tend to be more comfortable speaking in smaller groups.
- Students develop stronger bonds with other students in the class, which may increase their interest in attending.
- An environment of "positive competition" among groups is developed when sev-eral groups are asked to solve the same problem—as long as the instructor clari-fies that the purpose is for the good of all.
- Students in groups tend to develop leadership skills.
- Students learn to work with others.

College students may learn as much from peers as they do from instructors and readings. When students work effectively in a supportive group, the experience can be a powerful one. Interviews with college students at Harvard revealed that nearly every senior who had been part of a study group considered this experience to be crucial to his or her success.

Making Learning Teams Productive

Not all learning groups are effective. Sometimes teamwork fails to reach its potential because no thought was given to how the group should be formed or how it should function. Use the following strategies to develop high-quality learning teams that work.

- Remember that learning teams are more than study groups. Effective student learning teams collaborate regularly for other academic tasks besides test review sessions.
- In forming teams, seek students who will contribute quality and diversity to the group. Look for fellow students who are motivated, attend class regularly, are attentive and participate actively in class, and complete assignments. Include teammates from different ethnic, racial, or cultural backgrounds, different age groups, and different personality types and learning styles. Include males and females. Choosing only your friends will make it more likely that the group will get off track or lack the diversity it needs or both.
- Keep the group small (four to six). Smaller groups allow for more face-to-face interaction and eye contact and less opportunity for any individual to shirk responsibility. Also, it's much easier for small groups to meet outside class.

If two heads are better than one, four heads may be even better at examining course content.

- Consider choosing an even number of teammates (four or six), so you can work in pairs in case the team decides to divide its work.
- Hold individual team members personally accountable for their own learning and for contributing to the learning of their teammates. Research on study groups at Harvard indicates that they are effective only if each member has done the required work in advance of the group meeting (for example, completing required readings and other assignments). One way to ensure accountability is to have each member come to group meetings with specific information to share with teammates as well as questions to ask the group. Or have individual members take on different roles or responsibilities, such as mastering a particular topic, section, or skill to be taught to others.

Connecting with Your College Teachers

Your college instructors will encourage you to develop new ways of thinking, to realize there may be many acceptable answers as opposed to one, to question existing knowledge, to take issue with something they might say, to ask questions in class, and to offer possible solutions to problems. You may be surprised to find that most college teachers do not fit the stereotype of the ivory tower scholar.

Though many college instructors still must spend time doing scholarship and performing service for the institution, a majority of them admit they love teaching most of all, and for good reason: Motivating students like you to do their best in class can give a good teacher an amazing high.

Teachers may also do things your high school teachers never did, such as

- Supplementing textbook assignments with other information
- Giving exams covering both assigned readings and lectures
- Questioning conclusions of other scholars
- Accepting several different student opinions on a question
- Never checking to see if you are taking notes or reading the text
- Demanding more reading of you in a shorter period of time

It is very important to convince your students of the merits of team learning. Tell them you realize that their previous educational history may not have prepared them to work this way, but that doesn't make it right. Explain that students who participate in study groups get higher grades, stay in college longer, and are more likely to graduate.

It's important that students understand the difference between helpful collaboration (working together openly on a project, seeking criticism from others, etc.) and cheating (having someone else write a paper for you, getting quiz answers in advance, plagiarizing material and calling it yours, etc.).

SEE INTERNET EXERCISE 3.2 YOUR TEACHERS'– AND YOUR OWN– RESPONSIBILITIES

One of the best ways to discover what college instructors expect is to analyze their course syllabi. Ask students to check syllabi for statements of expectations, how they will be evaluated, opportunities for discussion, what requirements demand "active" behaviors, and so on. Use your syllabus for this course as an example of how to analyze other courses.

- Giving fewer quizzes or many more quizzes
- Expecting you to be familiar with topics related to their field
- Being sympathetic to difficulties you may have while holding firm to high standards of grading

You may be on friendly terms with your instructor and find you have received a low grade because you missed too many classes, did not complete all required work, or simply failed to produce acceptable work. A college teacher may tell you that although your grades may be unacceptable, this is not necessarily a reflection on your character.

To make the most of a student–teacher relationship:

1. **Attend class regularly and on time.** And participate in discussions; you'll learn more if you do. If you miss a class, you might get another student's notes, but that isn't the same thing as being present during class. Learning is easier when you're there every day.

2. **Save your cuts for emergencies.** When you know you will be absent, always let your instructor know in advance. It could make a big difference in your teacher's attitude toward you. And it's one way of introducing yourself.

3. **Sit near the front.** Studies indicate that students who do so are more free of distractions and tend to earn better grades.

4. **Speak up.** Ask questions when you need clarification, and voice your opinion when you disagree. Your teacher should respond favorably as long as your comments or questions are relevant.

5. **See your instructor outside class when you need help.** Instructors are required to keep office hours for student appointments. Make an appointment by phone, email, or at the end of class.

6. **Share one or more "1-minute papers,"** either in writing or through email, with your instructor. It could be the start of an interesting dialog.

Academic Freedom in the Classroom

College instructors believe in the freedom to speak out, whether it be in a classroom discussion about economic policy or at a public rally on abortion or gay rights. What matters more than what instructors believe is their right to proclaim that belief to others without fear. Colleges and universities have promoted the advancement of knowledge by granting scholars virtually unlimited freedom of inquiry, as long as human lives, rights, and privacy are not violated.

Stressing the importance of attendance may sound pretty basic, but remember this is the first time many students have had the freedom to choose whether to attend class or not. Do a reality check. Ask students if they know what the official attendance policy is and where they can find it. Remind them of your attendance policy. Verify that they have noted the policy in each of their other courses. Tell them it's always best to be there.

In this world of technology, distance learning, and the World Wide Web, we believe it's more important than ever to remind students that the human touch inherent in teaching is a vital element in their learning. This could lead to a discussion of "Why have class if you can read the book, watch videos, surf the Net?"

Ask students what they have encountered so far from their college instructors that is different and how they are reacting to and coping with these differences. Compare their comments to the list in this section of the chapter. Encourage them to suspend judgment on some of these differences until they have had time to adjust to them.

Critical Thinking

What Do College Teachers Expect of Students?

Look back over the differences between high school and college teachers. Then list five to ten qualities and behaviors you believe college teachers want in their students. Compare your response with those of several classmates. Consider asking one of your teachers to comment as well.

Some teachers may insult or speak sarcastically about a politician you admire. Although you need not accept such ideas, you must learn to evaluate them for yourself, instead of basing your judgments on what others have always told you is right.

Academic freedom also extends to you. In college, you will have more freedom than in high school to select certain research topics or to pursue controversial issues. You will also have the right to disagree with the instructor, but be certain you can support your argument with reliable published or personal evidence. Done with respect, such queries can enrich learning for the entire class.

When Things Go Wrong Between You and a Teacher

What If You Can't Tolerate a Particular instructor? Arrange a meeting to try to work things out. Getting to know the teacher as a person may help you cope with the way he or she teaches the course. If that fails, check the "drop/add" date, which usually falls at the end of the first week of classes. You may have to drop the course altogether and pick up a different one. If it's too late to add a class, you may still want to drop before the "drop date" later in the term and avoid a penalty. See your academic advisor or counselor for help.

If you are still having trouble with the instructor and need to stay in the class, consider seeing the head of the department. If you are still dissatisfied, move up the administrative ladder until you get a definite answer. Never allow a bad instructor to sour you on college. Even the worst course will be over in a matter of weeks.

What If You're Not Satisfied with Your Grade? First, make an appointment to see the instructor and discuss the assignment. Your teacher may give you a second chance because you took the time to ask for help. If you get a low grade on an exam, you might ask the instructor to review certain answers with you. Never insist on a grade change, as this will most likely backfire. Keep in mind that no one other than your teacher—not even the president of your campus—can change a grade. Your teacher's freedom to grade is sacrosanct.

What if You're Dealing with Sexual Harassment or Sexism? Sexual harassment is a serious offense and a cause for grievance. See your department chair if an instructor makes inappropriate or threatening remarks of a sexual nature. No instructor should ask for a date or otherwise pressure students to become involved in personal relationships, because the implied threat is that if you refuse, you may fail the course.

Sexism refers to statements or behaviors that demonstrate a belief in the greater general worth of one gender over the other. Comments such as "I don't know why girls take chemistry" are not only insulting but may cause women to lose confidence in their abilities. The same rules apply to defamatory remarks about one's ethnic group. Your campus has specific procedures to follow if you believe you are being harassed sexually; take advantage of them.

As an active learner and critical thinker, you should find it easier to admire both your teacher and your subject deeply, just as your teacher will learn to admire you.

This would be a good time to give students a brief history of academic freedom. You might want to bring in your faculty handbook and read the official statement describing academic freedom. You could also relate it to the concept of tenure and explain why campuses award tenure.

SEE INTERNET EXERCISE 3.3 FINDING FACULTY EMAIL ADDRESSES

SEE EXERCISE 3.9 INTERVIEWING A TEACHER

Explain your campus's policies on academic appeals and grievances, sexual harassment, and so on. Better still, supply them with copies.

SEE INTERNET EXERCISE 3.4 RESEARCHING CRITICAL THINKING AND ACTIVE LEARNING

SEE EXERCISE 3.10 A TEACHING EXPERIENCE

Internet Exercise 3.1 Critical Thinking Resources

The Center for Critical Thinking (http://www.criticalthinking.org/university/univclass/ Defining.html) offers resources and discussion of the fundamentals of critical thinking. (Go to http://success.wadsworth.com/book_resources/updated_links.html for the most up-to-date URLs.) Look up this site and read the discussion of what critical thinking is. Then compare it to the presentation in this chapter. Write a paper discussing the similarities and differences. Share your ideas with the class.

Internet Exercise 3.2 Your Teachers'—and Your Own—Responsibilities

A Like everyone else, teachers must juggle many responsibilities. Indicate what percentage of their working time you think faculty spend in each of the following activities:

Teaching   _____

Research/scholarship   _____

Administration   _____

Outside consulting   _____

Service/nonteaching activities   _____

Check your answers against the data in *The Digest of Educational Stastistics 1997*, Table 228: http://nces.ed.gov/pubs/digest97/d97t228.html (Go to http://success.wadsworth.com for the most up-to-date URLs.)

B Survey several of your teachers to find out how they spend their working time. Compare the results to the Internet figures. Remember that these percentages are averages for all faculty at all schools surveyed. The particular percentages at any school or for any particular faculty member may vary considerably.

Internet Exercise 3.3 Finding Faculty Email Addresses

Although email is often a poor substitute for an office visit, it is useful for specific questions, to explain why you missed class, or for other short messages. If you can't reach your teacher by phone, you might email to request an appointment by including your phone number in your message.

To send email, just as with regular mail, you must know someone's address. Find your instructors' email addresses on the campus network, or ask them for their email addresses on the first day of class. You may find their addresses in the course syllabus. If you are not familiar with sending and receiving email, ask another student to help you.

Additional Exercises

These exercises at the end of each chapter will help you sharpen what we believe are the critical skills for college success: writing, critical thinking, learning in groups, planning, reflecting, and taking action. Also check out the CD-ROM that came with your book—you will find more exercises there, as well as resources for this chapter.

Exercise 3.1 **Reflecting on Arguments**

Review the list of questions on page 47 of this chapter. Are they the kinds of questions that you tend to ask when you read, listen to, or take part in discussions? Each evening for the next week, revisit the list and think about whether you have asked such questions that day. Also try to notice whether people are stating their assumptions or conclusions.

Exercise 3.2 **The Challenge of Classroom Thinking**

Think about your experiences in each of your classes so far this term.

- Have your instructors pointed out any conflicts or contradictions in the ideas they have presented? Or have you noted any contradictions that they have not acknowledged?
- Have they asked questions for which they sometimes don't seem to have the answers?
- Have they challenged you or other members of the class to explain yourselves more fully?
- Have they challenged the arguments of other experts?
- Have they called on students in the class to question or challenge certain ideas?

How have you reacted to their words? Do your responses reflect critical thinking? Write down your thoughts for possible discussion in class. Consider sharing them with your instructors.

Exercise 3.3 **Hard or Easy?**

In your opinion, is it harder to think critically than to base your arguments on how you feel about a topic? What are the advantages of finding answers based on your feelings? Based on critical thinking? How might you use both approaches in seeking an answer?

Exercise 3.4 **Gathering Information for Decision Making**

In groups of four to six, choose a major problem on campus, such as binge drinking, cheating, date rape, parking, safety, class size, or lack of student participation in organizations. Between this class and the next, seek information and possible solutions by interviewing a campus authority on the topic, searching for articles on InfoTrac College Edition, searching campus library holdings, and/or conducting a survey of students. Next class, share your findings, citing your sources, with other members of the group. Try to reach consensus in the group on the best way to solve the problem. If any members of the group are using emotional rather than logical arguments, point it out to them.

Your Personal Journal

Here are several things to write about. Choose one or more, or choose another topic related to this chapter.

1. Based on the definitions in this chapter, do you believe you already are a critical thinker? If so, tell why. If not, tell how you plan to become one.

2. Think about one or more careers you hope you wind up in. They don't have to correlate with your academic major at this point, but they should be fields about which you have a passion. How might you use critical thinking in those fields? How would it help you do a better job?

3. We've stated that college teachers are different from high school teachers. Can you give an example or two of those differences, based on one of your high school teachers and one of your current college teachers? Whose style are/were you more comfortable with? Why? In which class do you believe you'll learn more? Why?

4. If you've tried collaborative learning, write about how that went. If you haven't tried it yet, write about why you haven't and whether you plan to do so in the near future.

5. An important part of active learning is student participation. What if some students are reticent about speaking in class (their learning styles may indicate they are introverted)? Should the teacher be flexible about this? If so, how? If not, what should he or she do?

6. What behaviors are you willing to change after reading this chapter? How might you go about changing them?

7. What else is on your mind this week? If you wish to share it with your instructor, add it to this journal entry.

_____

_____

_____

_____

_____

_____

_____

_____

_____

_____

_____

_____

_____

_____

_____

_____

Resources

One way to improve your critical thinking skills is to explore topics and issues you normally would not pay attention to. You might, for example, watch a PBS special on the Middle East instead of a major league baseball game. Or read a book containing new scientific evidence about the high fat content of fast foods instead of reading the latest fashion magazine. Or see a film with emotional depth instead of the new "blood and guts" thriller. Start making a list here.

	THE USUAL CHOICES	SOMETHING DIFFERENT
Movies		
TV		
Books		
Magazines		
Live Entertainment		

List the ones that seem the most interesting to you, and tell why.

....

....

....

....

....

....

....

....

....

Compare lists with friends.

Do a library or Internet search to come up with a list of articles about critical thinking. Choose one or two, read them, and reflect in writing on what you have learned.

....

....

....

....

....

....

....

....

....

You can learn a lot about your instructors both from the information they give you and from the information the school can give you. Connecting with your instructors inside and outside of class can make your college experience much more meaningful.

Enter the following information about your instructors this term.

Instructor's name .... Course name ....

Other courses he or she teaches ....

(You may want to take another class with him or her.)

Office hours .... Office location .... Phone ....

Home phone number .... Email address ....

　Is it okay to call this instructor at home? .... To send email? ....

Instructor's name .... Course name ....

Other courses he or she teaches ....

Office hours .... Office location .... Phone ....

Home phone number .... Email address ....

　Is it okay to call this instructor at home? .... To send email? ....

Instructor's name .... Course name ....

Other courses he or she teaches ....

Office hours .... Office location .... Phone ....

Home phone number .... Email address ....

　Is it okay to call this instructor at home? .... To send email? ....

Instructor's name .... Course name ....

Other courses he or she teaches ....

Office hours .... Office location .... Phone ....

Home phone number .... Email address ....

    Is it okay to call this instructor at home? .... To send email? ....

Instructor's name .... Course name ....

Other courses he or she teaches ....

Office hours .... Office location .... Phone ....

Home phone number .... Email address ....

    Is it okay to call this instructor at home? .... To send email? ....

Listening, Note Taking, and Participating

Getting the Most Out of Classes

Alvis Upitis/Getty Images/The Image Bank

IN THIS CHAPTER, YOU WILL LEARN

- How to assess your note-taking skills and how to improve them

- Why it's important to review your notes as soon as reasonable after class

- How to prepare to remember before class

- How to listen critically and take good notes in class

- Why you should speak up in class

- How to review class and textbook materials after class

This chapter was written with the expert assistance of Jeanne L. Higbee, University of Minnesota.

tune in

I can't believe it! I got a 65 on my first history test, and I thought I knew my lecture notes backward and forward. I was in class every day, but there were questions on the test about subjects I don't even remember! Maybe I just wasn't listening hard enough. Guess I'll have to write faster and take down everything the instructor says, or I'll never pass."

The information in this chapter is critical to college success. Emphasize that college courses differ significantly from high school courses and that effective listening, note taking, *and* participation in class are important. Remind students that many test questions on college exams are drawn from class lectures, not textbooks. Ask how many of their current courses are lecture based.

In virtually every college class you take, you'll need to master three skills to earn high grades: listening, note taking, and participating (one of the authors of this book was failing everything until he learned how to take lecture notes). Taking an active role in your classes—asking questions, contributing to discussions, or providing answers—will help you listen better and take better notes. That in turn will enhance your ability to learn: to understand abstract ideas, find new possibilities, organize those ideas, and recall the material once the class is over.

SELF-ASSESSMENT: LISTENING, NOTE TAKING, AND PARTICIPATING

Read each of the following statements and put a check mark in front of those that come close to describing you.

_____ 1. If I can't tell what's important in a lecture, I write down everything.

_____ 2. If an instructor moves through the material very fast, it might be a good idea to tape-record the lecture and not worry about paying attention in class.

_____ 3. If the instructor puts an outline on the board, I usually copy it right away.

_____ 4. Listening in a class that is mainly discussion is better than trying to take notes.

_____ 5. Most of my friends take notes in outline form; I guess I should do the same.

_____ 6. When the instructor says something I don't understand, I figure I'll get it from a friend later.

_____ 7. If I arrive early, I spend the time before class talking to my friends.

_____ 8. I rarely or never compare my notes with those of another student or a study group.

_____ 9. Whatever I miss in class, I'll catch up on in the textbook.

_____ 10. It's better to take notes than to raise my hand and ask a question.

One way to "imprint" these ten statements in the minds of your students is to create groups of five and assign three or four of the statements to each group. Ask if they can prove the statements are false and have them report their thoughts to the class. Be wary of item 7. Most students will claim it's their right to do whatever they please until the instructor begins class.

These skills are critical to your academic success because your college instructors are likely to introduce new material in class that your texts don't cover, and much of this material may resurface on quizzes and exams. By the way, none of the statements in the self-assessment inventory is considered good practice for the classroom. Instead, keep these suggestions in mind as you read the rest of this chapter.

1. Writing down everything the instructor says is probably not possible. If you are not sure what is important to remember, ask questions in class, go over your notes with a tutor, or compare your notes with a friend's.

2. Recording a lecture means you must sit through it at least twice in order to understand it. Unless you can concentrate on listening to the tape while commuting, this may not be the best use of your time. Instead, consider asking the instructor to speak more slowly or to repeat key points, or meet with a study group to compare notes. If there is a reason you do need to tape-record a lecture, be sure to ask the instructor's permission first.

3. Copying an outline immediately may not allow enough room for filling in the details. A good instructor will cover each point in sequence. Write down the first point and listen. Take notes. When the next point is covered, do the same.

4. During group discussion your instructor may take notes on what is said and could use it on exams. You should take notes as well as participate.

5. The same system won't work for everyone. If a formal outline works for you, fine. If it doesn't, consider other suggestions in this chapter for organizing your notes so you can understand them later.

6. Better yet, ask the instructor during or after class. Others may not have "gotten it" either or may have misunderstood the point the instructor was making.

7. As you'll learn in this chapter, when you chat with friends before class begins, you are wasting valuable review time.

8. Reviewing notes with one or two other students can be beneficial to all.

9. What the instructor says in class may not always be in the textbook. And vice versa.

10. Learning is a participatory sport. Speak up!

Short-Term Memory: Listening and Forgetting

Ever notice how easy it is to learn the words of a song? Yet you may read a few pages of a book several times or hear a lecture and find it difficult to retain the important ideas and concepts after a few hours. We remember songs and poetry more easily in part because they follow a rhythm and a beat, because we may repeat them— sometimes unconsciously—over and over in our heads, and because they often have a personal meaning for us—we relate them to something in our everyday lives. We remember prose less easily unless we make an effort to relate it to what we already know. And, because it is the most unstructured form of communication, and virtually impossible to relate to previous knowledge, we can hardly remember gibberish or nonsense words at all (see Figure 4.1).

When preparing for tests or for the next lecture, you may sometimes labor over your class notes, trying to figure out exactly what you wrote, what the notes mean, and what the central idea is. That's because most forgetting takes place within the first 24 hours after you see or hear something. So, if you do not review almost immediately after class, it will be difficult to retrieve the material later. In two weeks, you will have forgotten up to 70 percent of the material! Once you understand how to improve your ability to remember, you will retain information more easily and completely. Many instructors draw a significant proportion of their test items from their lectures; remembering what is presented in class is crucial to doing well on exams.

To demonstrate how easy it is to forget information, ask students to think back to a lecture they had the previous day and to write down as much of what they learned that they remember. For homework, ask them to compare what they just wrote to the notes they took while the class was in session.

**SEE EXERCISE 4.1
LISTENING AND MEMORY**

**SEE INTERNET
EXERCISE 4.1
STUDY SKILLS GUIDES
ON THE INTERNET**

If you still have your college notebooks, bring them to class and show your students where your notes were helpful to you and where they were not. Invite an upper-class student to talk about the importance of listening and getting good grades.

Using Your Senses in the Learning Process

You can enhance memory by using as many of your senses as possible while learning. How do you believe you learn most effectively?

FIGURE 4.1

Learning and Forgetting
Psychologists have studied human forgetting in many laboratory experiments. Here are the forgetting curves for three kinds of material: poetry, prose, and nonsense syllables. The shallower curves for prose and poetry indicate that meaningful material is forgotten more slowly than non-meaningful information. Because poetry contains internal cues such as rhyme and rhythm, it is forgotten less quickly than prose.

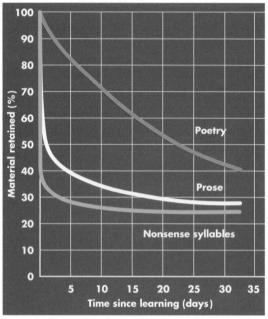

SOURCE: Used with permission from Wayne Weiten, *Psychology: Themes and Variations* (Pacific Grove, CA: Brooks/Cole, 1989, p. 254. Based on data from D. van Guilford, Van Nostrand, 1939).

Ask students to try to determine which of their senses they use most when sorting and learning material for class. Have them form groups by preferred sense. If some individuals are standing alone, put them in another group and have them explain their method as others explain theirs.

1. **Aural:** Are you an auditory learner? Do you learn by listening to other people talk, or does your mind begin to wander when listening passively for more than a few minutes?
2. **Visual:** Do you like reading? Do you learn best when you can see the words on the printed page? During a test, can you actually visualize where the information appears in your text? Can you remember data best when it's presented in the form of a picture, graph, chart, map, or video?
3. **Interactive:** Do you enjoy discussing coursework with friends, classmates, or the teacher? Does talking about information from lectures or the text help you remember it?
4. **Tactile:** Do you learn through your sense of touch? Does typing your notes help you remember them?
5. **Kinesthetic:** Can you learn better when your body is in motion? When participating in sports, dancing, or working out, do you know immediately if a movement feels right? Do you learn more effectively by doing it than by listening or reading about it?
6. **Olfactory:** Does your sense of taste or smell contribute to your learning process? Do you cook using a recipe or by tasting and adding ingredients? Are you sensitive to odors?

Two or three of these perceptual modes probably describe your preferred ways of learning better than the others. In college, many faculty members share information primarily via lecture and the text. Yet many students like to learn best through visual and interactive means, creating a mismatch between learning and teaching styles. This is only a problem if you do not learn how to adapt material conveyed by means of lecture and text to your preferred modes of learning.

In this chapter, you will learn some ways to do this. The following system will help you remember and understand lecture material better and relate information to other things you already know. It consists of three major parts: preparing to listen before class, listening and taking notes during class, and reviewing and recalling information after class.

Before Class: Prepare to Remember

Even if lectures don't allow for active participation, you can take a number of active learning steps to make your listening and note taking more efficient. Because many lectures constitute demanding intellectual encounters, you need to be intellectually prepared before class begins.

You would not want to walk in cold to give a speech, interview for a job, plead a case in court, or compete in sports. For each of these situations, you would want to prepare in some way. For the same reasons, you should begin active listening, learning, and remembering before the lecture.

1. **Do the assigned reading.** You may blame lecturers for seeming disorganized and confusing when in fact you may not have done the assigned reading necessary to follow what the lecturer is saying. Some instructors refer to assigned readings for each class session; others may hand out a syllabus and assume you are keeping up with the assigned readings. Completing the assigned readings on time will help you listen better, and critical listening (see page 68) promotes remembering.

2. **Warm up for class.** Read well and take good notes, or annotate, highlight, or underline the text. Then warm up by reviewing chapter introductions and summaries and by referring to related sections in your text and to your notes from the previous class period. This prepares you to pay attention, understand, and remember.

3. **Keep an open mind.** Every class holds the promise of discovering new information and uncovering different perspectives. Some teachers may intentionally present information that challenges your value system. One of the purposes of college is to teach you to think in new and different ways and to provide support for your own beliefs. Instructors do not necessarily expect you to agree with everything they or your classmates say, but if you want people to respect your values, you must show respect for them as well by listening to what they have to say with an open mind.

4. **Get organized.** Develop an organizational system. Decide what type of notebook will work best for you. Many study skills experts suggest using three-ring binders because you can punch holes in syllabi and other course handouts and

Give students a reading assignment and follow up with a related lecture in class. Then give them a quiz the next day, drawing about half the questions from the reading and the rest from your lecture. Which group of questions did students miss most?

David Gonzales

You'll get more out of a lecture if you prepare ahead of time. Stay abreast of the readings. Get your own ideas flowing by reviewing notes from the previous lecture. What questions were left unanswered? Where should today's session begin?

keep them with class notes. If you prefer using spiral notebooks, consider buying multisubject notebooks that have pocket dividers for handouts, or be sure to maintain a folder for each course. Create a recording system to keep track of grades on all assignments, quizzes, and tests. Retain any papers that are returned to you until the term is over and your grades are posted on your transcript. That way, if you need to appeal a grade because an error occurs, you will have the documentation you need to support your appeal. If you keep your notes and other course materials organized throughout the term, you will be aware of where you stand going into final exams and be prepared to review efficiently.

During Class: Listen Critically

Listening in class is not like listening to a TV program, listening to a friend, or even listening to a speaker at a meeting. Knowing how to listen in class can help you get more out of what you hear, understand better what you have heard, and save time.

1. **Be ready for the message.** If you have done the assigned reading, you will know what details are already presented in the text and to what extent you can focus your notes on key concepts during the lecture. You will also be aware of what information is not covered in the text and will be prepared to pay closer attention when the instructor is presenting unfamiliar material.

2. **Listen to the main concepts and central ideas, not just to fragmented facts and figures.** Although facts are important, they will be easier to remember and make more sense when you can place them in a context of concepts, themes, and ideas. You want to understand the material, not just memorize it!

3. **Listen for new ideas.** Even if you are an expert on the topic, you can still learn something new. Do not assume that college instructors will present the same information you learned in a similar course in high school.

4. **Really hear what is said.** Hearing sounds is not the same as hearing the intended message. Listening involves hearing what the speaker wants you to understand. Don't give in to distractions, such as doodling, daydreaming, or looking at other students. Try not to pass quick judgment on what is being said. As a true critical thinker, note questions that arise in your mind as you listen but save the judgments for later.

5. **Repeat mentally.** Words can go in one ear and out the other unless you make an effort to retain them. Think about what you hear and make an active effort to retain it by restating it in your own words silently. If you cannot translate the information into your own words, that is a sign that you do not really understand it and need further clarification.

6. **Decide whether what you have heard is not important, somewhat important, or very important.** If it's really not important, let it go. If it's very important, make it a major point in your notes by highlighting or underscoring it, or use it as a major topic in your outline if that is the method you use for note taking. If it's somewhat important, try to relate it to a very important topic by writing it down as a subset of that topic.

7. **Ask questions.** Early in the term, determine whether the instructor is open to responding to questions during lecture. Some teachers prefer to save questions for the end or to have students ask questions during separate discussion sections or office hours. If your teacher is open to answering questions as they arise, do not hesitate to ask if you did not hear or understand what was said. It is best to clarify things immediately, if possible, and other students are likely to have the same questions. If you can't hear another student's question, ask that the question be repeated.

As an experiment, tell students *not* to take notes, but to listen for the main points as you give a 5-minute lecture. Then ask them to write down those main points and compare them in small groups with other students. Finally, ask each group to report to the class. To encourage and model active listening, ask students to paraphrase the main points from the last speaker before presenting their reports.

Take time in class to ask and answer questions. Explain how to take notes during question-and-answer sessions. Point out the value of student questions. Show overhead transparencies two ways: first with some of the material covered, then by showing the entire overhead, and discuss with your class how this affects how much they are retaining.

8. **Listen to the entire message.** Concentrate on "the big picture," but also pay attention to specific details and examples that can assist you in understanding and retaining the information.

9. **Respect your own ideas and those of others.** Your own thoughts and ideas are valuable, and you need not throw them out just because someone else's views conflict with your own. At the same time, you should not reject the ideas of others too casually.

10. **Sort, organize, and categorize.** When you listen, try to match what you are hearing with what you already know. Think of your own examples to illustrate key ideas. Take an active role in deciding how best to recall what you are learning.

During Class: Take Effective Notes

You can make class time more productive by using your listening skills to take effective notes. Here's how.

1. **Decide on a system.** One method to assist you in taking and organizing notes is referred to as the Cornell format. One feature that makes this method so popular among new students is that it enables them to keep using whatever system has worked for them in the past—whether outlining, indenting, marking major ideas, or some other method. To start, create a recall column on each page of your notebook by drawing a vertical line about 2 to 3 inches from the left border. As you take notes during lecture, using whatever style you prefer, write only in the wider column on the right and leave the left-hand recall column blank. We'll return to the recall column later.

   You may also want to develop your own system of abbreviations. For example, when taking notes you might write "inst" instead of "institution" or "eval" instead of "evaluation." Just make sure you will be able to understand your abbreviations when it's time to review.

2. **Identify the main ideas.** Good lectures always contain certain key points. The first principle of effective note taking is to identify and write down the most important ideas around which the lecture is built. Although supporting details are important as well, focus your note taking on the main ideas. These main ideas may be buried in details, statistics, anecdotes, or problems.

   Some instructors announce the purpose of a lecture or offer an outline, thus providing you with the skeleton of main ideas, followed by the details. Others develop overhead transparencies or PowerPoint presentations and may make these materials available on a class Web site before lecture. If so, you can enlarge them, print them out, and take notes right on the teacher's outline.

> With students taking notes, lecture for about 20 minutes. Have students pair off and explain your lecture to one another. Or ask students to work individually to capture the essence of the lecture in a single phrase or word (sometimes called a "word journal"). Then have them pair up and discuss how their encapsulating word or phrase helps them retain information. Finally, ask them how successful this technique was.

Examining Values

A student is overheard saying, "These lectures are *so* boring. I just sit there and doodle to make the time pass. It's not as though this is a class in my major." Another student says, "You know, I read the assignment two days ago, but all this stuff he's talking about doesn't connect to the book at all!" A third student says, "Well, this isn't the most exciting material on earth, but I want to get a good grade, so I've practiced focusing on the lecture and asking questions when I don't understand something. I may need to know this stuff in the future." How would you characterize the values of each student? Or, said another way, what things does each student value most? Least?

Some lecturers change their tone of voice or repeat themselves at each key idea. Some ask questions or promote discussion. These are all clues to what is important. If a lecturer repeats something, it is probably essential information. Ask yourself, "What does my instructor want me to know at the end of today's session?"

3. **Don't try to write down everything.** Because of insecurity or inexperience, some first-year students stop being thinkers and become stenographers. Learn to avoid that trap. If you're an active listener, you will ultimately have shorter but more useful notes.

   As you take notes, leave spaces so that you can fill in additional details later that you might have missed. But remember to do it as soon after class as possible; remember the forgetting curve.

Discuss kinds of courses and topics that would be difficult to outline. Ask students how they might supplement their regular note taking in these situations.

4. **Don't be thrown by a disorganized lecturer.** When a lecture is disorganized, you need to try to organize what is said into general and specific frameworks. When this order is not apparent, you'll need to take notes on where the gaps lie in the lecturer's structure. After the lecture, you may need to consult your reading material or classmates to fill in these gaps.

   You might also consult your instructor. Most instructors have regular office hours for student appointments. You can also raise questions in class. Asking such questions may help your instructor discover which parts of his or her presentation need more attention and clarification.

5. **Return to your recall column.** The recall column is essentially the place where you write down the main ideas and important details for tests and examinations as you sift through your notes as soon after class as feasible, preferably within an hour or two. This is a powerful study device that reduces forgetting, helps you warm up for class, and promotes understanding in class.

Lecture to the class and ask students to take notes. Then give them 5 minutes to revise and complete their notes. Collect and review their notes. Or prepare a handout in which you have taken notes and used a recall column. Discuss the differences and similarities between their notes and yours. Use overhead transparencies to show how you made notes within the assigned reading materials.

   If you are a visual learner, dividing the page creates a visual image that makes it easier to picture key concepts. If you are an interactive learner, study in pairs or with a group. Test one another on the key words or phrases you have jotted down in the recall column to see how much of the material presented in lecture you can remember. If you are an aural learner, look at the recall column while you cover the rest of the page and recite out loud what you remember from your notes. Keep in mind that you want to use as many of your five senses as possible to enhance memory.

   The recall column is a critical part of effective note taking. In addition to helping you listen well, your notes become an important study device for tests and examinations.

Note Taking in Nonlecture Courses

Group discussion is becoming popular in college because it involves active learning. On your campus you may also have Supplemental Instruction (SI) classes that provide further opportunity to discuss the information presented in lectures.

Ask students which critical thinking methods can help them take notes in nonlecture courses. Should students learn to synthesize ideas on their own? Find possibilities in class discussions? Voice those possibilities during class? Is an organized note-taking system more essential in nonlecture courses?

How do you keep a record of what's happening in such classes? Assume you are taking notes in a problem-solving group assignment. You would begin your notes by asking yourself "What is the problem?" and write down the answer. As the discussion progresses, you would list the solutions offered. These would be your main ideas. The important details might include the positive and negative aspects of each view or solution.

The important thing to remember when taking notes in nonlecture courses is that you need to record the information presented by your classmates as well as by the instructor and to consider all reasonable ideas, even though they may differ from your own.

When a course has separate lecture and discussion sessions, you will need to understand how the discussion sessions augment and correlate with the lectures. If different material is covered in lecture than in discussion, you may need to ask for guidance in organizing your notes. If similar topics are covered, be sure to combine your notes so that you have comprehensive, unified coverage of each topic.

How to organize the notes you take in a class discussion depends on the purpose or form of the discussion. But it usually makes good sense to begin with a list of issues or topics that the discussion leader announces. Another approach is to list the questions that participants raise for discussion. If the discussion is exploring reasons for and against a particular argument, divide your notes into columns or sections for pros and cons. When conflicting views are presented in discussion, record each perspective and the rationale behind it. Your teacher may ask you to defend your own opinions in light of those of others.

Comparing and Recopying Notes

You may be able to improve your notes by comparing notes with another student or with a study group or learning community. Knowing that your notes will be seen by someone else will prompt you to make your notes well organized, clear, and accurate.

See whether your notes are as clear and concise as the other person's and whether you agree on the important points that should be included in the recall column. Share how you take and organize your notes and see if you get new ideas for using abbreviations. Take turns testing one another on what you have learned. By doing this, you are predicting exam questions and determining whether you will be able to answer them.

Incidentally, comparing notes is not the same as copying somebody else's notes. You simply cannot learn as well from someone else's notes, no matter how good they are, if you have not attended class. What you'll miss is how the teacher interprets the information and much more. Your campus may have a note-taking service. If so, ask your instructor about making use of it. If you decide to use such a service, keep in mind that the notes are not a substitute for going to class.

Some students choose to copy their own notes as a means of review, or because they think their notes are too messy and that they will not be able to understand them later. Unless you are a tactile learner, copying or typing your notes may not help you learn the material. A more profitable approach might be summarizing your notes in your own words.

Finally, have a backup plan in case you do need to be absent due to illness or a family emergency. Exchange phone numbers and email addresses with other students so that you can contact them to learn what you missed and get a copy of their notes. Also contact your instructor to explain your absence and set up an appointment during office hours to make sure you understand what you missed.

> Talk about comparing notes for the purpose of learning versus plagiarism and cheating. Show how sharing notes can be a good practice for comparing what each person thought was important and how sharing notes can be counterproductive when students use someone else's notes because they missed class or failed to take good notes themselves.

> Explain why outlines are used by teachers. Talk about other kinds of notes you have used and why you used them.

The Value of Good Class Notes

Good class notes can help you complete homework assignments. Take 10 minutes to review your notes as soon after class as possible. Put a question mark next to anything you do not understand at first reading. Draw stars next to topics that warrant special emphasis. Try to place the material in context: What has been going on in the course for the past few weeks? How does today's class fit in?

Before doing your homework, look through your notes again. Use a separate sheet of paper to rework examples, problems, or exercises. If there is related assigned material in the textbook, review it. Go back to the examples. Cover the solution and attempt to answer each question or complete each problem. Look at the author's work only after you have made a serious personal effort to remember it.

SEE "OTHER KINDS
OF NOTES"

SEE EXERCISE 4.2
COMPARING NOTES

Explain how the mind can rejuvenate
itself if a person completes the easy
part of a quiz or assignment, takes a
brief break, and then tears into the
more difficult parts, which suddenly
may not seem as difficult.

Ask how many students take class notes
on laptops. Have them talk about the
advantages and drawbacks. Ask if they
must modify their original notes before
they can study for exams.

SEE EXERCISE 4.3
MEMORY: USING A
RECALL COLUMN

SEE EXERCISE 4.4
APPLYING AN ACTIVE
LISTENING AND
LEARNING SYSTEM

Do any assigned problems and answer any assigned questions. As you read each question or problem, ask: What am I supposed to find or find out? What is essential and what is extraneous? Read the problem several times and state it in your own words. The last sentence may be where you will find the essential question or answer. Work the problem without referring to your notes or the text, as though you were taking a test.

Don't give up too soon. When you encounter a problem or question that you cannot readily handle, move on only after a reasonable effort. After you have completed the entire assignment, come back to those items that stumped you. Try once more, then take a break. Let your unconscious mind take over. Inspiration may come when you are waiting for a stoplight or just before you fall asleep.

You may be thinking, That sounds good, but who has the time to do all that extra work? In reality, this approach can actually save you time. Try it for a few weeks. You will find that you can diminish the frustration that comes when you tackle your homework cold and that you will be more confident going into exams.

Computer Notes in Class?

Computers are often poor tools for taking notes in class. Computer screens are not conducive to making marginal notes, circling important items, or copying diagrams. And although most students can scribble coherently without watching their hands, few are really good keyboarders.

Entering notes on a computer after class for review purposes may be helpful, especially if you are a tactile learner. Then you can print your notes and highlight or annotate, just as you would handwritten notes. On the other hand, if you enter everything the lecturer says during class or merely copy what you wrote in class, you may be wasting time that could be spent more productively.

After Class: Respond, Recite, Review

Don't let the forgetting curve take its toll on you. As soon after class as reasonable, review your notes and fill in the details you remember, but missed writing down, in those spaces you left in the right-hand column.

Relate new information to other things you already know. Organize similar kinds of information. Fit new facts into your total system of knowledge. Make a conscious effort to remember. One way is to recite important data to yourself every few minutes; if you are an aural learner, repeat it out loud. Another approach is to tie one idea to another idea, concept, or name, so that thinking of one will prompt recall of the other. Or you may want to create your own poem, song, or slogan using the information. Keep in mind that it may be easier to remember when it has a rhythm or beat.

For interactive learners, the best way to learn something may be to teach it to someone else. You will understand something better and remember it longer if you try to explain it. Asking and answering questions in class also provides you with the feedback you need to make certain your understanding is accurate.

Now you're ready to embed the major points from your notes into your memory. Use these three important steps for remembering the key points in the lecture:

1. **Write the main ideas in the recall column.** For 5 or 10 minutes, quickly review your notes and select key words or phrases that will act as labels or tags for main ideas and key information in the notes. Highlight the main ideas and write them in the recall column next to the material they represent (Figure 4.2).

2. **Use the recall column to recite your ideas.** Cover the notes on the right and use the prompts from the recall column to help you recite *out loud* a brief

version of what you understand from the class in which you have just participated. If you don't have a few minutes after class when you can concentrate on your notes, find some other time during *that same day* to review what you have written. You might also want to ask your teacher to glance at your recall column to determine whether you have noted the proper major ideas.

3. **Review the previous day's notes just before the next class session.** As you sit in class the next day waiting for the lecture to begin, use the time to quickly review the notes from the previous day. This will put you in tune with the lecture that is about to begin and also prompt you to ask questions about material from the previous lecture that may not have been clear to you.

A good way to reinforce the skills of active listening and effective note taking is to give mini-lectures throughout the course, requiring students to take notes. After each lecture, give students time to write down recall cues. Then pass out a set of model notes to demonstrate the importance of discerning between main ideas and supporting details.

Sept. 21   How to take notes

Problems with lectures	Lecture *not* best way to teach. Problems: Short attention span (may be only 15 minutes!). Teacher dominates. Most info is forgotten. "Stenographer" role interferes with thinking, understanding, learning.
Forgetting curves	Forgetting curves critical period: over ½ of lecture forgotten in 24 hours.
Solution: Active listening	Answer: Active listening, really understanding during lecture. Aims— (1) immediate understanding (2) longer attention (3) better retention (4) notes for study later
Before: Read Warm up	BEFORE: Always prepare. Read: Readings parallel lectures & make them meaningful. Warm up: Review last lecture notes & readings right before class.
During: main ideas	DURING: Write main ideas & some detail. No steno. What clues does prof. give about what's most important? Ask. Ask other questions. Leave blank column about 2½" on left of page. Use only front side of paper.
After: Review Recall Recite	AFTER: Left column for key recall words, "tags." Cover right side & recite what tags mean. Review / Recall / Recite

FIGURE 4.2 Sample Lecture Notes

These three engagements with the material will really pay off later, when you begin to study for your exams.

What if you have three classes in a row and no time for recall columns or recitations between them? Recall and recite as soon after class as possible. Review the most recent class first. Never delay recall and recitation longer than one day; if you do, it will take you longer to review, make a recall column, and recite. With practice, you can complete your recall column quickly, perhaps between classes, during lunch, or while riding a bus.

SEE EXERCISE 4.5
LOOKING BACK
ON YOUR NOTES

Participating in Class: Speak Up!

Learning is not a spectator sport. You won't learn much just by sitting in classes listening to teachers, memorizing readings and notes, and regurgitating answers on exams. To really learn, you must talk about what you are learning, write about it, relate it to past experiences, and make what you learn part of yourself.

Participation is the heart of active learning. We know that when we say something in class, we are more likely to remember it than when someone else does. So when a teacher tosses a question your way, or when you have a question to ask, you're actually making it easier to remember the day's lesson.

Naturally, you will be more likely to participate in a class where the teacher emphasizes discussion, calls on students by name, shows students signs of approval, and avoids shooting you down for an incorrect answer. Often, answers that are not quite correct can lead to ones that are.

Unfortunately, many classes, especially large ones of 100 or more, force instructors to use the lecture method. And large classes can be intimidating. If you speak up in a class of 100 and feel you've made a fool of yourself, 99 people will know it. Of course, that's somewhat unrealistic, since you've probably asked a question that they were too timid to ask, and they'll silently thank you for doing so. If you're lucky, you might even find that the instructor of such a class takes time out to ask or answer questions. To take full advantage of these opportunities in all classes, try using these techniques:

1. **Take a seat as close to the front as possible.** If you're seated by name and your name is Zoch, plead bad eyesight or hearing—anything to get moved up front.
2. **Keep your eyes trained on the teacher.** Sitting up front will make this easier for you to do.
3. **Raise your hand when you don't understand something.** But don't overdo it! The instructor may answer you immediately, ask you to wait until later in the class, or throw your question to the rest of the class. In each case, you benefit. The instructor gets to know you, other students get to know you, and you learn from both the instructor and your classmates.

Critical Thinking

Divide a piece of looseleaf paper as shown in Figure 4.2. In one of your classes other than this one, take notes on the right side of the paper, leaving the recall column and the last few lines on the page blank. As soon after class as possible, use the critical thinking process to abstract the main ideas and write them in the recall column. Use the blank lines at the bottom to write a summary sentence or two for that page of notes. Also use the recall column to jot down any thoughts or possibilities that occur to you. Examples might be "I wonder what I can attach this information to so I can recall it later?" or "Maybe if I break my American lit notes into small chunks, they'll be easier to remember."

Speaking of Careers

It should be pretty obvious that the skills of listening, note taking, and participating apply to the world of work as well as to the world of the classroom. To prepare for a meeting, you probably will have to read a memo, a recommendation, or other materials. Marking the major issues and writing questions in the margins will help prepare you to participate. Even though someone may be assigned to take notes for the group, you may want to jot down a few relevant reminders for yourself. See? College is so much more than your major field of study!

4. **Never feel that you're asking a stupid question.** If you don't understand something, you have a right to ask for an explanation. And never say, "This is a stupid question, but . . ."

5. **When the instructor calls on you to answer a question, don't bluff.** If you know the answer, give it. If you're not certain, begin with, "I think . . . , but I'm not sure I have it all correct." If you don't know, just say so.

6. **If you've recently read a book or article that is relevant to the class topic, bring it in.** Use it either to ask questions about the piece or to provide information that was not covered in class. Of course, you'll want to do this in a way that doesn't suggest your instructor has forgotten something important!

SEE INTERNET EXERCISE 4.2 RESEARCHING LISTENING AND LEARNING

Next time you have the opportunity, speak up. Class will go by faster, you and your fellow students will get to know one another, your instructor will get to know you, and he or she will in all likelihood be grateful to have the participation.

Search Online!

Internet Exercise 4.1 Study Skills Guides on the Internet

The Internet can be a major source of study skills and self-help materials prepared by many college learning centers. Check out the following:

- The CaiREN Project, a series of tips and exercises to help develop better study strategies and habits especially in the sciences: http://www.wpunj.edu/icip/see/STSERVstudy/htm
- Dartmouth Study Skills Guide Menu: http://www.dartmouth.edu/admin/acskills/index.html
- Study Tips, a collection of some of the handouts used at the University of Texas at Austin Learning Skills Center: http://www.utexas.edu/student/lsc/handouts/stutips.html
- Virginia Polytechnic Institute Study Skills Self-Help Information: http://www.ucc.vt.edu/stdysk/stdyhlp.html

What information did you find that you will be able to use? (Go to http://success.wadsworth.com for the most up-to-date URLs.)

Internet Exercise 4.2 Researching Listening and Learning

Using InfoTrac College Edition, try these phrases and others for key-word and subject-guide searches: "study skills," "note taking," "recalling information." Select a number of articles to read and synthesize their content. But don't stop there. Do a library search of books and periodicals for more information. If your teacher requires a short research paper, use the information you've gathered to write one, making sure you cite sources properly.

Additional Exercises

These exercises at the end of each chapter will help you sharpen what we believe are the critical skills for college success: writing, critical thinking, learning in small groups, planning, reflecting, and taking action. Also check out the CD-ROM that came with your book—you will find more exercises as well as resources for this chapter.

Exercise 4.1 **Listening and Memory**

Form groups of five and chat about the importance of listening, how well students listen in class, and what they should do to improve their listening. Each student who speaks after the first speaker must use at least one word from the *last* sentence spoken by the last speaker. The first speaker should do the same after the last student has spoken. How did this affect the quality of your listening? How can you apply it to the classroom?

Exercise 4.2 **Comparing Notes**

Pair up with another student and compare your class notes for this course. Are your notes clear? Do you agree on what is important? Take a few minutes to explain to each other your note-taking systems. Agree to use a recall column during the next class meeting. Afterward, share your notes again and check on how each of you used the recall column. Compare your notes to see what each of you deemed important.

Exercise 4.3 **Memory: Using a Recall Column**

Suppose the information in this chapter had been presented to you as a lecture rather than a reading. Using the system described previously, your lecture notes might look like those in Figure 4.2. Cover the right-hand column. Using the recall column, try reciting in your own words the main ideas from this chapter. Uncover the right-hand column when you need to refer to it. If you can phrase the main ideas from the recall column in your own words, you are well on your way to mastering this note-taking system for dealing with lectures. Does the system seem to work? If not, why not?

Exercise 4.4 **Applying an Active Listening and Learning System**

Write down your study schedule for this week or the coming week.
Before you begin, answer the following questions:

1. Where should you build in time for using the recall column?

   _____

   _____

   _____

2. What problems might you have in performing review/recall/recite as soon after class as possible?

   _____

   _____

   _____

3. How might you address and solve these problems?

   _____

   _____

   _____

   Share your answers with other students in a small group.

Your Personal Journal

Here are several things to write about. Choose one or more, or choose another topic related to this chapter.

1. Think of a course in which you're having trouble taking useful notes. Now write down some ideas from this chapter that may help you improve your note taking in that course.
2. How might a study group help you improve your note taking and other study habits? Is there a possibility that you might join one? Jot down the names of students in your classes whom you admire for their academic achievements. Ask one of them if he or she is interested in forming a group. If that person already belongs to a group, ask if you can join.
3. What behaviors are you willing to change after reading this chapter? How might you go about changing them?
4. What else is on your mind this week? If you wish to share it with your instructor, add it to your journal entry.

_____

_____

_____

_____

_____

_____

_____

_____

_____

_____

_____

_____

_____

_____

_____

_____

_____

_____

_____

_____

_____

_____

_____

Resources

Throughout this book, we stress how study groups can groom you for success in college. Use this Resources page to list names, phone numbers, and email addresses for students in the study group(s) you are in. Keep the list handy, especially close to test time. If you are not in a study group, list potential study group members and contact them.

Study group .... **meets** ....

Name	**Phone number**	**Email**

Study group .... **meets** ....

Name	**Phone number**	**Email**

Study group .... **meets** ....

Name	**Phone number**	**Email**

Libraries

Library	**Regular hours**	**Hours during finals**	**Phone number**	**Web address**

Reading
to Remember

Strategies for Understanding and Retaining Material

IN THIS CHAPTER, YOU WILL LEARN

- How to "prepare to read"
- How to preview reading material
- How to read your textbooks efficiently
- How to mark your textbooks
- How to review your reading
- How to adjust your reading style to the material
- How to develop a more extensive vocabulary

CORBIS

This chapter was written with the expert assistance of Jeanne L. Higbee, University of Minnesota.

crack the code

*"*ive pages down, thirty to go! This stuff is so boring! I have no idea what I just read. Oh well, at a page a minute I should be done in half an hour.*"*

Reading college textbooks is more challenging than reading high school texts or reading for pleasure. College texts are loaded with concepts, terms, and complex information that you are expected to learn on your own in a short period of time. To do this, it will help to use a studying and reading method such as the one presented in this chapter.

The four-step plan we suggest for textbook reading—previewing, reading, marking, and reviewing—will increase your focus and concentration, promote greater understanding of what you read, and prepare you to study for tests and exams.

Previewing

The purpose of previewing is to get the "big picture," to understand how the information in your text is connected to what you already know and to the material the instructor will cover in class. Begin by reading the title of the chapter. Ask yourself, "What do I already know about this subject?" Next, quickly read through the introductory paragraphs, then turn to the end of the chapter and read the summary (if one is there). Finally, take a few minutes to page through the chapter headings and subheadings. Note any study exercises at the end of the chapter.

As part of your preview, note how many pages the chapter contains. It's a good idea to decide in advance how many pages you can reasonably expect to cover in your first 50-minute study period. This can help build your concentration as you work toward your goal of reading a specific number of pages. It may take a few weeks before you can predict the number accurately.

SELF-ASSESSMENT: EVALUATING YOUR READING STRENGTHS AND WEAKNESSES

Read each of the following statements and put a check mark in front of those that come close to describing you.

_____ I skim or "preview" a chapter before I begin to read.

_____ I lose concentration while reading a text.

_____ I wait to underline, highlight, or annotate the text until *after* I read a page or section.

_____ I take notes after I read.

_____ I pause at the end of each section or page to review what I have read.

_____ After reading, I recite key ideas to myself or with a partner.

_____ I review everything I have read for a class at least once a week.

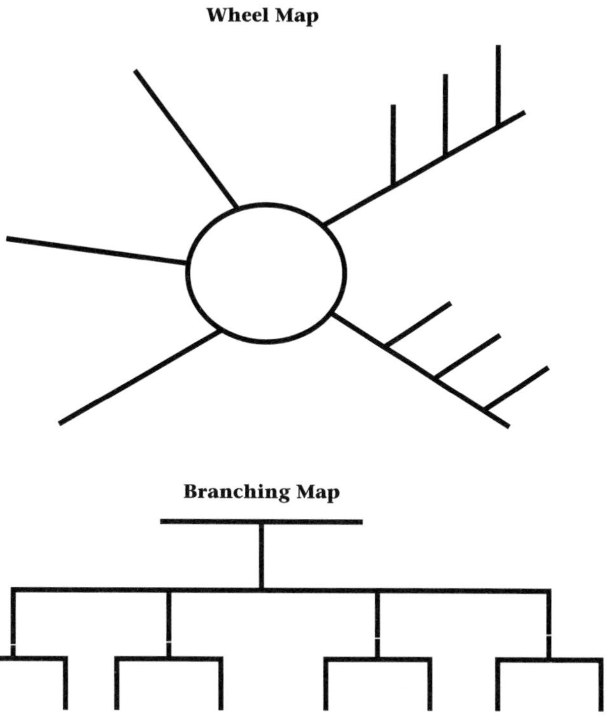

Wheel Map

FIGURE 5.1
Wheel and Branching Maps

Branching Map

Keep in mind that different types of textbooks may require more or less time to read. For example, depending upon your interests and previous knowledge, you may be able to read a psychology text more quickly than a logic text that presents a whole new symbol system.

Mapping

Mapping the chapter as you preview it provides a visual guide to how different chapter ideas fit together. Because about 75 percent of students identify themselves as visual learners, visual mapping is an excellent learning tool that will be useful for test preparation as well as active reading.

SEE EXERCISE 5.1
PREVIEWING AND
CREATING A VISUAL MAP

How do you map a chapter? While you are previewing, use either a wheel or a branching structure (Figure 5.1). In the wheel structure, place the central idea of the chapter in the circle, place secondary ideas on the spokes emanating from the circle, and place offshoots of those ideas on the lines attached to the spokes. In the branching map, the main idea goes at the top, followed by supporting ideas on the second tier, and so forth. Fill in the title first. Then, as you skim through the rest of the chapter, use the headings and subheadings to fill in the key ideas.

Alternatives to Mapping

Perhaps you prefer a more linear visual image. Then consider making an outline of the headings and subheadings in the chapter. You can fill in the outline after you read. Or make a list. Making a list can be particularly effective when dealing with a text that introduces lots of new terms and their definitions. Set up the list with the terms in the left column and fill in definitions, descriptions, and examples on the right after you read. Divide the terms on your list into groups of five, seven, or nine,

In response to the inevitable complaint that a systematic reading method takes too much time, emphasize that:
1. Because students will understand more of the chapter using this method, they will not have to spend additional time rereading.
2. This reading method is also a study method. Writing recall cues followed by recitation is a way of learning the material well.

and leave white space between the clusters so that you can visualize each group in your mind. This practice is known as "chunking." Research indicates that we learn material better in chunks of five, seven, or nine.

If you are an interactive learner, make lists or create a flash card for each heading and subheading. Then fill in the back of each card after reading each section in the text. Use the lists or flash cards to review with a partner or to recite the material to yourself.

Previewing, combined with mapping, outlining, or flash cards, may require more time up front but will save you time later. Here's why: You will have created an excellent review tool for quizzes and tests; and you will be using your visual learning skills as you create "advance organizers" to help you associate details of the chapter with the larger ideas. Such associations will be essential later.

As you preview the text material, look for connections between the text and the lecture material. Call to mind the related terms and concepts that you recorded in lecture. To warm up, ask yourself, "Why am I reading this? What do I want to know?"

Reading Your Textbook

Now you are ready to read the text actively. With your skeleton map or outline, you should be able to read more quickly and with greater comprehension. To avoid marking too much or marking the wrong information, read first without using your pencil or highlighter. When you have reached the end of a section, stop and ask yourself, "What are the key ideas in this section? What do I think I'll see on the test?" Then decide what to underline or highlight. Or you may want to try a strategy known as annotating the text. In your own words, write key ideas in the margins of the text.

Two common problems students have with textbooks are trouble concentrating and not understanding the content. Many factors may affect your ability to concentrate and understand texts, such as the time of day, your energy level, your interest in the material, and your study location.

To help you improve your reading ability:

Ask students to choose two or more of the tips for building concentration and understanding and to practice them during the next few days. Then have them report on what worked for them and what didn't—and why.

- Find a study location, preferably in the library if you are on campus, that is removed from traffic and distracting noises.
- Read in 50-minute blocks of time, with short breaks in between. By reading for 50 minutes more frequently during the day instead of cramming all your reading in at the end of the day, you should be able to understand and remember material more easily.
- Set goals for your study period, such as "I will read 20 pages of my psychology text in the next 50 minutes." Reward yourself with a 10-minute break after each 50-minute study period.
- If you are having trouble concentrating or staying awake, take a quick walk around the library or down the hall. Stretch or take some deep breaths and think positively about your study goals. Then go back and resume studying.
- Jot study questions in the margin, take notes, or recite key ideas. Reread confusing parts of the text and make a note to ask your instructor for clarification.
- Experiment with your reading rate. Try to move your eyes more quickly over the material by focusing on phrases, not individual words.
- Pay attention to the first and last sentences of paragraphs and to words in italics or bold print. They're probably important.
- Use the glossary in the text to define unfamiliar terms.

Monitoring

An important step in textbook reading is monitoring your comprehension. As you read, ask yourself, "Do I understand this?" If not, stop and reread the material. Look up words that are not clear. Try to clarify the main points and how they relate to one another.

Another way to check comprehension is to try to recite the material aloud to yourself or your study partner. Using a study group to monitor your comprehension gives you immediate feedback and can be highly motivating. One way that group members can work together is to divide up a chapter for previewing and studying and get together later to teach the material to one another.

Have students practice this method of monitoring with a study partner and ask them to share the results with you and the rest of the class.

Marking Your Textbook

Some students report that marking is an active reading strategy that helps them concentrate on the material as they read. In addition, most students expect to use their text notations when studying for tests. To meet these goals, some students like to underline, some prefer to highlight, and others use margin notes or annotations. Look at Figure 5.2 on pages 84–85 for examples of different methods of marking. You can also combine methods.

Out of habit, new college students may hesitate to mark their texts. It's important to stress how effective this is in helping them remember the main topics of a chapter.

Critical Thinking

Reading to Question, to Interpret, to Understand

Turn one statement in this chapter into a question. It might come from the very first sentence in the chapter: "Why is reading college textbooks more challenging than reading high school texts or reading for pleasure?" Then use the critical thinking process to find an explanation. You might answer by saying, "Because when I read for pleasure, I do not have to be concerned with remembering little details" or "My textbooks are less likely to keep my interest because I cannot relate to the material." Moving to stage 2 of the critical thinking process, you might write, "I wonder if I can make the textbook more interesting and remember more by thinking of experiences from my own life as examples of what I'm reading. Then it won't be so hard." Then brainstorm such examples. Finally, sift through your ideas and choose one or more that seem to work. Explain your process to other students and your instructor.

Here are other questions to choose from:

- Why should I take the time to read the title of the chapter and ask myself what I already know about the subject?

- Why should I spend extra time creating a map of this chapter?

- Is there a relationship between lack of concentration and complexity of material? If so, what is the relationship, and how can understanding it help me overcome my difficulties with concentrating and understanding?

- Why is "reading before you mark" and "thinking before you mark" more useful than marking as you read?

- Any other question you can construct from this chapter.

CONCEPT CHECKS

7. *Some students who read a chapter slowly get very good grades; others get poor grades. Why?*

8. *Most actors and public speakers who have to memorize lengthy passages spend little time simply repeating the words and more time thinking about them. Why? (Check your answers on page 288.)*

People need to monitor their understanding of a text to decide whether to keep studying or whether they already understand it well enough. Most readers have trouble making that judgment correctly.

SELF-MONITORING OF UNDERSTANDING

Whenever you are studying a text, you periodically have to decide, "Should I keep on studying this section, or do I already understand it well enough?" Most students have trouble monitoring their own understanding. In one study, psychology instructors asked their students before each test to guess whether they would do better or worse on that test than they usually do. Students also guessed after each test whether they had done better or worse than usual. Most students' guesses were no more accurate than chance (Sjostrom & Marks, 1994). Such inaccuracy represents a problem: Students who do not know how well they understand the material will make bad judgments about when to keep on studying and when to quit.

(why)

Even when you are reading a single sentence, you have to decide whether you understand the sentence or whether you should stop and reread it. Here is a sentence once published in the student newspaper at North Carolina State University:

(How)

He said Harris told him she and Brothers told French that grades had been changed.

Ordinarily, when good readers come to such a confusing sentence, they notice their own confusion and reread the sentence or, if necessary, the whole paragraph. Poor readers tend to read at their same speed for both easy and difficult materials; they are less likely than good readers to slow down when they come to difficult sentences.

Although monitoring one's own understanding is difficult and often inaccurate, it is not impossible. For example, suppose I tell you that you are to read three chapters dealing with, say, thermodynamics, the history of volleyball, and the Japanese stock market.

Later you will take tests on each chapter. Before you start reading, predict your approximate scores on the three tests. Most people make a guess based on how much they already know about the three topics. If we let them read the three chapters and again make a guess about their test performances, they do in fact make more accurate predictions than they did before reading (Maki & Serra, 1992). That improvement indicates some ability to monitor one's own understanding of a text.

A systematic way to monitor your own understanding of a text is the SPAR method: Survey, Process meaningfully, Ask questions, and Review and test yourself. Start with an overview of what a passage is about, read it carefully, and then see whether you can answer questions about the passage or explain it to others. If not, go back and reread.

SPAR
Survey
Process
Ask
Review

Also decide about larger units?

THE TIMING OF STUDY

Other things being equal, people tend to remember recent experiences better than earlier experiences. For example, suppose someone reads you a list of 20 words and asks you to recall as many of them as possible. The list is far too long for you to recite from your phonological loop; however, you should be able to remember at least a few. Typically, people remember items at the beginning and end of the list better than they remember those in the middle.

That tendency, known as the **serial-order effect**, includes two aspects: The *primacy effect* is the tendency to remember the first items; the *recency effect* refers to the tendency to remember the last items. One explanation for the primacy effect is that the listener gets to rehearse the first few items for a few moments alone with no interference from the others. One explanation for the recency effect is that the last items are still in

Cause of primacy effect

FIGURE 5.2 Sample Marked Pages

Cause of recency effect

the listener's phonological loop at the time of the test.

The phonological loop cannot be the whole explanation for the recency effect, however. In one study, British rugby players were asked to name the teams they had played against in the current season. Players were most likely to remember the last couple of teams they had played against, thus showing a clear recency effect even though they were recalling events that occurred weeks apart (Baddeley & Hitch, 1977). (The phonological loop holds information only for a matter of seconds.)

So, studying material—or, rather, *reviewing* material—shortly before a test is likely to improve recall. Now let's consider the opposite: Suppose you studied something years ago and have not reviewed it since then. For example, suppose you studied a foreign language in high school several years ago. Now you are considering taking a college course in the language, but you are hesitant because you are sure you have forgotten it all. Have you?

Harry Bahrick (1984) tested people who had studied Spanish in school 1 to 50 years previously. Nearly all agreed that they had rarely used Spanish and had not refreshed their memories at all since their school days. (That is a disturbing comment, but beside the point.) Their retention of Spanish dropped noticeably in the first 3 to 6 years, but remained fairly stable from then on (Fig-

ure 7.18). In other words, we do not completely forget even very old memories that we seldom use.

In a later study, Bahrick and members of his family studied foreign-language vocabulary either on a moderately frequent basis (practicing once every 2 weeks) or on a less frequent basis (as seldom as once every 8 weeks), and tested their knowledge years later. The result: More frequent study led to faster learning; however, less frequent study led to better long-term retention, measured years later (Bahrick, Bahrick, Bahrick, & Bahrick, 1993).

The principle here is far more general than just the study of foreign languages. *If you want to remember something well for a test,* your best strategy is to study it as close as possible to the time of the test, in order to take advantage of the recency effect and decrease the effects of retroactive interference. Obviously, I do not mean that you should wait until the night before the test to start studying, but you might rely on an extensive review at that time. You should also, ideally, study under conditions similar to the conditions of the test. For example, you might study in the same room where the test will be given, or at the same time of day.

However, *if you want to remember something long after the test is over,* then the advice I have just given you is all wrong. To be able to remember something whenever you want, wherever you are, and whatever you are doing, you should study it under as varied circumstances as possible. Study and review at various times and places with long, irregular intervals between study sessions. Studying under such inconsistent conditions will slow down your original learning, but it will improve your ability to recall it long afterwards (Schmidt & Bjork, 1992).

Studying for Test vs. Studying for long term

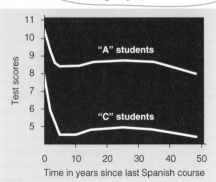

FIGURE 7.18
(Left) Spanish vocabulary as measured by a recognition test shows a rapid decline in the first few years but then long-term stability. (From Bahrick, 1984.) (Right) Within a few years after taking your last foreign-language course, you may think you have forgotten it all. You have not, and even the part you have forgotten will come back (through relearning) if you visit a country where you can practice the language.

CHAPTER 7
MEMORY

284

FIGURE 5.2 *(continued)*

SOURCE: Pages adapted with permission from James W. Kalat, *Introduction to Psychology*, 4th ed. (Pacific Grove, CA: Brooks/Cole, 1996).

**SEE EXERCISE 5.2
PREPARING TO READ,
THINK, AND MARK**

If students complain that a marked book won't get a high "buyback" price, ask them to consider what they value most—the cash or the better grade. Ask that they check buyback policies at local bookstores to find out how much they will "lose" by marking in their books.

Suggest that flash cards, lists, and outlines may also include their reactions to the material or questions they need to ask about it.

No matter what method you prefer, remember these two important guidelines:

1. **Read before you mark.** Finish reading a section before you decide which are the most important ideas and concepts. Only mark those ideas.
2. **Think before you mark.** When you read a text for the first time, everything may seem important. Only after you have completed a section and reflected on it will you be ready to identify key ideas. Ask yourself, "What are the most important ideas? What will I see on the test?" This can help you avoid marking too much material. Avoid marking entire pages; that won't help you find the main issues. Instead, take notes, create flash cards, make lists, or outline textbook chapters. These methods are also practical if you intend to review with a friend or study group.

Highlighting or underlining may provide you with a false sense of security. You may have determined what is most important without testing yourself on your understanding of the material. When you force yourself to put something in your own words when taking notes, you are not only predicting exam questions but assessing whether you can answer them! Although these active reading strategies take more time initially, they can save you time in the long run because they promote concentration as you read and make it easy to review. You probably won't have to pull an all-nighter before an exam.

Recycle Your Reading

**SEE INTERNET
EXERCISE 5.1
READING WEB PAGES
CRITICALLY**

Encourage students to use their learning center's reading resources to improve their reading rate and to master various methods of remembering material.

After you have read and marked or taken notes on key ideas from the first section of the chapter, proceed to each subsequent section until you have finished the chapter. After you have completed each section—*before* you move on to the next section—again ask, "What are the key ideas? What will I see on the test?" At the end of each section, try to guess what information the author will present in the next section. Good reading should lead you from one section to the next, with each new section adding to your understanding.

Reviewing

The final step in effective textbook reading is reviewing. Many students believe that they can read through their text material one time and be able to remember the ideas four, six, or even twelve weeks later at test time. More realistically, you will need to include regular reviews in your study process. Here is where your notes,

Examining Values

After reading this chapter, one of your classmates tells you, "I don't have the time to go over my assigned readings like this. I work every night from 6 to midnight." Another classmate tells you, "I'll try this in a few weeks, but my calendar is busy right now with social things. I'm making tons of new friends!" As they walk away, you start thinking about the choices they just made. What's your reaction to them?

Tom Jorgenson/Photo courtesy of University of Iowa

Write as you read. Taking notes on your reading helps you focus on the key ideas and summarize as you go. You take in and digest the material rather than skim it.

study questions, annotations, flash cards, visual maps, or outlines will be useful. Your study goal should be to review the material from each chapter every week.

Consider ways to use your senses to review. Recite aloud. Tick off each item in a list on one of your fingertips. Post diagrams, maps, or outlines around your living space so that you will see them often and will be able to visualize them while taking the test.

Adjusting Your Reading Style

With effort, you can improve your reading dramatically, but remember to be flexible. Assess the relative importance and difficulty of the assigned readings and adjust your reading style and the time you allot accordingly. Connect one important idea to another by asking yourself, "Why am I reading this? Where does this fit in?" When the textbook material is virtually identical to the lecture material, you can save time by concentrating mainly on one or the other. It takes a planned approach to achieve understanding and recall of textbook materials and other assigned readings.

SEE EXERCISE 5.3
HOW TO READ FIFTEEN
PAGES OF A TEXTBOOK
IN AN HOUR OR LESS

SEE INTERNET
EXERCISE 5.2
RESEARCHING HOW
TO READ TEXTS

Speaking of Careers

Obviously, any career will require that you do some reading in order to know what's going on in your organization and in your career field. But reading newspapers and magazines for enjoyment and to keep abreast of current happenings can also contribute to a successful career as well as to a more interesting life. In the information/technology age, information really *is* power. Someone once said, "If I ever stop learning, I'll be dead." Think about that the next time you wish college were over!

Developing Your Vocabulary

Textbooks are full of new terminology. In fact, one could argue that learning chemistry is largely a matter of learning the language of chemists and that mastering philosophy or history or sociology requires a mastery of the terminology of each. Because words are such a basic and essential component of our knowledge, follow these basic vocabulary strategies:

- During your overview of the chapter, notice and jot down unfamiliar terms. Make a flash card for each term, or a list of all of them.
- When you encounter challenging words, consider the context. See if you can predict the meaning of an unfamiliar term by using the surrounding words.
- If context by itself is not enough, try analyzing the term to discover the root or other meaningful parts of the word. For example, *emissary* has the root "to emit" or "to send forth," so we can guess that an emissary is someone sent forth with a message. Similarly, note prefixes and suffixes. For example, *anti-* means "against" and *pro-* means "for."
- Use the glossary/index of this text, a dictionary, or www.m-w.com/netdict.htm (The Merriam-Webster Dictionary online) to locate the definition. Note any multiple definitions and search for the meaning that fits this usage.
- Take every opportunity to use these new terms in your writing and speech. If you come across a new term, make sure you know it!

**SEE EXERCISE 5.4
EXPANDING YOUR
VOCABULARY**

Search Online!

Internet Exercise 5.1 Reading Web Pages Critically

Since anyone can publish on the Internet, you should read material on the Internet with a critical eye.

Examine the "Checklist for an Informational Web Page" offered by the Widener University Wolfgram Memorial Library, http://www2.widener.edu/Wolfgram-Memorial-Library/webevaluation/examples.htm. This page offers questions to ask about an informational Web page. (Go to http://success.wadsworth.com for the most up-to-date URLs.) Evaluate that Web page using its own five criteria:

1. What evidence is there to indicate how authoritative the site is?

    _____

    _____

2. What confirms that the information is accurate?

    _____

    _____

3. What leads you to believe the site is objective? Biased?

    _____

    _____

4. How current is the information on the site? How can you tell?

    _____

    _____

5. How complete is the coverage of the topic as cited in the page title?

    _____

    _____

Also see "Evaluating World Wide Web Information" by the Libraries of Purdue University: http://thorplus.lib.purdue.edu/library_info/instruction/gs175/3gs175/evaluation.html, which includes an Internet evaluator checklist, and "Thinking Critically About World Wide Web Resources" at http://www.library.ucla.edu/libraries/college/instruct/web/critical.htm.

Internet Exercise 5.2 Researching How to Read Texts

Using InfoTrac College Edition, try these phrases and others for key-word and subject-guide searches: "reading," "college reading." Select a number of articles to read and synthesize their content. But don't stop there. Do a library search of books and periodicals for more information. Interview experts on the topic, perhaps a study skills teacher at your academic skills center or a businessperson who might tell you how she absorbs material in reports. If your teacher requires a short research paper, use the information you've gathered to write one, making sure you cite your sources properly.

Additional Exercises

These exercises at the end of each chapter will help you sharpen what we believe are the important skills for college success: writing, critical thinking, learning in groups, planning, reflecting, and taking action. Also check out the CD-ROM that came with your book—you will find more exercises as well as resources for this chapter.

Exercise 5.1 Previewing and Creating a Visual Map

Preview this chapter and create a visual map, noting the following information: title, key points from the introduction, any graphics (maps, charts, tables, diagrams), study questions or exercises built into or at the end of the chapter, introduction and summary paragraphs. Create either a wheel or a branching map as shown in Figure 5.1. Add spokes or tiers as necessary. In a small group, compare your work. Now, arrange the same information in outline form. Which seems to work better for you? Why?

Exercise 5.2 Preparing to Read, Think, and Mark

Choose a reading assignment for one of your classes. After previewing the material as described earlier in this chapter, begin reading until you reach a major heading or until you have read at least a page or two. Then stop and write down what you remember from the material:

_____

_____

_____

_____

_____

_____

Next, go back to the same material and mark what you believe are the main ideas (don't fall into the trap of marking too much) and list four of those main ideas here:

1. _____

2. _____

3. _____

4. _____

Your Personal Journal

Here are several things to write about. Choose one or more, or choose another topic related to this chapter.

1. How can you use the suggestions in this chapter, along with those in the chapter on taking notes in class, to improve your study skills?

2. This chapter makes a number of suggestions for reading textbooks. Which ones strike you as most important? Which will be toughest for you to follow? Explain.

3. Try following some of the suggestions in this chapter. Then write how it felt to use them.

4. What behaviors are you willing to change after reading this chapter? How might you go about changing them?

5. What else is on your mind this week? If you wish to share it with your instructor, add it to this journal entry.

_____

_____

_____

_____

_____

_____

_____

_____

_____

_____

_____

_____

_____

_____

_____

_____

_____

_____

_____

_____

_____

_____

Resources

The only way to improve your reading is to read more. The more reading you do on your own—for pleasure, unrelated to school or study—the more you will begin to learn about writing, presentation, and vocabulary, in addition to what the material is about. Reading anything (almost) can contribute to your success in college—as long as you keep up with your homework assignments as well. Use this space to brainstorm a list of extracurricular reading materials. Use the second half of the page to list 10-minute rewards that you can give yourself when you finish a 50-minute homework reading session.

Things I would enjoy reading for pleasure: Need ideas? Wander through the library or a good bookstore. (Try spending at least one hour a week reading something just for you. Reading for pleasure before going to sleep at night is a great way to relax and take your mind off your studies and other sources of stress.)

FICTION BOOKS	NONFICTION BOOKS	MAGAZINES	NEWSPAPERS	INTERNET PAGES

Make a list of 10-minute rewards that you can give yourself after a 50-minute study reading session. Include a few bigger rewards for a week of successful studying.

10-minute rewards:

....

....

....

....

End-of-the-week rewards:

....

....

....

....

Taking Exams and Tests

Be Prepared, Confident, and Calm

IN THIS CHAPTER, YOU WILL LEARN

- How cheating hurts you, your friends, and your college

- How to prepare for an exam

- How study groups can help you prepare

- How to devise a study plan for an exam

- What to do while you're actually taking the exam

- Some memory techniques to help you study

This chapter was written with the expert assistance of Jeanne L. Higbee, University of Minnesota.

William Saliaz/CORBIS

reach the top

"Three tests in the next two days! I am never going to live through this week. I studied hard, and I never gave a thought to cheating. Now here I am walking into class and my mind is a total blank. Help!"

Now that you've learned how to listen and take notes in class and how to read and review your notes and assigned readings, you're ready to use those skills to do your best on exams. To begin with, certain study methods are more effective depending on your preferred learning style. This chapter will help you prepare physically, academically, and emotionally for exams.

Regardless of the study method you use, your goal always will be to seek the truth. Many students may believe that every problem has a single right answer, and the instructor or the textbook is always a source of truth. Yet most college instructors know that some questions have multiple answers, and they welcome as many valid interpretations as possible.

Since college instructors expect you to use higher-level thinking skills, they continually ask for reasons, for arguments, for the assumptions on which a given position is based, and for the evidence that confirms or discounts it. They want you to be able to support your opinions, to see how you think. You can cough up a list of details from lecture notes or readings, but unless you can make sense of them, you probably won't get much credit.

A good way to start talking about this critical chapter is to ask your students if they realize that most of their instructors will choose the same 1- or 2-week period to give exams. Might there be a better way? How does timing of exams relate to the drop date?

SELF-ASSESSMENT: BEING READY, CALM, AND CONFIDENT

Place a check mark in front of the items that best describe you. After completing the chapter, come back to this list and choose three or more items that you did not check but are willing to work on.

_____ I always study for essay tests by predicting possible questions and outlining the answers.

_____ I always begin studying for an exam at least a week in advance.

_____ I usually study for an exam with at least one other person.

_____ I usually know what to expect on a test before I go into the exam.

_____ I usually finish an exam early or on time.

_____ I usually know that I have done well on an exam when I finish.

_____ I usually perform better on essay tests than on objective tests.

_____ I usually perform better on objective tests than on essay tests.

Your approach and attitude toward an exam can affect how well you perform:

APPROACH	ATTITUDE	DECISION	OUTCOME
The easy way out	I don't know why I had to take this course. I learned nothing. (*I skipped a few classes and didn't take notes or read the assignments.*)	So I'll get the answers from someone who took the test earlier.	Not only did I bomb this one, but I didn't learn one thing in this class—except never to cheat again.
The defeatist approach	This course has been rough. I've been getting so-so grades. I can't seem to understand anything. (*I never joined a study group or asked my teacher for help.*)	So I'll cram the night before and hope for the best.	Blew the exam and barely passed the course. Didn't learn much. (*Only have myself to blame, I guess.*)
The sensible approach	I'm here to learn all I can. Who knows what I'll need for a job? Anyway, it's expensive to go to college.	My schedule lets me study longer for my toughest classes. And I've been reviewing my notes all term.	Got a great grade! Besides, studying with groups helped me understand things I might have missed.

On a test that requires you to think rather than memorize, it is much more difficult to cheat. However, cheating has even more important consequences for you, your classmates, and your college.

Have students role-play the three approaches in groups of three. One should take "the easy way out," another takes "the defeatist approach," while the third takes "the sensible approach." Ask what insights came through as they listened to each speaker.

Academic Honesty

Imagine where society would be if researchers reported fraudulent results that were then used to develop new machines or medical treatments. Integrity is a cornerstone of higher education, and activities that compromise that integrity damage everyone: your country, your community, your college, your classmates, and yourself.

Colleges and universities have policies or honor codes that clearly define cheating, lying, plagiarism, and other forms of dishonest conduct, but it is often difficult to know how those rules apply to specific situations. Is it really lying to tell an instructor you missed class because you were "not feeling well" (whatever "well" means) or because you were experiencing vague "car trouble"? (Some people think car trouble includes anything from a flat tire to difficulty finding a parking spot!)

Types of Misconduct

Institutions vary widely in how they define broad terms such as *lying* or *cheating*. One university defines cheating as "intentionally using or attempting to use unauthorized materials, information, notes, study aids or other devices . . . [including] unauthorized communication of information during an academic exercise." This would apply to looking over a classmate's shoulder for an answer, using a calculator when it is not authorized, procuring or discussing an exam (or individual questions from an exam) without permission, copying lab notes, purchasing term papers over the Internet, watching the video instead of reading the book, and duplicating computer files.

Plagiarism, or taking another person's ideas or work and presenting them as your own, is especially intolerable in academic culture. Just as taking someone else's property constitutes physical theft, taking credit for someone else's ideas constitutes intellectual theft.

Ask how your students would view each of the behaviors listed here. Ask if they know the campus policies regarding such conduct. Then tell how you deal with these behaviors. Find citations that will teach students how to avoid plagiarism. Be certain they know the difference between citing a source and writing as if they had created information that came from another source.

SEE INTERNET ACTIVITY 6.1 EXAMINING INSTITUTIONAL VALUES

On most tests, you do not have to credit specific individuals. (But some instructors do require this; when in doubt, ask!) In written reports and papers, however, you must give credit any time you use (1) another person's actual words, (2) another person's ideas or theories—even if you don't quote them directly, and (3) any other information not considered common knowledge.

Many schools prohibit other activities besides lying, cheating, unauthorized assistance, and plagiarism. For instance, the University of Delaware prohibits intentionally inventing information or results; the University of North Carolina outlaws earning credit more than once for the same piece of academic work without permission; Eastern Illinois University rules out giving your work or exam answer to another student to copy during the actual exam or before the exam is given to another section; and the University of South Carolina prohibits bribing in exchange for any kind of academic advantage. Most schools also outlaw helping or attempting to help another student commit a dishonest act.

Reducing the Likelihood of Problems

To avoid becoming intentionally or unintentionally involved in academic misconduct, consider the reasons it could happen.

- **Ignorance.** In a survey at the University of South Carolina, 20 percent of students incorrectly thought that buying a term paper wasn't cheating. Forty percent thought using a test file (a collection of actual tests from previous terms) was fair behavior. Sixty percent thought it was all right to get answers from someone who had taken an exam earlier in the same or in a prior semester. What do you think?
- **Cultural and campus differences.** In other countries and on some U.S. campuses, students are encouraged to review past exams as practice exercises. Some campuses permit sharing answers and information for homework and other assignments with friends. Others don't.
- **Different policies among instructors.** Because there is no universal code that dictates such behaviors, ask each instructor for clarification. When a student is caught violating the academic code of a particular school or teacher, pleading ignorance of the rules is a weak defense.
- **A belief that grades—not learning—are everything,** when actually the reverse is true. This may reflect our society's competitive atmosphere. It also may be the result of pressure from parents, peers, or teachers. In truth, grades are nothing if one has cheated to earn them.
- **Lack of preparation or inability to manage time and activities.** Before you consider cheating, ask an instructor to extend a deadline.

Here are some steps you can take to reduce the likelihood of problems:

1. **Know the rules.** Learn the academic code for your school. Study course syllabi. If a teacher does not clarify his or her standards and expectations, ask.
2. **Set clear boundaries.** Refuse to "help" others who ask you to help them cheat. In test settings, keep your answers covered and your eyes down, and put all extraneous materials away.
3. **Improve time management.** Be well prepared for all quizzes, exams, projects, and papers. This may mean unlearning habits such as procrastination.
4. **Seek help.** Find out where you can obtain assistance with study skills, time management, and test taking. If your methods are in good shape but the content of the course is too difficult, see your instructor, join a study group, or visit your campus learning center or tutorial service.

SEE "DOES CHEATING HURT ANYONE?"

Ask students to role-play how they would say no to someone who asks for academic help. Have several others do the same. Then have the class discuss the ideal way to handle situations like this.

Ask what it would take to cause a student to withdraw from a course or from college for a full term. Have one or more students role-play how they would explain this to their parents or families.

5. **Withdraw from the course.** Your school has a policy about dropping courses and a last day to drop without penalty. Some students may choose to withdraw from all classes and take time off before returning to school if they find themselves in over their heads or if a long illness, a family crisis, or other unexpected occurrence has caused them to fall behind. When withdrawing, it is important to know campus policies as well as how withdrawing could affect any federal financial aid and other scholarship programs. See your advisor or counselor.

6. **Reexamine goals.** Stick to your own realistic goals instead of giving in to pressure from family or friends to achieve impossibly high standards. You may also feel pressure to enter a particular career or profession of little or no interest to you. If so, sit down with counseling or career services professionals or your academic advisor and explore alternatives.

Exams: The Long View

You actually began preparing for a test on the first day of the term. All your lecture notes, assigned readings, and homework were part of that preparation. As the test day nears, you should know how much additional time you will need to review, what material the test will cover, and what format the test will take.

Three things will help you study well: good communication with your instructor, effective time management, and organization of materials.

- **Ask your instructor.** Have you learned from your instructor the purpose, conditions, and content of the exam? Talked with your instructor to clarify any misunderstandings you may have about the content of the course?

- **Manage time wisely.** Have you laid out a schedule that will give you time to review effectively for the exam, without waiting until the night before? Is your schedule flexible, allowing for unexpected distractions?

- **Sharpen your study habits.** Have you created a body of material from which you can effectively review what is likely to be on the exam? Is that material organized in a way that will allow you to study efficiently? If you are an interactive learner, have you collaborated with other students in a study group or as study partners to share information? If you are a visual learner, have you created maps, lists, diagrams, flash cards, tables, or other visual aids that will enhance memory?

Have students talk about previous midterm and final exam experiences. Ask them to write down all of the materials they will need as they prepare for an exam.

Examining Values

Review "Does Cheating Hurt Anyone?" on your CD-ROM. Imagine what the world would be like if the majority of college students decided to cheat. How would this affect

1. Your values as a college student?
2. Your thoughts about the purpose of a college education?
3. Your values about society in general?
4. Your values with regard to friends or someone you love very much?
5. Your perceptions of the relative importance of honesty and truth?

Planning Your Approach

Physical Preparation

1. **Maintain your regular sleep routine.** Don't cut back on your sleep in order to cram in additional study hours. In an exam, you must have all your brain power available. Especially during final exam weeks, it is important to be well rested in order to remain alert for extended periods of time.

2. **Maintain your regular exercise program.** Walking, jogging, swimming, or other aerobic activities are effective stress reducers and provide positive—and needed—breaks from studying.

3. **Eat right.** Avoid drinking more than one or two caffeinated drinks a day or eating foods high in sugar or fat. Be sure to eat a light breakfast before a morning exam. Avoid greasy or acidic foods that might upset your stomach. Eat fruits, vegetables, and foods that are high in complex carbohydrates so that you won't experience energy highs and lows. Consider a banana, a slice of cantaloupe, or other foods that are high in potassium to help prevent muscle cramps. Ask the instructor if you may bring a bottle of water to the exam.

Emotional Preparation

1. **Know your material.** If you have given yourself adequate time to review, you will enter the classroom confident that you are in control. Study by testing yourself or quizzing one another in a study group so you will be sure you really know the material.

Ask the class which of the three suggestions appeals most to them. Have students with the same choices form groups and discuss when they experienced such positive or negative feelings before an exam and how it affected their performance.

2. **Practice relaxing.** Some students experience upset stomachs, sweaty palms, racing hearts, or other unpleasant physical symptoms before an exam. See your counseling center about relaxation techniques. If you have trouble getting to sleep the night before an exam, try mental imagery. Create your own peaceful scene. It can be real or imaginary—the beach, the woods, the mountains—as long as it is a setting in which you would feel completely relaxed. Use your five senses to take yourself there—what would you see, hear, taste, smell, and feel?

3. **Use positive self-talk.** Instead of telling yourself "I never do well on math tests" or "I'll never be able to learn all the information for my history essay exam," make positive statements, such as "I have attended all the lectures, done my homework, and passed the quizzes. Now I'm ready to pass the test!"

Speaking of Careers

How many of the suggestions in this chapter apply to the workplace? Nearly all of them: Honesty, knowing the rules, seeking help, getting sleep and exercise, eating properly, knowing how to handle an emergency, reviewing information, finding a system of memorizing. It might be interesting to interview someone who holds a job and ask him or her to react to this list.

Find Out About the Test

Ask your instructor whether it will be essay, multiple choice, true/false, or another kind of test. Ask how long the test will last and how it will be graded. Some instructors may let you see copies of old exams, so you can see the types of questions they use. Never miss the last class before an exam, because your instructor may summarize valuable information.

Most college instructors would agree that essay exams measure learning far better than objective exams. Explain why so many of the latter are given to students (large classes, efficiency of grading, and so on).

Design an Exam Plan

Use the information about the test as you design a plan for preparing. Build that preparation into a schedule of review dates. Develop a "to do" list of the major steps you need to take in order to be ready, such as joining a study group.

The week before the exam, set aside a schedule of 1-hour blocks for review, along with notes on what you specifically plan to accomplish during each hour.

SEE EXERCISE 6.1
DESIGNING
AN EXAM PLAN

Join a Study Group

Study groups can help students develop better study techniques. In addition, group members can benefit from different views of instructors' goals, objectives, and emphasis; have partners to quiz them on facts and concepts; and gain the enthusiasm and friendship of others to help sustain their motivation.

Ask your instructor, advisor, or campus tutoring or learning center to help you identify interested students and decide on guidelines for the group. Study groups can meet all semester, or they can review for midterms or final exams. Group members should complete their assignments before the group meets and prepare study questions or points of discussion ahead of time. If your study group decides to meet just before exams, allow enough time to share notes and ideas. Together, devise a list of potential questions for review. Then spend time studying separately to develop answers, outlines, and mind maps (discussed below). The group should then reconvene shortly before the test to share answers and review.

SEE EXERCISE 6.2
FORMING A STUDY GROUP

Ask small groups to brainstorm pros and cons of study groups. Have one member from each team report the pros, with another member reporting the cons. List them on the board. Now restructure groups by teaming students who are taking other courses together, who have the same academic major, or the same intended field of study. Ask groups to brainstorm strategies for changing the cons into pros. Finally, discuss strategies from each team and conclude by encouraging students to form study groups in your class and other classes.

Tutoring and Other Support

Often excellent students seek tutorial assistance to ensure their A's. In the typical large lecture classes for first-year students, you have limited opportunity to question instructors. Tutors know the highlights and pitfalls of the course.

Many tutoring services are free. Ask your academic advisor or counselor or campus learning center. Most academic support centers or learning centers have computer labs that can provide assistance for coursework. Some offer walk-in assistance for help in using word processing, spreadsheet, or statistical computer programs.

Often computer tutorials are available to help you refresh basic skills. Math and English grammar programs may also be available, as well as access to the Internet.

Have students locate and share information about various learning centers on campus, including those that offer computer assistance.

Now It's Time to Study

Review Sheets, Mind Maps, and Other Tools

To prepare for an exam covering large amounts of material, you need to condense the volume of notes and text pages into manageable study units. Review your materials with these questions in mind: Is this one of the key ideas in the chapter or unit?

SEE "EMERGENCY?
YOUR INSTRUCTOR
NEEDS TO KNOW"

Will I see this on the test? As indicated in Chapter 4, you may prefer to highlight, underline, or annotate the most important ideas, or you may create outlines, lists, or visual maps containing the key ideas.

Sheets summarizing main ideas can be organized chapter by chapter or according to the major themes of the course. Look for relationships between ideas. Try to condense your review sheets down to one page of essential information. Key words on this page can bring to mind blocks of information.

A *mind map* is essentially a review sheet with a visual element. Its word and visual patterns provide you with highly charged clues to jog your memory. Because they are visual, mind maps help many students recall information more easily.

Figure 6.1 shows what a mind map might look like for a chapter on listening and learning in the classroom. See if you can reconstruct the ideas in the chapter by following the connections in the map. Then make a visual mind map for this chapter and use it to help you remember the material.

Have students work with a partner to review the mind map in Figure 6.1. Then have them create mind maps on sections in this or other chapters. Transfer the best ones to transparencies and share them with the class.

FIGURE 6.1
Sample Mind Map on Listening and Learning in the Classroom

While you're taking an exam, your only focus should be on that task and that alone.

In addition to review sheets and mind maps, you may want to create flash cards or outlines. Also, do not underestimate the value of using the recall column from your lecture notes to test yourself or others on information presented in class.

Taking the Test

1. **Write your name on the test** (unless directed not to) and answer sheet.
2. **Analyze, ask, and stay calm.** Take a long, deep breath and slowly exhale before you begin. Read all the directions so that you understand what to do. Ask for clarification if you don't understand something. Be confident. Don't panic.
3. **Make the best use of your time.** Quickly survey the entire test and decide how much time you will spend on each section. Be aware of the point values of different sections of the test. Are some questions worth more points than others?
4. **Answer the easy questions first.** Expect that you'll be puzzled by some questions. Make a note to come back to them later. If different sections consist of different types of questions (such as multiple choice, short answer, and essay), complete the type of question you are most comfortable with first. Be sure to leave enough time for any essays.
5. **If you feel yourself start to panic or go blank, stop whatever you are doing.** Take a long deep breath and slowly exhale. Use positive self-talk—you will be fine! You do know your stuff! You can do well on this test! Then take another deep breath. If necessary, go to another section of the test and come back later to the item that triggered your anxiety.
6. **If you finish early, don't leave.** Stay and check your work for errors. Reread the directions one last time. On a scantron answer sheet, make sure that all answers are bubbled completely.

SEE "SUMMARIES"

SEE EXERCISE 6.3
WRITING A SUMMARY

Essay Questions

Although you will take objective (multiple-choice, matching, and true/false) exams in college, many college teachers, including the writers of this book, have a strong preference for the essay exam because it promotes higher-order critical thinking. Generally, the closer you are to graduation, the more essay exams you'll take. To be successful on essay exams, follow these guidelines:

Ask students to write a paper linking the four steps in the critical thinking process to an approach for studying for essay exams. They should answer these questions:

1. What were the main issues covered in text and class lectures/discussions? (Making abstractions from a large amount of information.)
2. What essay questions might be asked from such issues? (Finding new possibilities.)
3. Which are the most likely to be asked? (Organizing logically.)

1. **Budget your exam time.** Quickly survey the entire exam and note the questions that are the easiest for you, along with their point values. Take a moment to estimate the approximate time you should allot to each question and write the time beside each number. Be sure you know whether you must answer all the questions or choose among questions. Start with the questions that are easiest for you and jot down a few ideas before you begin to write. Remember, it can be a costly error to write profusely on easy questions of low value and take up precious time you may need on more important questions. Wear a watch so you can monitor your time, including time at the end for a quick review.

2. **Develop a very brief outline of your answer before you begin to write.** Then use your first paragraph to introduce the main points and subsequent paragraphs to describe each point in more depth. If you begin to lose your concentration, the outline can help you regain your focus. If you find that you cannot complete an essay, at the very least provide an outline of key ideas. Since instructors usually assign points based on coverage of the main topics, you will usually earn more points by responding to all parts of the question briefly than by addressing just one aspect in detail.

3. **Write concise, organized answers.** Be sure to address all the subquestions that may be embedded in a single essay item. Many well-prepared students write fine answers to questions that may not have been asked because they did not read a question carefully or did not respond to all parts of the question. Others hastily write down everything they know on a topic. Answers that are vague and tend to ramble will probably be downgraded.

4. **Know the key task words in essay questions.** Being familiar with the key word in an essay question will help you answer it more specifically. The following key task words appear frequently on essay tests. Take time to learn them.

Divide the class into groups of four to five and ask them to prepare several potential essay questions from their notes, using a variety of these key task words. Have each student prepare a mind map of one of the questions to share with other students.

Analyze To divide something into its parts in order to understand it better. Show how the parts work together to produce the overall pattern.

Compare To look at the characteristics or qualities of several things and identify their similarities or differences. Do not just describe the traits; be sure you define how the things are alike and how they are different.

Contrast To identify the differences between things.

Criticize/Critique To analyze and judge something. Criticism can be positive, negative, or both. A criticism should generally contain your own judgments (supported by evidence) and those of other authorities who can support your point.

Define To give the meaning of a word or expression. Giving an example sometimes helps to clarify a definition, but an example by itself is not a definition.

Describe To give a general verbal sketch of something, in narrative or other form.

Discuss To examine or analyze something in a broad and detailed way. Discussion often includes identifying the important questions related to an issue and attempting to answer these questions. A good discussion explores all relevant evidence and information.

Critical Thinking

Essay questions may require quite different responses, depending on their key task words. Answer and then discuss the following questions in class. In your discussion, include what each task word is asking you to do and how it differs from the other two listed here.

1. How would you *define* the purposes of this chapter?

_____

_____

_____

2. How would you *evaluate* the purposes of this chapter?

_____

_____

_____

3. How would you *justify* the purposes of this chapter?

_____

_____

_____

Evaluate To discuss the strengths and weaknesses of something. Evaluation is similar to criticism, but the word *evaluate* places more stress on the idea of how well something meets a certain standard or fulfills some specific purpose.

Explain To clarify something. Explanations generally focus on why or how something has come about.

Interpret To explain the meaning of something. In science, you might explain what an experiment shows and what conclusions can be drawn from it. In a literature course, you might explain—or interpret—what a poem means beyond the literal meaning of the words.

Justify To argue in support of some decision or conclusion by showing sufficient evidence or reasons in its favor. Try to support your argument with both logic and concrete examples.

Narrate To relate a series of events in the order in which they occurred. Generally, you will also be asked to explain something about the events you are narrating.

Outline To present a series of main points in appropriate order. Some instructors want an outline with roman numerals for main points, followed by letters for supporting details. If in doubt, ask the instructor.

Prove To give a convincing logical argument and evidence in support of some statement.

Review To summarize and comment on the main parts of a problem or a series of statements. A review question usually also asks you to evaluate or criticize.

Summarize To give information in brief form, omitting examples and details. A summary is short yet covers all important points.

Trace To narrate a course of events. Where possible, you should show connections from one event to the next.

On overheads, show some typical college essay questions. Incorporate key task words in such items. Show how essay items generally require conceptual thinking rather than memorization of specifics, although both skills will be of use in writing the answers.

Multiple-Choice Questions

Expose students to all types of exams—essay, multiple choice, true/false, and matching. Explain you will deliberately attempt to mislead them on the multiple-choice and true/false items.

Preparing for multiple-choice tests requires you to actively review all of the material covered in the course. Reciting from flash cards, summary sheets, mind maps, or the recall column in your lecture notes is a good way to review such large amounts of material.

Take advantage of the many cues that multiple-choice questions contain. Careful reading of each item may uncover the correct answer. Always question choices that use absolute words such as *always, never,* and *only.* These choices are often incorrect. Also, read carefully for terms such as *not, except,* and *but* that are introduced before the choices. Often the answer that is the most inclusive is correct. Generally, options that do not agree grammatically with the stem of the question are incorrect.

Some students are easily confused by multiple-choice answers that sound alike. The best way to respond to a multiple-choice question is to read the stem and then predict your own answer before reading the options.

If you are totally confused by a question, leave it and come back later, but be sure that you answer the remaining questions in the correct spaces on your answer sheet. Always double-check that you are bubbling in the answer for the right question! Sometimes another question will provide a clue for a question you are unsure about. If you have absolutely no idea, and there is no penalty for guessing, look for an answer that at least contains some shred of information that sounds familiar to you.

True/False Questions

Remember, for the question to be true, every detail of the question must be true. Questions containing words such as *always, never,* and *only* are usually false, whereas less definite terms such as *often* and *frequently* suggest the statement may be true. Read through the entire exam to see if information in one question will help you answer another. Do not doubt your answers because a sequence of questions are all true or all false.

Memory "tricks" can be invaluable at times like these.

© Matthew McVay/Stock, Boston Inc./PictureQuest

Matching Questions

The matching question is the hardest to answer by guessing. In one column you will find the term, in the other the description of it. Before answering any question, review all of the terms or descriptions. Match those terms you are sure of first. As you do so, cross out both the term and its description, and then use the process of elimination to assist you in answering the remaining items. Flash cards and lists (remember to "chunk" in groups of five, seven, or nine) are excellent ways to prepare for matching questions.

Aids to Memory

Anecdotal evidence suggests that elephants, which possess the largest brain of any land animal, are intelligent creatures with impressive memories. The animals can learn up to 100 commands. After mastering tricks, circus elephants seem able to recall them indefinitely. Other animals, including the domesticated dog, have the capacity to associate human words with actions.[1] When you say, "Gracie, sit!" Gracie usually sits.

Remind students of the differences between memorization and learning.

Cal Fussman tells of discovering a simple way to remember things:

> *My eureka came at the library when I stumbled onto a book called* Total Recall *by Joan Minninger. I fixed on a phrase on the jacket that read, "How to Remember 20 Things in Less Than Two Minutes." The book suggests associating the first ten things you want to remember with body parts, starting at the top of your head and going down to your forehead, nose, mouth, throat, chest, belly button, hips, thighs, and feet.*
>
> *I was determined to memorize a list of twelve white wines, going roughly from lightest to weightiest. I tapped the top of my head. That would be the two lightest whites, Soave and Orvieto. Then my forehead —that'd be Riesling. Nose: Muscadet. Mouth: Champagne. Throat: Chenin blanc. . . . I tapped each corresponding body part, saying the name of the wine aloud. By the fifth time, without even trying, crazy associations began to invade my mind. As I tapped the top of my head, I thought, Start Out, and the S made me think of Soave and the O of Orvieto. I touched my forehead, thought, Reeeemember, and the Reeee brought Riesling off my tongue. I tapped my nose and smelled musk cologne, which triggered Muscadet, then tapped my lips and blew a kiss as if I'd just tasted Dom Perignon champagne. . . . Took me less than three minutes—and it solved my problems.[2]*

Another way to "peg" words goes like this: As you're driving to campus, relate any landmarks along the way to something from your class notes or readings. The white picket fence might remind you of "work 15 hours or less a week," while the tall oak tree on the next block reminds you to "work on campus if at all possible."

SEE INTERNET EXERCISE 6.2 MORE MEMORY DEVICES

---

[1]Steve Nadis, "Who You Calling Dumbo? (Memory in Elephants)," *Omni,* June 1993 v15 n8 p20(1).

[2]Cal Fussman, "Thanks for the Memory," *Esquire,* Feb 1999 v131 i2 p142(1).

Remember How You Remember Best

Have you ever had to memorize a speech or lines from a play? One actor records her lines as well as the lines of others on a cassette and listens to them in her car to and from work each day. Another actor records only others' lines and leaves blank time on the tape so that he can recite his lines at the proper moments. Another remembers lines by visualizing where they appear in the script: left-hand page, top; right-hand page, middle; and so forth. And another simply reads and rereads the script over and over until it becomes branded on her brain.

You can apply similar approaches to remembering material for exams. But although knowing certain words will help, remembering concepts and ideas may be much more important. To embed such ideas in your mind, ask yourself as you review your notes and textbooks:

1. What is the essence, or main point, of the idea?
2. Why does this idea make sense? (What is the logic behind it?)
3. What arguments against the idea could there be?
4. How does this idea connect to other ideas in the material?

Good listening, good note taking, and good study habits add up to good grades. You need not study every waking hour of the day or night; that can be disastrous. At the same time, we hope you won't be tempted to party on the evening when studying matters most. The time to celebrate is after you know you've aced the exam. You've earned it!

SEE "MORE AIDS TO MEMORY"

SEE INTERNET EXERCISE 6.3 RESEARCHING GOOD STUDY HABITS

Search Online! 《●》

Internet Exercise 6.1 Examining Institutional Values

Many colleges and universities post campus rules and regulations on their Internet sites. For example, the student code of conduct for Southern Methodist University can be found at http://www2.smu.edu/studentlife/PCL_04_HC.html.

A Search this page to see how SMU defines the following infractions and what the penalties are for committing them.

- Academic sabotage
- Cheating
- Fabrication
- Facilitating academic dishonesty
- Plagiarism
- Failing to cooperate with the council

B Compare SMU's regulations with the document "Statement of Student Academic Integrity for Faculty Members" (http://www.brooklyn.cuny.edu/serindex.htm). What are the differences in philosophy, and which one would you feel more comfortable with?

C Now compare both codes of conduct with those on your campus. How do your rules differ, and with which do you feel more comfortable? (Go to http://success.wadsworth.com for the most up-to-date URLs.)

(continued)

Search Online!   《●》

Internet Exercise 6.2 More Memory Devices

Use the Internet to improve your memory. Go to "The Memory Page" (http://www.premiumhealth.com/memory). Try one of the tips and tricks or memory games. Report back to the class how the memory trick you tried worked and how you might make it even more effective. (Go to http://success.wadsworth.com for the most up-to-date URLs.)

Internet Exercise 6.3 Researching Good Study Habits

Using InfoTrac College Edition, try these phrases and others for key-word and subject-guide searches: "mnemonics," "memory," "examinations," "cheating in college," "academic integrity," "truth," "honesty," "public speaking." Select some articles to read and synthesize their content. But don't stop there. Do a library search of books and articles for more information. Interview a study skills expert on your campus. If your teacher requires a short research paper, use this information to write one, making sure you cite your sources properly.

Additional Exercise

These exercises at the end of each chapter will help you sharpen what we believe are the critical skills for college success: writing, critical thinking, learning in groups, planning, reflecting, and taking action. Also check out the CD-ROM that came with your book—you will find some selected exercises as well as resources for this chapter.

Exercise 6.1 Designing an Exam Plan

Use the following guidelines to design an exam plan for one of your courses:

1. What are the characteristics of the exam?

   What material will be covered?

   What type of questions will it contain?

   How many questions will there be?

   What is the grading system?

2. Identify the approach you intend to use to study for this exam.

3. How much time and how many study sessions will you need?

4. Using your "to do" list format, list all material to be covered.

_____

What still needs to be read?

_____

5. Create a study schedule for the week prior to the exam, allowing as many 1-hour blocks for review as you need and specifically stating what you need to do.

Your Personal Journal

Here are a number of topics to write about. Choose one or more, or choose another related to this chapter.

1. If you are facing any issues related to academic honesty, what are they? What are you doing about them?
2. If you knew you could get away with cheating on an exam, would you do it? Explain.
3. Assuming you have taken an exam, what strategies did you use to prepare? How did they work? If you haven't taken an exam, what strategies do you plan to use? Why?
4. It has been said that exams only measure how well you can memorize information, and that since some people have a natural-born talent for memorization, exams aren't fair. What holes can you punch in this argument?
5. What behaviors are you thinking about changing after reading this chapter? How will you go about changing them?
6. What else is on your mind this week? If you wish to share it with your instructor, add it to this journal entry.

_____

_____

_____

_____

_____

_____

_____

_____

_____

_____

_____

_____

_____

_____

_____

_____

_____

_____

_____

_____

_____

_____

_____

Resources

Now that you've had time to think about academic integrity and organizing your study time, here are a few more things that will help you appreciate the value of studying well. To learn more about cheating and values, find and read several articles on cheating from InfoTrac College Edition. After reading them, condense their messages into a well-written paragraph.

....

....

....

....

Interview one or more of your teachers about cheating. Besides the obvious answer you will get about cheating being a dishonorable character trait, ask them to be more specific about what harm cheating can cause. Write those thoughts down.

....

....

....

....

....

....

Make a list of your exams, quizzes, and papers. Add a way to celebrate when you've finished each one.

Class and Exam Date	Reward

Know Yourself!

Strategies for Success

TAKE CHARGE OF LEARNING!

- Show up for class
- Have work done on time
- Set up a daily schedule
- If full-time student, limit work week to 15 hours; work on campus if possible
- If stressed, enroll part-time
- Assess how you learn best

HONE YOUR SKILLS!

- Improve your reading, note taking, and study habits
- Improve your writing
- Develop critical thinking skills
- Participate in class
- Practice giving presentations
- Learn how to remember more from every class
- Learn from criticism
- Choose instructors who favor active learning
- Study with a group
- Take workshops on how to study
- Get to know your campus library and other information sources
- Embrace new technologies

KNOW YOURSELF!

- Get to know at least one person on campus who cares about you
- Get involved in campus activities
- Learn about campus helping resources
- Meet with your instructors
- Find a great academic advisor or counselor
- Visit your campus career center
- Take advantage of minority support services
- Enlist support of your spouse, partner, or family
- Take your health seriously
- Have realistic expectations
- Learn how to be assertive, yet tactful
- Be proud of your heritage

Developing Values

Choosing Unique Pathways

Lisette Le Bon/SuperStock

**IN THIS CHAPTER,
YOU WILL LEARN**

- How to define *values*

- Some of the different
  usages of the term *values*

- Distinctions between moral
  values and aesthetic and
  performance values

- Distinctions between
  instrumental and intrinsic
  values

- How societal values are
  in conflict

- How changes in American
  society have forced
  changes in societal values

- The difficulties of basing
  our behaviors on certain
  societal values

This chapter was written with
the expert assistance of John M.
Whiteley and James B. Craig,
University of California, Irvine.

reveal yourself

"It amazes me to hear people talk about what's important to them. Two of my friends think nothing of spending the night together. Someone else I know admits to cheating on an exam to raise his grade. Another friend feels guilty if he misses church, and someone else says she plagiarized material for her term paper. I thought people here were going to act more like I do."

Students may ask, "Where do people come up with their screwball ideas?" It's vital that you explain that this chapter does not deal with "right" or "wrong" values but is an examination of how values are formed and acted upon.

Ask students to write their own definitions of values. Write them on the board as your students call them out. Then ask the class to determine which definitions come close to explaining what values are and why.

Unlike most chapters in this text, this chapter deals with an abstract concept—the concept of values. Like it or not, values are an integral part of who you are. By understanding how your values and the values of others may conflict with one another, we hope you will gain a greater understanding of yourself, your friends, your family, and society at large.

The word *values* means different things to different people. For some, the word refers to specific views a person holds on controversial moral issues such as capital punishment. For others, it refers to whatever is most important to a person, such as a good job, a fancy car, or the welfare of one's family. For still others, it refers to abstractions such as truth, justice, or success. In this chapter, we offer definitions of values, provide a framework for thinking about values, and explore ways to discover your values and apply them not only to the college experience but to life after college as well.

SELF-ASSESSMENT: VALUES

The choice of values to live by will guide your actions throughout your life, but the choices you make are not made in a vacuum. They are influenced in direct and subtle ways by the values of your society and by those of your parents, friends, and significant others. Read the following statements and check those that apply to you. Read them again at the end of the chapter and compare your answers.

_____ 1. I am under pressure from family and friends to make the "right" value choices.

_____ 2. So far, college life is not challenging my existing values.

_____ 3. I am concerned about the continuing changes in society that are affecting family values.

_____ 4. Based on what I've seen of other relationships (those of my family and friends), I am pretty sure about the values I will seek in a "significant other."

_____ 5. I believe our country is doing its best for the poor and disabled who cannot take care of themselves.

_____ 6. There is no excuse for poverty. Anyone can find a job if he or she really makes an effort. We should not support poverty by giving free handouts.

_____ 7. If two people choose to have a sexual relationship, it's nobody's business but their own.

_____ 8. I know some people cheat in school. That's why I don't feel so bad about cheating—that is, if I have to for a good grade.

Challenges to Personal Values in College

Most students find that college life challenges their existing personal and moral values. New students are often startled at the diversity of personal moralities found on campus. For instance, you may have been taught that it is wrong to drink alcohol, yet you find that friends whom you respect and care about see nothing wrong with drinking. At the same time, students from more liberal backgrounds may be astonished to discover themselves forming friendships with classmates whose personal values are very conservative.

When you don't approve of some aspects of a friend's way of life, do you try to change his or her behavior, pass judgment on the person, or withdraw from the relationship? Often, part of the problem is that the friend demonstrates countless good qualities and values that make the troublesome conduct seem less significant. In the process, your own values may begin to change under the influence of a new kind of relativism: "I don't choose to do that, but I'm not going to make any judgments against those who do."

In cases where a friendship is affected by differing values, tolerance is generally a good goal. Tolerance for others is a central value in our society and one that often grows during college. Even so, it is easy to think of cases in which tolerance gradually becomes an indulgence of another's destructive tendencies. It is one thing to accept a friend's responsible use of alcohol at a party and quite another to fail to challenge a drunk who plans to drive you home. Sexual intimacy in an enduring relationship may be one thing; a never-ending series of one-night stands is quite another. Remember, the failure to challenge destructive conduct is no sign of friendship.

Your challenge is to balance your personal welfare, your tolerance for diversity, and your freedom of choice. It can be very enriching and rewarding to talk about values with those whose values seem to be in conflict with your own. What are the other person's true values (consciously identified, freely chosen, and actively expressed)? Do his or her current behaviors correspond to those values? Each of you can learn a great deal from talking about why you value what you do. Many people flee from diversity and fail to confront conflicting value systems when, realistically speaking, the values of our society change over time, and many deeply held societal values are in serious conflict. Adopting a set of values that truly make sense to you can help you move ahead with your life and enable you to consciously analyze and reflect on what is taking place in society.

This interesting use of the word "tolerance" begs discussion. How much annoying behavior should one tolerate from someone he or she likes? At what point should one speak up about such behavior? What are the risks of doing so? Of not doing so?

If it is very enriching and rewarding to talk about values with those whose values are in conflict with yours, why don't most people do it? Ask if any students will attempt to have such a conversation with someone they admire but whose values are in conflict with theirs. Ask them later to tell how it went.

Defining Values

SEE EXERCISE 7.1
FRIENDS AND VALUES

Perhaps we can best define a value as an important attitude or belief that commits us to take action, to do something. We may not necessarily act in response to others' feelings, but when we truly hold a value, we act on it.

For instance, we might watch a television program showing starving people and feel sympathy or regret but take no action whatsoever. If our feelings of sympathy cause us to take action to help those who are suffering, those feelings qualify as values.

Actions do not have to be overtly physical. They may involve thinking and talking continually about a problem, trying to interest others in it, reading about it, or sending letters to officials regarding it. The basic point is that when we truly hold a value, it leads us to do something.

We can also define values as beliefs that we accept by choice, with a sense of responsibility and ownership. Much of what we think is simply what others have taught us. Many things we have learned from our parents and others close to us will count as our values, but only after we fully embrace them ourselves.

SEE "DICTIONARY
DEFINITIONS OF VALUES"

SEE EXERCISE 7.2
EVIDENCE OF VALUES

Check to see if your students understand the importance of choice, affirmation, and action here. For example, ask how many believe in democracy. Then ask how many have ever voted in any kind of election and how many have openly affirmed to others how they feel about the issues or candidates. Finally, ask if they have expressed these values in action by volunteering to work for the candidate of their choice.

Make a list on the board of "smuggled values" that college students probably have received from their families. Have students call out the values. Then go through the list with them and determine which values might still apply in this day and age and which are outmoded. Ask why.

Are there such things as correct values? Your class could have quite a disagreement about this, especially if you define "correct values" as values that apply to everyone.

Finally, the idea of affirmation or prizing is an essential part of values. We should be proud of our values and the choices to which they lead, and want others to know it. We also should find ourselves ready to sacrifice for them and to establish our priorities around them.

In summary, then, our values are those important attitudes or beliefs that we (1) accept by choice, (2) affirm with pride, and (3) express in action.

When Australian actor Russell Crowe was being interviewed backstage at the 2001 Academy Awards ceremony after having won the best actor award for his role in *Gladiator,* he recalled some advice he had received from his father: "You know, I'd really like you to do something at a technical college or do some kind of apprenticeship—to fall back on." Such advice from a father is not atypical. Crowe's father was reflecting the hope that his son would always have the skills to support himself and his family, and would not have to worry about where the proverbial "next meal" was coming from. This valuing of security and of developing skills to help a young person fit productively into society is an example of the values that one generation, with the best of intentions and beliefs, attempts to pass on to the next. But for the next generation, these are "smuggled values."

As you know, Russell Crowe chose to reject his father's advice. He chose his own direction for life in terms of his own hierarchy of values, which were different from those of his father. He recalled that he told his father, "Mate, I'm really certain in my life that I'm gonna fall on my face, but it's highly unlikely that I'm ever gonna fall back." At a pinnacle of success in his career as an actor, he was expressing quite a different set of values for himself in defining his own uniqueness.

This chapter will help you discern your own unique values in the context of a society whose basic institutions "smuggle" or put pressure on you to choose what they believe are the "correct" values when in fact those correct values are often in conflict with your own.

Pressures from family and friends to make the "right" value choices often come with the best of intentions. But within a democratic free society, a basic human right is to choose your own values. This chapter will empower you to understand more about the origins and forms of pressures on you to make particular value choices.

The nature of the human condition is that we are like all other people in some respects, we are like some other people in many respects, and we are like no one else in our special uniqueness. How we choose to establish values different from those of our friends, our family, our society, and its institutions is what helps us become unique.

Another Way of Looking at Values

The word *values* is used so differently in scientific and popular literature that we need to explain how we are using the concept. Values define what is deemed desirable and describe the standards someone employs to determine future directions and evaluate past actions. J. P. Shaver and W. Strong state: "Values are our standards and principles for judging worth. They are the criteria by which we judge 'things' (people, objects, ideas, actions, and situations) to be good, worthwhile, desirable; or, on the other hand, bad, worthless, despicable; or of course, somewhere in between these extremes."[1] Milton Rokeach, an important researcher whose field is the nature of values, believes that the ultimate function of human values is to provide "a set of

[1] J. P. Shaver and W. Strong, *Facing Value Decisions: Rationale-Building for Teachers,* New York: Teachers College Press, 1982, pp. 17–34.

As you clarify your values in college, you can choose activities that affirm several of them at the same time. What different values can you guess are important to this student volunteer? (Two seem obvious; what others do you see?)

Photo by Angela Mann

standards to guide us in all our efforts to satisfy our needs and at the same time maintain and, insofar as possible, enhance self-esteem."[2]

Conceived in this way, values are central to determining human behavior and to influencing public and private action. Because values can be organized into hierarchies that help guide individual decisions about occupational goals and educational interests, values are basic to understanding the many differences in how both people and institutions choose to act. On the institutional level, values guide decisions about where resources ought to be allocated, what policies should be formulated, and what directions institutions ought to pursue.

One thing that strikes us here is that the values of those in charge are determining what policies institutions choose to pursue. What do your students think of that? Is there any way to prevent policies that are not in the public interest from being instituted?

Types of Values

To help you with the process of analysis, there are a number of useful ways of thinking about values. One approach is to distinguish among moral values, aesthetic values, and performance values. Another is to consider ends versus means.

SEE "SEVENTEEN CHANGES IN AMERICAN SOCIETY"

Moral Values

Moral values are those values that we generally do not believe should be imposed on others but that are of immense importance to ourselves as individuals. These moral values are used to justify our own behavior toward others (as well as to privately judge others). The college years represent a significant opportunity to focus on the choice of moral values to live by, often for the first time away from the influences of parents, siblings, and previous peer groups. For example, "I think cheating is wrong."

[2] M. Rokeach, *Understanding Human Values: Individual and Societal,* New York: The Free Press, 1979.

Aesthetic Values

Aesthetic values are the standards by which we judge beauty. Beauty, as used here, refers to a broad set of judgments about nature, art, music, literature, personal appearance, and so on. For example, people make different value judgments about music, about what is of value artistically, and about what types of books are worth reading. Within society, vast differences of opinion exist about the definition of proper aesthetic values and how to judge beauty—or even what beauty is. For example, "I think NSync is just a lot of noise."

Performance Values

Ask students why there is comparatively less difference of opinion about performance values and why they are termed "nonmoral."

There is comparatively less difference of opinion about nonmoral performance values, or how well a person performs to some standard, at least within most campus and other institutional cultures. The definition of performance may vary from person to person or context to context, but representative performance values are accuracy, speed, accomplishment, reward, and discipline.

Performance values influence college students through the expectations of important people in their lives. No example is closer to home for college students than the expectations of parents and teachers for a high level of academic performance. For example, "I think it's good to be able to resist drinking too much."

Means Values Versus Ends Values

Values may also be classified as means values versus ends values. Ends, or *intrinsic values,* refer to the ultimate goals toward which it is worth striving. Rokeach identified a list of eighteen ends values that included a world at peace, a comfortable life, freedom, wisdom, and true friendship. Means, or *instrumental values,* are values that are used to help one attain other values. Rokeach identified eighteen means values ranging from responsible, obedient, loving, and imaginative to ambitious, independent, and honest.[3]

SEE "ENDS VALUES AND MEANS VALUES"

SEE INTERNET EXERCISE 7.1 OBLIGATIONS TO SOCIETY

When you think about your values, you should realize that values do not always separate clearly into means and ends categories. The fundamental American value of equality of opportunity, for example, is frequently offered as an intrinsic value of our society and one of the values that distinguishes the United States from totalitarian countries. But equality of opportunity can also be instrumental to the achievement of other intrinsic values, such as the enhancement of human dignity, the realization of human potential, and the liberation of the human spirit, putting it in the category of a means value.

Societal Values in Conflict: Value Dualisms

Poverty is deplorable and should be abolished.

But: There never has been enough to go around, and the Bible tells us that "The poor you have always with you."[4]

In small groups, have students come up with value dualisms, or values in conflict. For example: Running is a good way to stay in shape. But if you are having such a good time that you miss your class, it isn't so good. Or, you should study 2 to 3 hours for every hour of class. But if that means going without sleep some nights, it isn't going to be of much help.

A basic reality of analyzing values is that the values held by a society are not necessarily consistent. And individuals do not easily recognize value conflicts in themselves. Therefore, it is useful to understand that the process of choosing your values does not exist apart from the culture in which you live and that the values in your culture and in the broader society are frequently in conflict.

[3] Ibid.

[4] Robert S. Lynd, *Knowledge for What?* Princeton, NJ: Princeton University Press, 1939, p. 62.

Your conflicting beliefs, or *value dualisms*, may derive from many different experiences occurring from childhood through adolescence and into adulthood. This prolonged period of time, coupled with the very different sources from which your value dualisms derive, may help explain why such conflicts remain largely unexamined. Formal education apparently has little effect on helping you reconcile your value dualisms.

Two of the conflicting value assumptions identified by Robert Lynd relate to poverty and welfare. You read the first one at the beginning of this section. Here is another:

No man deserves to have what he hasn't worked for. It demoralizes him to do so.

But: You can't let people starve.[5]

Now apply this dualism to a contemporary problem in American society. Children under 18 years of age living in poverty reached nearly 17 percent in 1999, up from 14 percent in 1970. Also in 1999 nearly 10 percent of adults over age 65 were living below the poverty level. Given the immense wealth of the United States, to leave substantial percentages of its most vulnerable populations, children and the aged, to subsist in poverty is simply not a rational value choice. Yet no one has reached a consensus on how to solve the problems of poverty and welfare or demonstrated the political will to insist that the problems be solved.

Another pair of assumptions cited by Lynd refer to America's view of its place in the world and the role of individualism:

The United States is the best and greatest nation on earth and will always remain so.

Individualism, "the survival of the fittest," is the law of nature and the secret of America's greatness; and restrictions on individual freedom are un-American and kill initiative.

But: No man should live for himself alone; for people ought to be loyal and stand together and work for common purposes.[6]

The reality of the United States in the world of the 21st century is that it is far from approaching its potential and has a long way to go before it becomes the "best and greatest nation on earth."

The value of individual freedom is essentially synonymous with the values of the United States. When seen from the perspective of people in China for example, where the rights of the state take precedence over the rights of the individual, the contrast is striking and clear. It is less clear when one examines what is happening in American society.

The values embedded in Americans working for common purposes is documented in the *Index of Social Health,* a composite measure of these sixteen indices:

These could be viewed as fightin' words. Does this country have a long way to go? On what issues? What values are inherent in these issues?

SEE EXERCISE 7.3
TWENTY KEY
ASSUMPTIONS ABOUT
AMERICAN LIFE

1. Infant mortality
2. Child abuse
3. Children in poverty
4. Teen suicide
5. Drug abuse
6. High school dropouts
7. Average weekly earnings
8. Unemployment
9. Health insurance coverage
10. The elderly in poverty
11. Health insurance for the elderly
12. Highway deaths due to alcoholism
13. Homicides
14. Food stamp coverage
15. Housing
16. The gap between rich and poor

Since 1970, social health in the United States has declined more than 45 percent, with eleven of the sixteen indices worsening over this time period, including child

[5] Ibid., p. 62.

[6] Ibid., p. 60.

Can your students explain how one of the richest societies in the world still has so many people who fall between the cracks of being well-to-do and being destitute?

abuse, unemployment, health insurance coverage, average weekly earnings, poverty over 65, out-of-pocket health costs over 65, and the gap between rich and poor.[7]

Four of these problems (child abuse, health insurance coverage, average weekly earnings, and the income gap between rich and poor) reached their lowest levels since such records have been kept. If value dualisms within American society contribute to the failure of needed reforms, what are those dualisms?

Changing Society, Changing Values

Changes in society dramatically affect both individual values and the values of society. Change was the hallmark of the 20th century. With the information technology revolution and globalization already bringing fundamental changes to the worlds of business and education, there is every reason to believe that change will be even more rapid in the 21st century.

Consider the changes identified in the book *America at Century's End.*[8] Using the 1950s and 1960s as a baseline, Alan Wolfe and his colleagues document a series of changes in some of the fundamental institutions of American society, including family, religion, education, and the place of the United States in the global marketplace. He reminds us that these changes will have the most profound implications for values and value change in both individuals and society.

You might recall for your students how children of your generation were urged to do better than their parents *by* their parents—and often did. What factors may have caused that situation to change?

For example, one of the major changes in American society over the past half century has been a new demographic profile due to immigration from Latin America and Asia as well as a population shift to the South and West. Another major area of change has been the extensive political realignments and major transformations in American and world economies. Social and technological changes have reinforced each other in governing how people work, how they use their leisure time, and how they travel. Both upward and downward mobility have increased to create a larger middle class. For the first time we can remember, children may not achieve the economic level of their parents, and dual-career families have become a reality.

Moreover, agreement at the local level may contrast sharply with values held at state and national levels. New ethical challenges affecting moral values are coming from such diverse sources as surrogate mothering, computer hacking, AIDS, white-collar crime, abortion, and the bioethical implications of genetic engineering.

Examining Values

Robert S. Lynd's original insights into value dualisms in American culture were formulated more than half a century ago. Is the basic insight relevant to the college campus and college student culture of today? We believe the answer is yes, and offer this example:

> Earning excellent grades in college is critical to success in life.

But: The most important decision you make in college is about the kind of person you want to be.

Comment on this dualism. Do you find yourself holding both values? Your friends? What should you (they) do about it? What other value dualisms exist in your campus culture?

---

[7] *Index of Social Health: Monitoring the Social Well-Being of the Nation,* New York: Fordham Institute for Innovation in Social Policy, 1994.

[8] A. Wolfe (Ed.), *America at Century's End,* Berkeley: University of California Press, 1991.

© Michael Newman/PhotoEdit

Next time you bemoan the lack of time to get everything done, think about what this student mom is going through!

If values did not (or could not) change with the changing societal structure, we would never have progress. At the same time, it is all the more difficult to define enduring values. For example, in the institutions of business and the economy, "conditions at work have been almost completely transformed."[9] One implication is that the wife, rather than staying at home as she did in the majority of cases in the 1950s, now works full-time. Wolfe notes that "for more and more Americans, everything about work is negotiated constantly—between husbands and wives and between employees and employers." From these new situational changes spring profound value dilemmas.

The traditional family of an earlier generation does not serve as a model for society today. In 1950, 60 percent of American households contained male breadwinners and female homemakers, with or without children. By 1986, more than 60 percent of married women with children under 18 were in the labor force, and only 7 percent of households fit the previous pattern. In attempting to characterize the nature of the family in the United States, J. Stacey calls it "diverse, fluid, and unresolved."[10] By inference, one might conclude that family values possess similar characteristics.

In a companion chapter, Kathleen Gerson reports that women still retain responsibility for the lion's share of household labor but also experience discrimination in the workplace. As a result, "the structural conflicts between family and work continue to make it difficult for either women or men to combine child rearing with sustained employment commitment."[11] Although some women have gained access to highly rewarding careers, most women are constrained within ill-rewarded, female-dominated occupations, while most men continue to enjoy significant economic advantages. Yet many women have joined the workforce as a result of a higher divorce rate as well as stagnant wages for their husbands. Ironically, gender inequality at work makes domesticity an inviting alternative for those women who cannot

Ask what value changes have caused the spurts in more two-income families and more working women. Tell them to ignore the need for money and look for basic changes in our thinking that are directly related to this revolution in the workplace.

[9] Ibid., p. 4.

[10] J. Stacey, "Backward Toward the Postmodern Family: Reflections on Gender, Kinship, and Class in the Silicon Valley," in Alan Wolfe (Ed.), *America at Century's End,* Berkeley: University of California Press, 1991.

[11] K. Gerson, "Coping with Commitment: Dilemmas and Conflicts of Family Life," in Alan Wolfe (Ed.), *America at Century's End,* Berkeley: University of California Press, 1991.

earn a decent wage. Despite all the talk about women's rights, the data indicate that women have a long way to go.

If continuing changes in society are affecting values within families, what are the implications for today's college students? What do we mean by a "generation gap" between this generation of college students and the generation represented by their parents and the parents of their friends? If men's and women's experiences with family continue to change, how does someone in college decide what enduring values will "work" for him or her? What enduring values should you be seeking in a significant other?

Implementing Societal Values

In his book *The State of the Nation,* Derek Bok, President Emeritus of Harvard University, offers a historical and comparative assessment of how well the United States is doing in meeting the goals of its citizens.[12] He contends that "Americans remain surprisingly united on what the basic goals of the society ought to be." One of the values they say they cherish most is individual freedom in the exercise of political and personal liberties. Accepting such a value carries with it a responsibility to respect the legitimate rights and interests of others. When polled, most Americans say they want to help the poor, are concerned that the sense of individual responsibility is eroding, and point to the controversy over the value of particular social welfare programs.

Bok observes that a distinguishing feature of Americans' treatment of freedom is the contrast between the "elaborate protection given to political, intellectual and artistic freedoms on the one hand, and the absence of any affirmative constitutional rights" to such basic necessities as food, jobs, shelter, and health care on the other. He notes that the constitutions of Japan and Germany, for example, make explicit mention of such rights. The Swedish constitution states that "the personal, economic and cultural welfare of the individual shall be the fundamental aims of the community. In particular, it shall be incumbent on the community to secure the right to work, to housing and to education, and to promote social care and security as well as favorable living experience."

Bok observes that the percentage of American adults who say they trust other people dropped by one-third from the 1960s to the 1990s. Three-fourths of Americans are unhappy with the "honesty and ethical standards of other citizens." The statement that "most Americans try to avoid taking responsibility for their actions" is endorsed by 75 percent of respondents under 20 years of age and 70 percent of respondents between 30 and 44.

Values and the Family

The family is an important institution for considering social values in the United States, notes Bok, because of the inherent basic obligations it entails toward others and the bridge that the family provides between social and personal values. Do fathers have a basic obligation to their children? If so, how is that obligation reflected in behavior? A study of 1000 teenage children of divorced parents found that more than 40 percent had not seen their fathers in more than a year. Only half of all divorced mothers received any child support, an issue of both personal and social values. Of that half, just over half received the full amount due.

**SEE EXERCISE 7.4
YOUR VALUES AND YOUR
FAMILY'S VALUES**

[12] D. C. Bok, *The State of the Nation: Government and the Quest for a Better Society,* Cambridge, MA: Harvard University Press, 1996. Excerpts reprinted by permission of the publisher. Copyright © 1996 by Derek Bok.

Values and the Community

Bok also explores how the United States has been doing on such fundamental indices of responsibility to the community as voting in elections and contributing time to community organizations. In 1960, 63 percent of potential voters cast ballots. In the sharply contested presidential election of 2000, the percentage was around 50 percent of potential voters. In contrast, Bok reports that the average turnout among eighteen European nations from 1945 to 1989 ranged between 80 and 85 percent.

A long and valued tradition in the United States is volunteer participation. This was noted in 1835 by Alexis de Tocqueville in *Democracy in America,* and its continued presence is documented by Bok, who cited evidence that nearly half of all adult Americans engaged in some form of volunteer activity. Robert Putman provides conflicting evidence in a controversial article called "Bowling Alone: America's Declining Social Capital,"[13] in which he reports that membership in the League of Women Voters has declined by 42 percent since 1969, and Boy Scout volunteers have declined by 26 percent. Thus, there is conflicting evidence on this dimension of the intersection of personal and societal values.

Values and Personal Responsibility

In assessing changes in various aspects of American life from the early 1960s through the early 1990s, Bok found that these six dimensions of personal responsibility had worsened:

- Obeying the law
- Children born out of wedlock
- Cheating on exams
- Income given to charity
- Community service
- Voting rates

Bok notes that some of the value problems that concern society today—such as the environment, poverty, and gender discrimination—went largely unrecognized from World War II until the 1960s. He compared progress in the United States on selected values dimensions with that of six other industrial democracies: Canada, France, West Germany, Japan, Sweden, and the United Kingdom. Among these seven democracies, the United States scored only average. On the dimension of providing for the poor and disadvantaged—percentage of population with incomes

---

Critical Thinking

Smuggled Values

A problem in choosing your own values is that the pressure from individuals (parents, teachers, peers) and social institutions to choose the "right" values is often masked. Using your analytical framework of moral, aesthetic, performance, and means and ends values, write a short paper that identifies and examines the principal "smuggled" values evident in the important people and institutions of your life and how your own values agree or differ.

---

[13] Robert Putman, "Bowling Alone: America's Declining Social Capital," *Journal of Democracy, 65,* 1995.

below the poverty line, severity of poverty, and effectiveness of government transfer programs—the United States was "at or near bottom." On the percentage of children born out of wedlock, the U.S. score was average (in absolute terms, 28 percent of U.S. children are born out of wedlock). The United States was also "at or near the bottom" on the following critical dimensions:

- Violations of criminal laws (57.6 crimes per 1000 people)
- Incidence of teenage pregnancy (64 pregnancies per 1000 girls ages 15–19)
- Voting rates

Bok's summary of this evidence was not encouraging:

Whether one looks at stealing, cheating on exams, paying taxes, charitable giving, paying child support, voting, births out of wedlock, or community service, it is hard to find a single case in which our record today is as strong as it was in 1960.

SEE EXERCISE 7.5
VALUES IN CONFLICT

SEE INTERNET
EXERCISE 7.2
RESEARCHING VALUES

SEE "CHANGES IN
VALUES OVER FOUR
YEARS OF COLLEGE"

SEE EXERCISE 7.6
SHARED VALUES?

Values and You

With all of this in mind, what value goals do present-day college students hold for a society in which you soon will play a leadership role? Does your generation of college students want to unravel some of the value dualisms discussed in this chapter? If you were to revisit some of the same issues fifty years from now, what social values would you like to see more fully actualized in practice? What dominant social values do you want to bequeath to your children? College offers a time to reflect on the purpose of learning and on the uses to which you will put your knowledge. Values are a central element in this reflection. College is also a time to reflect on the ethical dilemmas that confront citizens individually and as members of society.

An essential goal of a college education is to cultivate a capacity for reflection about, and analysis of, issues of values in society and values in one's personal life. College is preparation for life as well as a career, and an opportunity for personal development, including—quite centrally—values development. It is vitally important to learn to integrate both intellectual development and personal values development. All too often, such an opportunity goes wasted.

In addressing a college graduating class, a character in *Doonesbury,* the creation of cartoonist Garry Trudeau, described them as "prematurely professionalized and chillingly competitive." The speaker chided students for their "obsessive concern for the future," seen as "the salient shaping influence on your attitudes during a very critical four years." He went on, "It could have been more than that. This

Speaking of Careers

Three basic elements in career are aptitude, personality, and values. Aptitude does not mean whether you are intelligent compared to people in general (college students are an elite group, after all), but what your special pattern of intellectual competencies is compared to other bright people. As for personality, salespeople are usually quite different from production engineers or financial managers in how they relate to people and problems. As for values, your career center can help you take a test that compares your pattern of values with those associated with different careers. Looking at the results may help you narrow your present list of career possibilities.

college offered you a sanctuary, a place to experience *process,* to *feel* the present as you moved through it, to *embrace* both the joys and sorrows of moral and intellectual maturation! It needn't have been just another waystation."[14]

The college years provide an essential opportunity to experience values development as part of what Trudeau called "process." Embracing values that will enhance your life will be one of the most important outcomes of your college experience. The first year of college is the optimal time to begin this process.

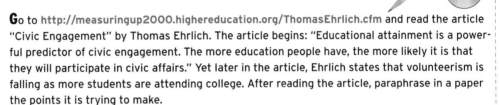

Search Online!

Internet Exercise 7.1 Obligations to Society

Go to http://measuringup2000.highereducation.org/ThomasEhrlich.cfm and read the article "Civic Engagement" by Thomas Ehrlich. The article begins: "Educational attainment is a powerful predictor of civic engagement. The more education people have, the more likely it is that they will participate in civic affairs." Yet later in the article, Ehrlich states that volunteerism is falling as more students are attending college. After reading the article, paraphrase in a paper the points it is trying to make.

Or visit http://www.acenet.edu/hena/issues/1999/10_25_99/opinion_dungy.html and read "Educators Must Promote Integrity Within the Academy" by Gwendolyn Jordan Dungy, Executive Director NASPA–Student Affairs Administrators in Higher Education. What is the main issue in her article? What values is she seeking to promote? Among whom?

Internet Exercise 7.2 Researching Values

Use InfoTrac College Edition as a starting point for researching values. Try these phrases and others for key-word and subject-guide searches: "values," "core values," "college students and values," "values clarification," "values and competition," "values and age," "values and gender," and "family values." Select a number of articles to read and synthesize their content. If you want to learn more, do a library search of books and periodicals. Interview experts on the topic, perhaps a teacher of philosophy or sociology on your campus. If your teacher requires a short research paper, use the information you've gathered to write one, making sure you cite your sources properly.

---

[14] G. B. Trudeau, *Doonesbury,* New York: Universal Press Syndicate, 1972, p.290.

Additional Exercises

These exercises at the end of each chapter will help you sharpen what we believe are the critical skills for college success: writing, critical thinking, learning in groups, planning, reflecting, and taking action. Also check out the CD-ROM that came with your book—you will find more exercises as well as resources for this chapter.

Exercise 7.1 **Friends and Values**

A   Consider several friends and think about their values. Pick one who really differs from you in some important value. Write about the differences.

B   In a small group, discuss this difference in values. Explore how it's possible to be friends with someone so different.

Exercise 7.2 **Evidence of Values**

One way to start discovering your values is by defining them in relation to some immediate evidence or circumstances. In the spaces below, list fifteen items in your room (or apartment or house) that are important or that symbolize something important to you.

_____   _____   _____

_____   _____   _____

_____   _____   _____

_____   _____   _____

_____   _____   _____

Now cross out the five items that are least important—the ones you could most easily live without. Of the remaining ten, cross out the three that are least important. Of the remaining seven, cross out two more. Of the remaining five, cross out two more.

Rank-order the final three items from most to least important. What has this exercise told you about what you value?

Your Personal Journal

Here are a number of topics to write about. Choose one or more, or choose another topic related to values.

1. If you had been in Russell Crowe's position with his father in talking about the next steps for your life, what values would you talk about to help the other person be more accepting?
2. What do you value most in potential significant others? Why? How do those values differ from your own?
3. How are your values different from those of your parents? How are they similar? What do you want to change about this? Why?
4. Values are reflected in the workplace in important ways. What values will you seek before accepting a position with an organization? What do you need to learn more about in terms of the values systems in different careers? Are there some pathways that appear potentially fulfilling for you? Some that turn you off?
5. What values in society do you find most at variance with your own?
6. What value choices do you wish to change after reading this chapter? How might you go about changing them?
7. What else is on your mind this week? If you wish to share it with your instructor, add it to this journal entry.

_____

_____

_____

_____

_____

_____

_____

_____

_____

_____

_____

_____

_____

_____

_____

_____

_____

_____

_____

_____

_____

_____

Resources

Where values are concerned, your best resource may be yourself. Each chapter of this book includes a feature called "Examining Values." In creating the list that follows, we've chosen some main topics from each chapter. Review the list and prioritize the chapter topics according to how important they are to you. Write that number alongside the statement, with 1 being most important and 20 being least important. Then reflect on your choices. What does your list tell you about yourself and your values?

.... Setting goals for myself

.... Mastering time management

.... Developing my critical thinking skills

.... Participating frequently in class discussion

.... Understanding my learning style and using its strengths and weaknesses

.... Working on my class notes after I leave class

.... Improving my comprehension of assigned readings

.... Developing a system for studying for exams

.... Improving my speaking and writing skills

.... Learning how to get what I need in the library

.... Learning everything I can about computers and how they can help me

.... Erasing the block I have about math and science courses

.... Realizing that all learning is related to my future career choice

.... Carefully choosing relationships that enhance, rather than endanger, my life

.... Making a concerted effort to know people from different cultural backgrounds

.... Proudly affirming my values to others

.... Finding a way to manage stress so that I can accomplish more

.... Making sensible decisions about sex

.... Making sensible decisions about alcohol and other drugs

.... Setting up a money management plan and sticking to it

List your top five items. Then decide if your choices are more or less similar to choices made by the rest of the class. Check "Similar" if you believe they are; "Dissimilar" if you believe they are not.

	Similar	Dissimilar
....	☐	☐
....	☐	☐
....	☐	☐
....	☐	☐
....	☐	☐

See if your instructor will collect the five top choices from each student and develop a composite "class values" list. If so, were your choices really similar to or different from the group's?

Careers and Courses

Making Sensible Choices

**IN THIS CHAPTER,
YOU WILL LEARN**

- How majors and careers are linked—but not always

- Surprising things about careers and liberal arts majors

- Factors in career planning and choosing a major

- How to prepare a résumé and cover letter

- How to choose a good academic advisor/ counselor

- How your college catalog can be a helpful reference

This chapter was written with the expert assistance of Philip Gardner, Michigan State University; Linda Salane, Columbia College; and Stuart Hunter, University of South Carolina.

Richard Cummins/CORBIS

ask for directions

"*Don't know why I chose English as a major. What will I do with it after I graduate? Off the top of my head, I can't think of any job that requires an English degree. Maybe Lila was right. She chose management—not because she's thrilled about it, but it sure will make her more marketable than me.*"

Sara entered college with thoughts of majoring in the sciences because she enjoyed working in a laboratory. Her concern for helping others led her to choose nursing as a major, a good career path that combined her two primary interests. Sara sailed through the first two years, excelling in her science classes. During her junior year, she began her nursing courses and spent more time observing nursing practice in her university's teaching hospital. After a summer working in various departments of her hometown hospital, Sara made an appointment with a career counselor. She confessed that she did not like being around sick people every day and wanted to change her major but had no idea what she wanted to do.

John explored several majors during his first two years in college by choosing his elective courses with careers in mind and talking to his friends. He settled on business as a major, focusing on finance. John had high aspirations of working for a Fortune 500 company and earning a six-figure salary within 5 years of graduation. He performed above average in his academic work, though he was occasionally slack with assignments and frequently missed class. He interned with two prominent companies and eventually accepted a position at a Fortune 500 company. To his surprise, he was laid off 9 months later because he was frequently late for work and on two occasions had missed important deadlines.

SELF-ASSESSMENT: CAREERS AND MAJORS

Place a checkmark next to the statements that best describe your present situation. Circle the items you need help with. Then come back to the inventory after reading this chapter and reflect on your answers.

_____ 1. I have made contact with my academic advisor.

_____ 2. I have found useful information about majors and careers in my college catalog.

_____ 3. I have declared a major, but am not sure how it will lead to a career.

_____ 4. I have declared a major, but I wonder if I made the right choice.

_____ 5. I'm not sure I have the necessary skills to pursue the major of my choice.

_____ 6. I know how to prepare a good résumé.

_____ 7. I know how to prepare an effective cover letter to accompany my résumé.

_____ 8. I chose my major primarily because of the potential to earn lots of money.

_____ 9. I chose my major primarily because I enjoy this subject.

Like Sara and John, students planning for careers frequently encounter bumps along the way. Choosing a career is a process of discovery, involving a willingness to remain open to new ideas and experiences. And many of the decisions you make during your first year in college will have an impact on where you end up in the workplace.

Careers and the New Economy

Throughout the 1990s, companies restructured and took on new shapes to remain competitive. As a result, major changes in how we work, where we work, and the ways we prepare for work have changed. The following characteristics in many ways define the economy of the early 21st century.

- **Global** Increasingly, national economies have gone multinational, not only moving into overseas markets, but seeking cheaper labor, capital, and resources abroad.

- **Boundaryless** Teams of workers within an organization need to understand the missions of other teams because they most likely will have to work together. You may be an accountant and find yourself working with the public relations division of your company, or a human resources manager who does training for a number of different divisions and in a number of different countries. You might even find yourself moved laterally— to a unit with a different function—as opposed to climbing up the traditional career ladder.

- **Customized** More and more, consumers are demanding products and services tailored to their specific needs. One example is health food supermarkets that have sprung up in many cities, offering complete grocery shopping for the segment of the market that demands natural/healthy foods.

- **Fast** When computers became popular, people rejoiced because they believed the computer would reduce their workloads. Actually, the reverse happened. Where secretaries and other support workers performed many tasks for executives, now executives are designing their own PowerPoint presentations because, as one article put it, "it's more fun to work with a slide show than to write reports."

SEE "CAREERS AND THE ECONOMY"

Send students, in small groups, to research a multinational company such as Procter & Gamble or Coca-Cola. Ask them what they found out about how the company is structured, what sorts of positions are listed in the company profile, and whether or not the company markets the same brands worldwide.

Finding a Major

It is perfectly fine to enter college as an undetermined major. Most college students change their majors at least once, and some change more often. It may even be better to shop around during your first year before you make the important decision.

Once you have explored your interests, you can begin to connect them to academic majors. If you're still not sure, take the advice of Patrick Combs, author of *Major in Success,* who recommends that you major in a subject that you are really passionate about.

Hold on. Choose something like history because I love history? Where will that put me in the job market? The reality is that most occupational fields do not require a specific major, and graduates have found a number of ways to use their majors. Today English majors are designing Web pages, philosophy majors are developing logic codes for operating systems, and history majors are sales representatives and business managers. You do not have to major in science to gain admittance to medical school. Of course, you do have to take the required science and math courses, but medical schools seek applicants with diverse backgrounds.

SEE "LIBERAL ARTS MAJORS ARE IN"

Some fields do require specific degrees, such as nursing, accounting, engineering, and pharmacy, because certification in these fields is directly tied to an academic degree.

Where to Go for Help

A visit to the career center can be both fascinating and useful. While there, students may (1) take the Strong Interest Inventory (named for Strong, as opposed to "strong interest") and have it interpreted and (2) seek information in those Holland areas in which they achieved high scores. For the latter, you might assign an essay in which each student profiles his or her favorite field in the high-scoring category and evaluates it in terms of interests, skills, aptitudes, personality, and life goals and work values.

- **Career center** Every college campus has a career center where you can obtain free counseling and information on careers. A career professional will work with you to help you define your interests, to interpret results of any assessment you complete, and to coach you on interview techniques and critique your résumé.

  It's important to schedule an appointment. Even though a career counselor may not be the first person you see on campus, by the end of your first year you should be familiar with the career center—where it is located and the counselor responsible for your academic major or interests.
- **Faculty** On many campuses, faculty take an active role in helping students connect academic interests to careers. A faculty member can recommend specific courses in this regard. Faculty in professional curricula, such as business and other applied fields, often have direct contact with companies and serve as contacts for internships. If you have an interest in attending graduate school, faculty sponsorship is critical to admission. Finding a faculty mentor can open doors in a number of ways.

Ask students to find out if there are student organizations related to their majors. As homework, have them attend the next meeting and report on it in class. Group your students by major and have them attend in those groups.

- **Upper-class students** Resident assistants and senior mentors can help you navigate courses and find important resources. They may also have practical experience from internships and volunteering. Their insights can extend the theoretical aspects of academic work into the practical realm. Since they have tested the waters, they can alert you to potential pitfalls or apprise you of opportunities.
- **Student organizations** Professional student organizations that focus on specific career interests meet regularly throughout the year. Join them now. Not only will they put you in contact with upper-class students, but their programs often include employer representatives, helpful discussions on searching for internships or jobs, and exposure to current conditions in the workplace.

Surviving in a Fast Economy

Ask students to find one or two examples of organizations that sponsor noncommercial causes. Ask them why they think companies sponsor such causes. How does a company choose a cause to sponsor?

According to *Fast Company* magazine, the new economy has changed many of the rules about work. Leaders are now expected to teach and encourage others as well as head up their divisions. Careers frequently zig-zag into other areas. People who can second-guess the marketplace are in demand. Change has become the norm. Workers are being urged to continue their learning, and companies are volunteering to play a critical role in the welfare of all people through sponsorship of worthy causes. With the lines blurring between work and personal life, workers need to find healthy balances in their lives. Bringing home work may be inevitable at times, but it shouldn't be the rule.

As you work, you'll be continually enhancing and expanding your skills and competencies. You can accomplish this on your own, by taking evening courses, or by attending conferences and workshops your employer sends you to. As you prepare over the next few years to begin your career, remember that

Talk about the amount of work you must bring home during the week and on weekends. Explain your attempts to strike a healthy balance between work and play. Ask students, in small groups, to discuss how their families handle "homework" and how they plan to handle this issue when they join the workforce. Ask for comments.

- **You are responsible for your career.** At one time, organizations provided structured "ladders" that an employee could climb in his or her moves to a higher professional level. In most cases, such ladders have disappeared. Companies may assist you with assessments and information on available positions in the industry, but the ultimate task of designing a career path is yours.

- **To advance your career, you must accept the risks that accompany employment and plan for the future.** Organizations will continually restructure, merge, and either grow or downsize in response to economic conditions. As a result, positions may be cut. Because you can be unexpectedly unemployed, it will be wise to keep other options in mind.

- **A college degree does not guarantee employment.** Of course, you'll be able to hunt through opportunities that are more rewarding, financially and otherwise, than if you did not have a degree. But just because you want to work at a certain organization doesn't mean there's a job for you there.

- **A commitment to lifelong learning will help keep you employable.** In college you have been learning a vital skill: how to learn. Your learning has just begun when you receive your diploma.

Now the good news. Thousands of graduates find jobs every year. Some may have to work longer to get where they want to be, but persistence pays off. If you start now, you'll have time to build a portfolio of academic and cocurricular experiences that will begin to add substance to your career profile. This Rudyard Kipling couplet from *The Just So Stories* (1902) is an easy way to remember how to navigate for career success:

> I keep six honest serving men
> (They taught me all I knew);
> their names are what and why and when
> and how and where and who.

The knowledge to manage your career comes from you (why, who, how) and from an understanding of the career you wish to enter (what, where, when).

- **Why** Why do you want to be a _____? Knowing your goals and values will help you pursue your career with passion and an understanding of what motivates you. Never say "because I'm a people person" or "because I like to work with people." Sooner or later, most people have to work with people. And your interviewer has heard this much too often!

Despite doomsday pundits, the real message is, "be realistic." Inform your students that even the good guys often get bumped, for reasons that have more to do with organization problems than an individual's performance. Most of all, assure them that those who persist and do the right things will find jobs.

Critical Thinking

Facing Reality

You may already have run into this dilemma. Imagine that you've set your sights on being a physician. You understand the rewards, both financial and personal. You also realize the long hours, the hard work, and the fact that every day people may be counting on you to make them healthier, even save their lives. Your parents support your decision; they're extremely proud of this noble goal. Then you take your first college chemistry course. It's a disaster for you. Your mind simply doesn't work like that. What are you going to do? How are you going to explain to your parents and acquaintances that you made a mistake?

Using the critical thinking process, write a "script" to help you explain logically why you are going to change your major from premed to liberal arts. What are your reasons for choosing liberal arts? Where will that lead? Try to leave emotion out of your argument. Check library sources if you think they might help.

- **Who** Network with people who can help you find out what you want to be. Right now, that might be a teacher in your major or an academic advisor or someone at your campus career center. Later, network with others who can help you attain your goal. Someone will always know someone else for you to talk to.
- **How** Have the technical and communications skills required to work effectively. Become a computer whiz. Learn how to do PowerPoint presentations. Take a speech course. Work on improving your writing. Even if your future job doesn't require these skills, you'll be more marketable with them.
- **What** Be aware of the opportunities an employer presents, as well as such potential obstacles as relocation overseas. Clearly understand the employment requirements for the career field you have chosen. Know what training you will need to remain in your chosen profession.
- **Where** Know the points of entry into the field. For example, you can obtain on-the-job experiences through internships, co-ops, or part-time jobs.
- **When** Know how early you need to start looking. Find out if certain professions hire at certain times of the year.

Starting Your Career-Planning Program

The process of making a career choice begins with understanding your values and motivations, identifying your interests, linking your personality and learning styles to those interests, and using this information to decide on an appropriate academic major. Next comes research into possible occupations that match your skills, your interests, and your academic major.

You will need to evaluate your strengths and weaknesses critically and then take steps to build on your strengths and develop those skills that are weak. Finally, you'll need to prepare a marketing strategy that sells you as a valued member of a professional team. The key tools in your marketing kit will be a résumé and a cover letter.

You won't have to do all these things at once. Table 8.1 (on your CD-ROM) provides a guide to what you should be doing during each year you are in college (if you are in a two-year program, you will have to do more during your second year than this table suggests).

You may proceed through these steps at a different pace than your friends. Don't worry! What you want is to develop your qualifications, make good choices, and be actively engaged in the opportunities available on campus. Keep your goals in mind as you select courses and seek employment, but also keep an eye out for unique opportunities; the route you think you want to take may not be the best one for you.

SEE TABLE 8.1 CHARTING YOUR CAREER COURSE

Do's and Don'ts: Factors to Consider

Some first-year students come to college with a strong sense of self-knowledge and a focus on a specific interest. Others have no idea what their interests might be and are in the process of sorting through their values, interests, and skills in an attempt to define themselves. Such self-definition is an ongoing experience that, for many of us, continues well beyond college. It helps to keep a journal of such thoughts because reviewing these early interests later in life may lead to long-forgotten career paths just when you need them.

As you start examining your aspirations and interests, keep in mind these simple do's and don'ts:

DO'S

1. Do explore a number of career possibilities and academic majors.
2. Do get involved through volunteering, study abroad, and student organizations—especially those linked to your major.
3. Do follow your passion. Learn what you love to do, and go for it.

DON'TS

1. Don't just focus on a major and blindly hope to get a career out of it. That's backward.
2. Don't be motivated by external stimuli, such as salary, prestige, and perks. All the money in the world won't make you happy if you hate what you're doing every day.
3. Don't select a cool major for that reason alone.
4. Don't choose courses simply because your roommate said they were easy. That's wasting your valuable time, not to mention tuition.

Factors Affecting Career Choices

Some people have a definite self-image when they enter college, but most of us are still in the process of defining (or redefining) ourselves throughout life. We can look at ourselves in several useful ways with respect to possible careers:

- **Interests** Interests develop from your experiences and beliefs and can continue to develop and change throughout life. You may be interested in writing for the college newspaper because you wrote for your high school paper. It's not unusual to enter Psych 101 with a great interest in psychology and realize halfway through the course that psychology is not what you imagined.
- **Skills** Skills are measured by past performance and can usually be improved with practice.
- **Aptitudes** Aptitudes are inherent strengths, often part of your biological heritage or the result of early training. They are the foundation for skills. We each have aptitudes we can build on. Build on your strengths.

On the other hand, we could also argue that focusing on a major in the liberal arts may lead to any number of careers. Tell students to try a major they think they like and see what develops but not to pin all their hopes on finding a career in that major alone.

Have students jot down five things they find interesting. Collect their responses and form small "interest groups" of students who listed similar things. Have groups identify what kinds of careers their similar interests might be useful for. For example, a passion for writing might lead to a career in communications but could also lead to a career in either business or information technology.

Ask students what they believe they come by naturally or what others have told them they are "a natural" at. Can they explain where such aptitudes came from?

© Bill Bachman/Stock, Boston, Inc./PictureQuest

Don't aim for a tech job unless you have an aptitude for the field and are genuinely interested in it.

Ask students, in groups of four, to take turns describing their personalities. Then ask the other three students to respond to that description. Do they see the students as those students see themselves? How can they account for the differences? Instruct students to avoid praise or criticism but to provide objective comments exclusively.

SEE "MISSION AND VISION"

SEE INTERNET EXERCISE 8.1 MISSION AND VISION

Have students try to determine which of the Holland categories seems to describe them best before they read the corresponding careers on page 137. Later, have them compare their guesses to the career list and the mosaic exercise (see CD-ROM). Which seems closest to the truth? Why?

SEE EXERCISE 8.1 WHAT ARE YOUR LIFE GOALS?

- **Personality** The personality you've developed over the years makes you *you* and can't be ignored when you make career decisions. The quiet, orderly, calm, detail-oriented person probably will make a different work choice than the assertive, outgoing, argumentative person.
- **Life goals and work values** Each of us defines success and satisfaction in our own way. The process is complex and very personal. Two factors influence our conclusions about success and happiness: (1) knowing that we are achieving the life goals we've set for ourselves and (2) finding that we gain satisfaction from what we're receiving from our work. If your values are in conflict with the organizational values where you work, you may be in for trouble.

Exploring Your Interests

Dr. John Holland, a psychologist at Johns Hopkins University, has developed a number of tools and concepts that can help you organize the various dimensions of yourself so that you can identify potential career choices.

Holland separates people into six general categories based on differences in their interests, skills, values, and personality characteristics—in short, their preferred approaches to life.[1]

Realistic (R) These people describe themselves as concrete, down to earth, and practical—as doers. They exhibit competitive/assertive behavior and show interest in activities that require motor coordination, skill, and physical strength. They prefer situations involving action solutions rather than tasks involving verbal or interpersonal skills, and they like to take a concrete approach to problem solving rather than relying on abstract theory. They tend to be interested in scientific or mechanical areas rather than cultural and aesthetic fields.

Investigative (I) These people describe themselves as analytical, rational, and logical—as problem solvers. They value intellectual stimulation and intellectual achievement and prefer to think rather than to act, to organize and understand rather than to persuade. They usually have a strong interest in physical, biological, or social sciences. They are less apt to be people oriented.

Artistic (A) These people describe themselves as creative, innovative, and independent. They value self-expression and relations with others through artistic expression and are also emotionally expressive. They dislike structure, preferring tasks involving personal or physical skills. They resemble investigative people but are more interested in the cultural aesthetic than the scientific.

Social (S) These people describe themselves as kind, caring, helpful, and understanding of others. They value helping and making a contribution. They satisfy their needs in one-to-one or small-group interaction using strong verbal skills to teach, counsel, or advise. They are drawn to close interpersonal relationships and are less apt to engage in intellectual or extensive physical activity.

Enterprising (E) These people describe themselves as assertive, risk-taking, and persuasive. They value prestige, power, and status and are more inclined than other types to pursue it. They use verbal skills to supervise, lead, direct, and persuade rather than to support or guide. They are interested in people and in achieving organizational goals.

Conventional (C) These people describe themselves as neat, orderly, detail oriented, and persistent. They value order, structure, prestige, and status and possess

---

[1]Adapted from John L. Holland, *Self-Directed Search Manual* (Psychological Assessment Resources: 1985). Copyright 1985 by PAR, Inc. Reprinted with permission.

a high degree of self-control. They are not opposed to rules and regulations. They are skilled in organizing, planning, and scheduling and are interested in data and people.

Holland's system organizes career fields into the same six categories. Career fields are grouped according to what a particular career field requires of a person (skills and personality characteristics most commonly associated with success in those fields) and what rewards those fields provide (interests and values most commonly associated with satisfaction). Here are a few examples:

Realistic (R) Agricultural engineer, electrical contractor, industrial arts teacher, navy officer, fitness director, package engineer, electronics technician, computer graphics technician

Investigative (I) Urban planner, chemical engineer, bacteriologist, flight engineer, genealogist, laboratory technician, marine scientist, nuclear medical technologist, obstetrician, quality control technician, computer programmer, environmentalist, physician, college professor

Artistic (A) Architect, film editor/director, actor, cartoonist, interior decorator, fashion model, graphic communications specialist, journalist, editor, orchestra leader, public relations specialist, sculptor, media specialist, librarian, reporter

Social (S) Nurse, teacher, social worker, genetic counselor, marriage counselor, rehabilitation counselor, school superintendent, geriatric specialist, insurance claims specialist, minister, travel agent, guidance counselor, convention planner

Enterprising (E) Banker, city manager, FBI agent, health administrator, judge, labor arbitrator, salary and wage administrator, insurance salesperson, sales engineer, lawyer, sales representative, marketing specialist

Conventional (C) Accountant, statistician, census enumerator, data processor, hospital administrator, insurance administrator, office manager, underwriter, auditor, personnel specialist, database manager, abstractor/indexer

To display the relationship between career fields and the potential conflicts people face as they consider them, Holland's model is commonly presented in a hexagonal shape (Figure 8.1). The closer the types, the closer the relationships among the career fields; the farther apart the types, the more conflict among the career fields.

Holland's model can help you address the problem of career choice in two ways. First, you can begin to identify many career fields that are consistent with what you know about yourself. Then you can use the career library at your college to get more information about those fields, such as daily activities for specific jobs, interests and abilities required, preparation required for entry, working conditions, salary and benefits, and employment outlook. Second, you can begin to identify the harmony or conflicts in your career choices, which will help you analyze the reasons for your career decisions and be more confident as you make those choices.

Make it clear that career inventories only provide general guidelines; an inventory simply matches their interests with those of professionals in certain fields. If students don't possess the aptitudes or interests in those fields, the match is probably not correct.

SEE EXERCISE 8.2
PERSONALITY MOSAIC

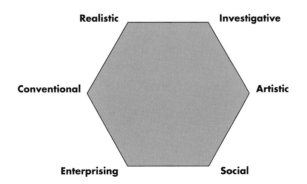

FIGURE 8.1
Holland's Hexagonal Model of Career Fields

SEE INTERNET
EXERCISE 8.2
INTERNET CAREER
RESOURCES

SEE EXERCISE 8.3
THE HOLLAND HEXAGON

SEE EXERCISE 8.4
FINDING YOUR
INTERESTS

Invite someone from your campus service learning office to visit your class to acquaint students with opportunities for service learning in the local area. Consider building a service learning requirement into your course.

Form four-member teams of students with the same academic major or who share similar career interests. One pair of students within each team can research internship opportunities related to their career interests while the other pair investigates related service learning opportunities. The group's final product would represent a composite of available "experiential learning" opportunities relevant to their particular academic majors or future career interests.

Holland's approach does not pigeonhole you into a career path you do not desire. If you find you do not fit the category you expected, the implication is to develop interests and skills in the area consistent with the area you desire. Never feel you have to make a decision simply on the results of one assessment. Career choices are complex and involve many factors; furthermore, these decisions are not irreversible. Take time to talk over your interests with a career counselor. Another helpful approach is to shadow an individual in the occupation that interests you to obtain a better understanding of what the occupation entails in terms of skills, commitment, and opportunity.

Getting Experience

Now that you have a handle on your interests, it's time to test the waters and do some exploring. Your campus has a variety of activities and programs in which you can participate to confirm those interests, check your values, and gain valuable skills. Here are some examples.

- **Volunteer/service learning** Some instructors build service into their courses as a learning device. Service learning allows you to apply academic theories and ideas to actual practice. Volunteering outside of class is a valuable way to encounter different life situations and to gain work knowledge in areas such as teaching, health services, counseling, and tax preparation. A little time each week can provide immense personal and professional rewards.
- **Study abroad** Spend a term studying in another country and learn about a different culture at the same time. Learn to adapt to new traditions and a different pace of life. Some study-abroad programs also include a service learning experience.
- **Internships/co-ops** Many employers now expect these work experiences. They want to see that you have experienced the professional workplace and gained an understanding of the skills and competencies necessary to succeed. Check with your academic department and your career center on the internships that are available in your major.
- **On-campus employment** On-campus jobs may not provide much income, yet this type of employment gives you a chance to practice good work habits. Some jobs have direct connections to employment. More important, on-campus employment brings you into contact with faculty and other academic professionals whom you can later utilize as mentors or references.

Speaking of Careers

Since this entire chapter is about careers, we want to shift the emphasis in this box to your next summer job. Certainly many of you will be working then to help offset the costs of college. But what if you could gain experience—even without pay—by working in your intended field? Can't afford it? Think again. Without the pressures of school, you might be able to work a limited number of hours interning in your field and use the remaining time to earn cash. Find the person in your major who runs internship or practicum programs and ask if he or she has any ideas. Even though you may not qualify for credit, the experience may help you decide whether or not you belong in this field. If you like it, you may be able to come back to that same person for a real internship or a job in the future.

- **Student projects/competitions** In many fields, students engage in competitions based on what they have learned in the classroom. Civil engineers build concrete canoes, and marketing majors develop market strategies, for example. They compete against teams from other schools. In the process, they learn teamwork, communication, and applied problem-solving skills.
- **Research** An excellent way to extend your academic learning is to work with a faculty member on a research project. Research extends your critical thinking skills and provides insight on a subject above and beyond your books and class notes.

Time for Action

In addition to being well educated, you'll also need

1. Communication skills that demonstrate solid oral, written, and listening abilities.
2. Presentation skills, including the ability to respond to questions and serious critiques of your presentation material.
3. Computer/technical aptitudes at the level required for the position being filled. Computer ability is now perceived as a given core skill, right up there with reading, writing, and mathematics. Expectations for computer knowledge and application continue to rise.
4. Leadership skills, or the ability to take charge or relinquish control according to the needs of the organization; closely aligned with possessing management abilities.
5. Team skills, the ability to work with different people while maintaining autonomous control over some assignments.
6. Interpersonal abilities that allow a person to relate to others, inspire others to participate, or mitigate conflict between coworkers.
7. Personal traits including showing initiative and motivation, being adaptable to change, having a work ethic, being reliable and honest, possessing integrity, knowing how to plan and organize multiple tasks, and being able to respond positively to customer concerns.
8. Critical thinking/problem solving—the ability to identify problems and their solutions by integrating information from a variety of sources and effectively weighing alternatives.
9. Intelligence and common sense.
10. A willingness to learn quickly and continuously.
11. Work-related experiences in college that provide an understanding of the workplace and allow you to apply classroom learning.

Refer students to Chapter 4 on listening and learning.

Refer students to Chapter 3 on critical thinking.

Building a Résumé

Before you finish college, you'll need a résumé—whether it's for a part-time job, for an internship or co-op position, or for a teacher who agrees to write a letter of recommendation for you. Note the two résumés in Figure 8.2. One is written in chronological format, and the other is organized by skills. Generally, choose the chronological résumé if you have related job experience and choose the skills résumé if you can group skills from a number of jobs or projects under several meaningful categories. Try for one page, but if you have a number of outstanding things to say and they run over, add a second page. Here are some other suggestions for good résumés:

- **Always put a contact block at the top.** This includes name, address, permanent address if applicable, email address, and telephone number.

SEE EXERCISE 8.5
WRITING A RÉSUMÉ
AND COVER LETTER

Students may wonder why they should do a résumé when they've just started college. The answer is: practice! These are general guidelines for most majors. In some majors, the résumé may be organized differently. If students have a question about this, suggest they contact a faculty member in their department.

SKILLS RÉSUMÉ

Sammie S. Skillful
Sskillful@infi.com

Present Address
2424 Main Street
Columbia, SC 29211
(803) 999-9999

Permanent Address
39 Sherman Avenue
Lake George, SC 29999
(803) 267-8989

OBJECTIVE
Seeking hospitality related managerial position utilizing sales, organizational, and supervisory experience.

EDUCATION
Bachelor of Arts in English, December 2003
University of South Carolina, Columbia, SC
• GPA: overall 3.87/major 4.0
• Financed 100% of educational expenses

SKILLS

Initiative
• Developed and promoted summer pool parties
• Established and managed in-home dining service
• Developed marketing strategy and arranged promotions

Organization
• Organized parties for up to 500 area residents
• Hired and trained staff of six
• Ordered supplies on a monthly basis

Supervision
• Supervised staff of ten hired for New Year's Eve party
• Hired and trained staff of four for own dining business

Computer
• Designed promotional materials using desktop publishing
• Created and maintained customer database

EXPERIENCE
Self-Employed, June 1996–August 1998
Diner's Delight, Columbia, SC

Self-Employed, August 1994–May 1996
Parties Plus, Columbia, SC

Bagger, May–August 1993
Wee Pig Food Store, Charleston, SC
• Received six monthly awards for most courteous service

HONORS
Sigma Tau Delta English Honor Society, Golden Key National Honor Society, Dean's List, Phi Beta Kappa

INTERESTS
Jogging, skiing, reading

REFERENCES
Available upon request

CHRONOLOGICAL RÉSUMÉ

Rita Résumé
3130 Appian Way
Columbia, SC 29229
(803) 989-0000, rway@infi.com

OBJECTIVE
Seeking entry-level position in finance utilizing analytical, supervisory, and organizational skills.

EDUCATION
Bachelor of Science in Business Administration, May 2003
University of South Carolina, Columbia, SC
• Major: Finance
• GPA: overall 3.2/major 4.0
• Financed 60% of educational expenses

RELATED EXPERIENCE
Intern, Bank of Carolina, Summer 1998, Columbia, SC
• Developed procedures manual for tellers
• Performed financial analysis for loan packages
• Supervised summer student staff

OTHER EXPERIENCE
Assistant Manager, Pop's Deli, September 1998–present, Columbia, SC
• Supervised wait staff of ten
• Ordered $1,000 in supplies weekly
• Trained twelve new employees
• Increased sales by 10%

Manager's Assistant, Aiken Pool, Summer 1997, Aiken, SC
• Assisted with supervision of aquatic facility used daily by 300 people
• Organized concession stand with $300 daily sales

ACTIVITIES
President, Zeta Zeta Zeta Sorority
University of South Carolina, Columbia, SC
• Organized and supervised work of ten committees
• Allocated annual budget of $15,000
• Interacted with university, city, and state officials
• Membership increased 10% during presidency

Chair, Panhellenic Council
University of South Carolina, Columbia, SC
• Convened and led weekly meetings
• Supervised work of all committees
• Organized fund-raising that raised $25,000
Delta Sigma Pi Business Fraternity
Water Skiing Club
Equestrian Club

INTERESTS
Golf, tennis, English literature

REFERENCES
Available upon request

FIGURE 8.2 Sample Résumés

- **State an objective if appropriate.** If you're seeking a specific position, absolutely state an objective. But be realistic. You're probably seeking an entry-level position at this stage. If you're applying for several different types of jobs, change your objective to fit each mailing.
- **List education to date.** As a first-year student, you can list under "Education" something like the following: "Enrolled in Bachelor of Arts, Psychology, University of Nebraska." When you're nearer to graduation and seeking full-time employment, state the degree and when you expect to receive it.
- **Give grade point average only if it's impressive.** What's important is that you demonstrate a balance between good grades and involvement in other areas of campus life.
- **Use action verbs in stating accomplishments.** "Developed bookkeeping system for company." "Organized special event that raised $5,000 for charity." "Supervised editorial staff of twelve."
- **Separate work experience related to your academic major from other work experience.** If you have no related work experience, simply list jobs under "Work Experience." Even though the job may not be related, it indicates someone thought enough of you to hire you and pay you.
- **Explain honors and awards thoroughly.** People will probably know what Phi Beta Kappa is, but how many will understand "Gold Monument Award from Callback Club"?
- **Include interests.** These tell employers that you have interests in life beyond your work. Few prospective employers seek workaholics.
- **Be sure you have obtained permission from your references if you state "references available upon request."** Let references know that a prospective employer may call. Nothing is more awkward—or harmful—than a reference getting a call and thinking "Who the heck is that?" when your name is mentioned.
- **Ask someone to review your résumé.** Ask your academic advisor, counselor, or someone else whose judgment you trust to look at your résumé before you put it into final form.

Writing a Cover Letter

Sending a résumé without a cover letter is somewhat like forgetting to put on your clothes over your underwear: You can do it, but people will notice something important is missing. In writing a cover letter, heed the following suggestions:

- **Find out whom to write to.** It's not the same in all fields. If you were seeking a marketing position at an advertising agency, you would write to the director of account services. If you were approaching General Motors regarding a position in their engineering department, you might write to either the director of human resources for the entire company or to a special HR director in charge of engineering. Your academic advisor or career counselor can help you here. So can the Internet.
- **Get the most recent name and address.** Advisors or counselors can guide you to references in your campus or career library. Never write "To whom it may concern."
- **Use proper format for date, address, and salutation,** as shown in Figure 8.3.

College students often view the choice of a career as a monumental and irreversible decision. But, in its broadest sense, a career is the sum of the decisions you make over a lifetime. There is no "right occupation" just waiting to be discovered. Rather, there are many career choices you may find fulfilling and satisfying. The question is, "What is the best choice for me now?"

Writing about yourself can be excruciating. Tell students to expect this as they draft a cover letter that accentuates the positives without bragging. One suggestion: pretend you're writing a close friend to tell him or her about some of your recent accomplishments and what you are thinking of doing after college and why.

If a student asks, "Why send a cover letter AND résumé?" the answer is simple: The résumé tells what you've done; the cover letter tells who you are. If your writing style is congenial, straightforward, organized, and commanding, it says you're a pretty solid individual.

SEE INTERNET
EXERCISE 8.3
RESEARCHING COURSES
AND CAREERS

FIGURE 8.3
Sample Cover Letter

Janet R. Mars
3130 Appian Way
Columbia, SC 29229

January 10, 2003

Mark B. Stoneridge
VP, Sales and Marketing
Ainsley Pharmaceuticals
3000 Appalachian Way
Pittsburgh, PA 49877

Dear Mr. Stoneridge:

(In your opening paragraph, tell why you are writing) When I receive my B.A. degree this spring, I would very much like to begin a career as a pharmaceutical salesperson.

(In the ensuing paragraphs, tell what makes you the right person for the job) I had no idea I would be interested in this field when I majored in speech. Then I chose a minor in marketing and discovered they fit together beautifully. The third part of the equation was knowing a friend of my mother who works for a pharmaceutical company in sales. I spent a good deal of time with her, shadowed her on calls, and decided this was the career I was meant for.

(In the last paragraph, tell what you will do next) I plan to visit Pittsburgh sometime around June 15 and would greatly appreciate a few moments of your time. If you have no openings at your company, perhaps you might refer me to other organizations. I will call you at least a week before I make my trip to see if you have time to visit with me.

(End with a proper closing)
Sincerely,

(signature) Janet R. Mars

Janet R. Mars

Your Academic Advisor

One person you can look to for advice on majors and careers is your academic advisor or counselor—one of the key individuals you will meet in college. This person can guide you through the complexities of choosing courses that follow your interests and meet the requirements of your major. He or she can also direct you to your campus career center for further research on career fields that interest you.

A mounting body of evidence suggests that poor academic advising is a major reason students leave college in the first year.

At most colleges, you will visit your advisor or counselor at least once a term to obtain approval for the courses you will take the following term. The advising period is usually widely publicized on campus. Beyond that time, your advisor or counselor is available whenever you need help—when you're having trouble in a course, when a medical emergency forces you to miss classes beyond the drop date, when you're doubtful about the major you have chosen, or for other academic or personal reasons that may affect your success in college.

At many colleges, academic advisors and counselors are full-time faculty. At some campuses, some may be professional staff. In many community colleges,

SEE EXERCISE 8.6 YOUR ACADEMIC ADVISOR/COUNSELOR

Have teams of students generate a list of academic or personal problems they need help with. Have them arrange those problems into categories and identify campus resources that can offer help. Each student in the group should now assume a special role in locating campus resources for each category. Have the group present its results in the form of a "concept map" that visually connects problem categories to related sources of campus assistance.

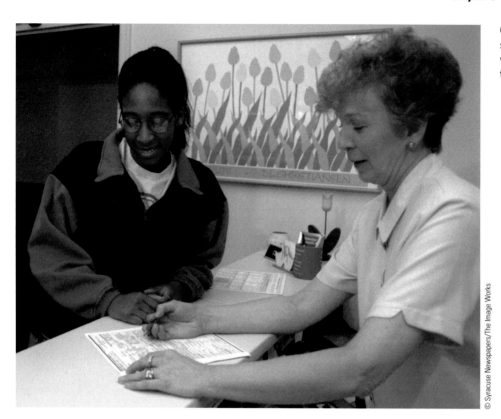

Choose your advisor or counselor carefully. He or she can be vitally helpful as you work through your college years.

academic advising is done by counselors in the counseling/advising center. These counselors are trained in and responsible for assisting students with both academic and personal issues. Your institution may not assign you to an advisor in your intended major until you are formally admitted to a program. In any event, your advisor should be familiar with the requirements of your program.

Preparing for Your Meeting

Your advising sessions will be more productive if you are familiar with your college catalog. Make a list of questions before your appointment and arrive with a tentative schedule of courses and alternate choices for the coming term.

Discuss any major decisions—adding or dropping a course, changing your major, or transferring or withdrawing from school—before making them. You may also choose to discuss personal problems with your advisor. If he or she can't help you, ask for referral to a professional on campus who can. Be sure to confirm that your advisor will respect your request for confidentiality on such matters.

Is Your Advisor/Counselor Right for You?

How comfortable do you feel with your advisor/counselor? Does this individual seem to take a personal interest in you, listen actively, provide enough time for you to have your say, and either make an effort to get you the information you request or tell you where you can find it yourself?

If not, find someone else. Ask one of your favorite instructors or check with your department head or dean's office. Never stay in an advising/counseling relationship that isn't working for you.

How can students find a great advisor? Tell them to visit their student services office or ask an upper-class student for a recommendation. Be certain they understand that they have every right to ask for a change of advisor/counselor if the relationship isn't working.

Your College Catalog

Have students use the catalog to check academic requirements for their major and share one or two things they learned. Have undeclared students choose a major they are considering. If any requirements are unclear, have them check with the college or department for clarification and report what they learned.

SEE EXERCISE 8.7 FINDING YOUR CATALOG AND STARTING A FILE

SEE "WHAT ARE YOU LOOKING FOR IN YOUR ACADEMIC ADVISOR?"

Ask students which items in the general information section seem most important. Have them become familiar with critical dates, such as the last day to register for a course, drop date, holiday break, and final exam schedule. Chances are your campus publishes this information on the Internet as well.

Assign the academic regulations section in the catalog as a "must read." Ask students to write about the regulations that
(1) they were surprised to discover,
(2) they need to know immediately, and
(3) they need to remember for future use.

College can be less complex if you treat your college catalog as a user's manual. Learn what's in your catalog—it can be a valuable resource throughout your college years. Moreover, your catalog is a legal contract between you and your school. It must honor what it promises, just as you must honor those obligations stated in the catalog.

Much of the information in your college catalog is probably online. Campus computer bulletin boards and Internet home pages are especially useful for information that is in constant flux or that has changed recently. In addition to lists of classes and prerequisites, office hours, and student services, you can often search listings of job opportunities, scholarships, schedules, and departmental telephone numbers and email addresses.

Publication Date and General Information

Colleges and universities are constantly changing admissions standards, degree requirements, academic calendars, and so on. But the catalog in use at the time of your matriculation (the day you enrolled for the first time) will generally stand as your individual contract with the institution.

Most college catalogs include a current academic calendar, which shows the beginning and ending dates of academic terms, holidays, and important deadlines. If you are not doing well in a particular class, you may want to drop the course rather than receive a failing grade, but you must do so before the deadline for withdrawal.

General Academic Regulations

Don't rely on secondhand grapevine information. Become familiar with general academic regulations directly from the catalog. If you don't understand something in the catalog, seek clarification from an official source, such as your academic advisor.

Academic Programs

By far the lengthiest part of most catalogs is the section on academic programs. It summarizes the various degrees offered, the majors within each department, and the requirements for each discipline. The academic program section also describes all courses offered at your institution: course number, course title, units of credit, prerequisites for taking the course, and a brief statement of the course content. For more detailed academic information, check with individual departments.

Examining Values

The relationship between an academic advisor/counselor and a student is a vital one. In a short paper, describe the values you would seek in such a person. Then explain why those values are important to you. For example, would you prefer an advisor who valued helping you find the right academic program? Or one who valued a close relationship with students? Or one who valued his or her expertise on academic matters? Or what?

Search Online!   《 ● 》

Internet Exercise 8.1 Mission and Vision

Get started on your vision statement by using the exercise available at the
Franklin Covey Web site, http://www.franklincovey.com/missionbuilder/index.html. Imagine
the life you wish to create and write down your images in the present tense.

_____

_____

_____

_____

From your vision, extract a short motivational sentence that will help you attain your vision.
Write down your images in the present tense.

_____

_____

_____

_____

Internet Exercise 8.2 Internet Career Resources

The Internet offers a variety of resources for choosing a career. These include Oakland
University's "Definitive Guide to Internet Career Resources" (http://phoenix.placement.
oakland.edu/career/guide.htm), an extensive listing of career sites; "The Catapult on Job Web"
(http://www.jobweb.org/catapult/catapult.htm), a major guide with links to career and job-
related sites; and "The Riley Guide to Employment Opportunities and Job Resources on the
Internet" (http://www.dbm.com/jobguide). Other Internet career resources include American
Career InfoNet Career Resources Library: http://www.acinet.org/resource/misc/#diverse;
Yahoo Business/Employment menu: http://www.yahoo.com/Business/Employment Career
Resources Center; http://www.careers.org; Advancing Women Career Center: http://www.
advancingwomen.com/awcareer.html; Peterson's Web site: http://www.petersons.com/;
What Color Is Your Parachute? The Net Guide: http://www.washingtonpost.com/parachute.
(Go to http://success.wadsworth.com for the most up-to-date URLs.) Describe the resources
available at four or more sites.

_____

_____

_____

_____

Of the sites you visited, which are better for gathering information about a future job? Which
are better for finding a job immediately?

_____

_____

Internet Exercise 8.3 Researching Courses and Careers

Use InfoTrac College Edition as a starting point for researching courses and careers. Try
these phrases and others for InfoTrac College Edition key-word and subject-guide searches:
"career planning," "careers," "new economy," "academic advisor," "college majors," "multinational organizations."

   Select a number of articles to read and synthesize their content. But don't stop there. Do
a library search of books and periodicals for more information. Interview experts on the topic,
perhaps a career counselor on your campus or a human resources manager at an area organization. If your teacher requires a short research paper, use the information you've
gathered to write one, making sure you cite your sources properly.

Additional Exercise

These exercises at the end of each chapter will help you sharpen what we believe are the critical skills for college success: writing, critical thinking, learning in groups, planning, reflecting, and taking action. Also check out the CD-ROM that came with your book—you will find more exercises as well as resources for this chapter.

Exercise 8.1 What Are Your Life Goals?

The following list includes some life goals that people set for themselves. This list can help you begin to think about the kinds of goals you may want to set. Check the goals you would like to achieve in your life. Next, review the goals you have checked and circle the five you want most. Finally, review your list of five goals and rank them by priority—1 for most important, 5 for least important. Be prepared to discuss your choices in class if your instructor asks.

_____ The love and admiration of friends

_____ Good health

_____ Lifetime financial security

_____ A lovely home

_____ International fame

_____ Freedom within my work setting

_____ A good love relationship

_____ A satisfying religious faith

_____ Recognition as the most attractive person in the world

_____ An understanding of the meaning of life

_____ Success in my profession

_____ A personal contribution to the elimination of poverty and sickness

_____ A chance to direct the destiny of a nation

_____ Freedom to do what I want

_____ A satisfying and fulfilling marriage

_____ A happy family relationship

_____ Complete self-confidence

_____ Other: _____

Note: Adapted from *Human Potential Seminar* by James D. McHolland, Evanston, IL, 1975. Used by permission of the author.

Your Personal Journal

Here are a number of topics to write about. Choose one or more, or choose another topic related to this chapter.

1. What internal (feelings, emotions) and external (parents, peers) influences have affected your thoughts about majors and careers? How has this affected your thinking?

2. What other majors and/or careers have you been thinking about? Why do these appeal to you? If you're not considering other careers and majors, why are you dead-set on the one you've chosen?

3. What factors are important to you in deciding on a major and a career?

4. Where do you want to be a year from now in your career-decision process?

5. What behaviors are you willing to change after reading this chapter? How might you go about changing them?

6. What else is on your mind this week? If you wish to share it with your instructor, add it to this journal entry.

_____

_____

_____

_____

_____

_____

_____

_____

_____

_____

_____

_____

_____

_____

_____

_____

_____

_____

_____

_____

_____

Resources

You may find that thinking about careers feels overwhelming, you may have a clear idea of your future career even now, or you may fall somewhere in between these extremes. Career interest information, academic program information, and major and course descriptions can sometimes seem abstract. One thing that can help you find the best fit for your talents and strengths is to talk to people who are taking the courses, following the majors, and pursuing the careers that you are interested in. Use this Resources form to find people you could interview for information about courses, majors, and careers. Be creative. Over the years, this list could grow into a major networking tool.

STUDENTS WHO COULD BE RESOURCES FOR MAJORS AND COURSES

Name	Major	Course(s)	Phone number

OTHER PEOPLE WHO COULD BE RESOURCES FOR CAREER AREAS

Don't forget your advisor, instructors, family, and friends. Also include people you may have met while volunteering.

Name	Career/job title	Phone number

Creating Diverse Relationships

All Kinds of People, All Kinds of Ideas

IN THIS CHAPTER, YOU WILL LEARN

- The value of sharing your uniqueness with others
- What colleges are doing to promote healthy diversity
- Who's off limits for dating, and why
- The stages of love
- The best options for long-distance relationships
- How to handle marriage and school
- What makes parents tick
- The pros and cons of electronic relationships
- How to deal with roommates
- The value of co-op programs and service learning
- How diversity in America has changed and is changing
- Why it isn't easy to label an individual as a member of a certain cultural group
- How to fight discrimination and prejudice on campus
- How the "old minority" is becoming the "new majority"

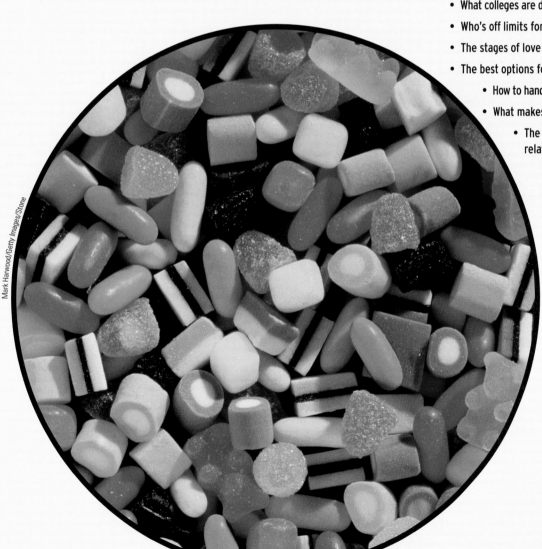

Mark Harwood/Getty Images/Stone

This chapter was written with the expert assistance of Tom Carskadon, Mississippi State University, J. Herman Blake, Iowa State University, and Joan Rasool, Westfield State College.

enjoy the variety

Enough said about diversity! We've worked out all the problems, and there's no point in any further discussion. I have friends who are Asian, African American, Hispanic, and disabled. Should I stick with people more like me, or try to make friends with different kinds of people? Might learn something from them. Then again, what I learn might not be so great, either. And I'm not as close to them as I am to people my own color, but that's normal, isn't it?"

SELF-ASSESSMENT: RELATIONSHIPS AND DIVERSITY

Check those statements that are true. Leave the others blank. After reading this chapter, come back to this inventory and place an *X* beside any item you now think differently about.

_____ 1. When in love, you should listen to your heart, not to other people.

_____ 2. If you date people you work with, you get the best of both worlds.

_____ 3. Homosexuals are sick, but they could choose to be normal.

_____ 4. The average person who is sexually active during 5 years of college and uses condoms for birth control has about a 50-50 chance of having a pregnancy.

_____ 5. Now that you are in college, asking your parents' advice is a good idea.

_____ 6. Roommates are like the weather: You hope for the best, but you take what you get with a smile.

_____ 7. Join a fraternity or sorority, and you will probably become a lot like the other people in it, if you aren't already. Same thing's true with the friends you run with: You're likely to end up a lot like them.

_____ 8. Service learning is charity where you help others; you should not go into it expecting any benefit for yourself.

_____ 9. Culture, ethnicity, and race all mean the same to me.

_____ 10. I am not part of any cultural, ethnic, or racial group.

_____ 11. I believe that "staying with your kind" puts less stress on friendships.

_____ 12. Older students have their own agendas. They don't seem to be interested in making friends with younger students like me.

_____ 13. Younger students have their own agendas. They don't seem to be interested in making friends with older students like me.

_____ 14. I tend to avoid speaking to physically disabled people because it might make them self-conscious about their disabilities.

_____ 15. People who have special privileges because they are "learning disabled" are usually faking it so they can have an easier time in college.

For years, the United States prided itself on being one nation united by a common culture. Subcultures (Hispanic, African American, Asian American, and others) were encouraged to shed much of their cultural identities and become part of the whole.

Then, in the wake of the civil rights movement, this concept of a melting pot vanished, replaced by an ideal called "diversity," where different ethnic groups would celebrate their own cultures as well as the general culture.

Many view diversity as a more tolerant ideal than the melting pot, claiming it allows people to preserve their identities instead of forcing them into assimilation.

As a new college student, you should understand that individuals belonging to various cultural, ethnic, and racial groups share common traits not only with others of their particular group but also with others beyond their group—and that, despite our ideal of the American Dream, the United States can look back on a long and painful history of discrimination.

For example, after Japanese bombers destroyed the U.S. fleet at Pearl Harbor on December 7, 1941, the U.S. government rounded up Japanese American families—in many cases, families who had lived in the United States all their lives—and placed them in detention camps for the duration of World War II. Many of these people not only had their lives interrupted but lost all of their worldly possessions. Other Asian Americans—Chinese, Koreans, and Filipinos, to name a few—were required to prove their ancestry in order to avoid the camps. Government officials found it difficult to tell that they were not Japanese simply by looking at them.

In the wake of the September 11, 2001, terrorist attacks, innocent Arabs and Muslims were beaten. What is it that causes such divisions among people? What did *you* learn about people who were different from you when you were growing up?

Throughout college you will begin and end a number of relationships. You can seek out people who pretty much grew up the way you did, or you can also seek out those from different races, ethnic groups, and cultures. You might become friends with a handicapped person or one with a sexual orientation different than yours. In any event, the most important thing in a relationship is the ability to get along. It's not our business to tell you which choice to make, but we do know that the more diverse your circle of friends, the better prepared you will be for the real world.

How did your students react to this grim reminder? Ask each student to make two lists. One should be a list of incidents in which they felt discriminated against, the other a list of incidents in which they practiced discrimination. Collect the lists without names and share them with the entire class. Ask for a reaction.

Have your students practice their library skills by finding out more about the Japanese internment during World War II. Have them compare what they learned to the portrayal of Japanese in movies about that war.

Have students gather news from the Internet on discrimination against Arabs and Muslims and analyze it.

Race, Ethnic Groups, and Culture

Before discussing relationships, it's helpful to know some definitions. The word *race* generally refers to a group of people who are distinct from other people in terms of certain inherited characteristics: skin color, hair color, hair texture, body build, and

SEE INTERNET EXERCISE 9.1 DIVERSITY IN THE POPULATION AND ON CAMPUS

Critical Thinking

Do a search for an article or articles on discrimination. It might be about something as local as a private club that does not admit people of certain races or religions or as devastating as the Holocaust, which saw 6 million Jews go to their deaths at the hands of Germany's Nazi Party. Even though it may be difficult for you, try to be neutral so that you can seek the underlying causes for such discrimination and hate. What overriding ideas lead to such situations? What do those ideas suggest? How can you organize your thoughts in a logical manner? Write a commentary on the situation you chose, attempting to provide a logical explanation for why some people choose to discriminate. Warning: Some of the logic may not make sense to you, but pursue it anyway, to better understand what fuels prejudice and hate.

Questions for students: What are some of the characteristics of "the American culture"? What is the culture of the area where your college or university is located? What is the culture of your campus? Use groups of three students and the "jigsaw" procedure, in which each student in the group assumes individual responsibility for answering one of these three questions. Then the three students convene to piece together their answers into a coherent whole that incorporates both the common themes and individual differences among their answers.

SEE "A CENTURY
OF CHANGE"

SEE EXERCISE 9.1
SHARING YOUR
BACKGROUND

As a variant to the exercise just described, each student could first meet with one member of another group who is responsible for answering the same question. After they discuss their responses to that question, they return to their teams to add their answer to the group's final product.

SEE "THE CHANGING
U.S. POPULATION"

SEE EXERCISE 9.2
CREATING COMMON
GROUND

Students of the majority often wonder why minority students find it necessary to create their own campus organizations. Can they—or you—explain why?

Is this student being too sensitive? Have students justify their responses.

SEE "THE MANY
DIMENSIONS OF
DIVERSITY"

SEE EXERCISE 9.3
DIVERSITY ON YOUR
CAMPUS

facial features. *Ethnic group* can refer to people of different races or to people of the same race who can be distinguished by language, national origin, religious tradition, and so on.

Culture refers to the material and nonmaterial products that people in a society create or acquire from other societies and pass on to future generations. Culture includes a society's beliefs, values, norms, and language. For example, many European societies believe children should learn to be independent and self-sufficient at an early age, whereas Hispanic cultures tend to place a high value on strong family ties. Culture may also include such tangible items as cell phones, futons, basketballs, and college yearbooks.

As people from different ethnic groups marry one another and have children, the word *race* is slowly becoming insufficient as a descriptor of individuals with mixed heritages, and many such people are refusing to fill in the line asking for "race" on numerous government and business forms, especially when their only choices are White, Black, Asian, Hispanic, and the ubiquitous "Other."

The Concept of Race on Campus

As you observe your campus environment, you will see clear evidence of the significance of race in the way students interact with one another and how they view others as well as themselves. This is a particularly intense experience for Black or African American students. Such groups as the Black Student Alliance (Union) as well as Black fraternities and sororities are crucial to the participation of Black students in predominantly White institutions.

Black students rarely seek to isolate themselves from the larger campus community but are seldom welcomed into the campus community based on their individual merits and special qualities. Instead, they are often seen and perceived as Black, with little understanding of who they really are. Whenever someone inquires "Why do all the Black students sit together in the cafeteria?" you might do well to ask if they have ever noticed that all the White students also sit together. Why does one group stand out and another escape notice? The compelling sense of race in American society is the reason.

Transcending the boundaries of race in college will require that all students become extremely sensitive to one another and aware of how race affects perceptions, understandings, and experiences. One student writes about her sentiments:

Many times in class I feel uncomfortable when White students use the term Black *because even if they aren't aware of it they say it with all or at least a lot of the negative connotations they've been taught goes along with Black. Sometimes it just causes a stinging feeling inside of me. Sometimes I get real tired of hearing White people talk about the conditions of Black people. I think it's an important thing for them to talk about, but still I don't always like being around when they do it. I also get tired of hearing them talk about how hard it is for them, though I understand it, and most times I am very willing to listen and be open, but sometimes I can't. Right now I can't.*[1]

To a profound degree, ideas of race affect how students perceive themselves and how they perceive others, and they may well affect the opportunities for shared activities. What's more, as we have seen, ideas of race are changing even though fun-

---

[1]Beverly Daniel Tatum, "Talking About Race, Learning About Racism," in Kathryn Geismar and Guitele Nicoleau (Eds.), *Teaching for Change: Addressing Issues of Difference in the College Classroom*, Cambridge, MA: Harvard Educational Review, 1993.

Most colleges make an effort to help students feel welcome, respected, and supported in every way that the students themselves feel is important.

damental notions of race persist. College is the one place where many of these concepts and their related structures can be bridged if students find common ground for interaction and cooperation.

The Importance of Relationships

Now that you're in college, your instructors and parents may think classes and studies are the first thing on your mind. But student journals suggest that what really takes center stage are relationships—with dates, lovers, or lifelong partners; with friends and enemies; with parents and family; with roommates, classmates, and coworkers; and with new people and new groups.

Relationships have outcomes far beyond your social life: They strongly influence your survival and success in college. Distracted by bad relationships, you will find it difficult to concentrate on your studies. Supported by good relationships, you will be better able to get through the rough times, reach your full potential, remain in college—and enjoy it.

Dating and Mating

Swiss psychiatrist Carl Gustav Jung identified a key aspect of love: We each have an idealized image of the perfect partner, which we unconsciously project onto potential partners we meet. The first task in any romantic relationship, then, is to look beyond the initial attraction and see that the person you are in love with really exists! Hormones make it even harder. Are you in love, or are you in lust? People in lust often sincerely believe they are in love, and more than a few will say almost anything to get what they want. But would you still want that person if sex were out of the question? Would that person still want you?

Folklore says love is blind. Believe it. Check out your perceptions with trusted friends. If they see a lot of problems that you do not, at least listen to them. Another good reality check is to observe the other person's friends. Exceptional people rarely surround themselves with jerks and losers. If the person of your dreams tends to collect friends from your nightmares, wake up!

If a prospective partner does not have the qualities you desire, don't pursue it, even if you feel some attraction. Look for the person you want in places where that kind of person is likely to be. Bars and wild parties may be poor fishing grounds.

Ask students how much time they have for relationships, how much relationships and other outside activities interfere with or help their studies, and whether they have a plan to balance the two. Remind them that throughout life they'll need to maintain this balance by setting priorities that make some sense to them.

Ask every student in the room to write—anonymously—the three most important qualities of his or her ideal lover. Have them pass their papers forward (without names, of course) and redistribute among the class. Make four columns on the board: physical, emotional, intellectual, other. As each student calls out the three qualities of another student's ideal lover, write them in the appropriate columns and ask the class to come up with a composite ideal lover. Then ask them how realistic that composite is. Note: You might want to scan the submissions for raw language.

Ask students why they are more likely to tell others that they love someone because "He's a hunk" or "She's got a great bod" instead of sharing more profound thoughts, such as, "I love his sense of humor," "She's as smart as they come," "He and I enjoy the same kinds of things," or "She makes me feel good about myself." Why is it easier to talk about physical or sexual characteristics than to share more realistic feelings?

Developing a Relationship

Because students may choose not to discuss their relationships, try role-playing instead. Ask students in teams of two or three to develop a brief scenario about a relationship and present it to the class. Half the class should focus on a relationship in the passionate stage while the other half focuses on a relationship in the companionate stage. Consider a variant of the fishbowl technique, in which groups take turns role-playing their scenarios in the middle of a circle while other classmates observe. Then have students rejoin their small groups to answer these questions: Which of the passionate relationships shows promise of lasting?

Usually, relationships develop in stages. Early in a relationship, you may be wildly "in love." You are likely to idealize the other person, yet you may overreact to faults or disappointments. If the relationship goes awry, your misery is likely to be intense, and the only apparent relief from your pain lies in the hands of the very person who rejected you. Social psychologist Elaine Walster calls this the stage of *passionate love.*

Most psychologists see the first stage as being unsustainable—and that may be a blessing! A successful relationship will move on to a calmer, more stable stage. At this next stage, your picture of your partner is much more realistic. Walster calls this more comfortable, long-lasting stage *companionate love.*

If a relationship is to last, it is vital to talk about it as you go along. What are you enjoying, and why? What is disappointing you, and what would make it better? If you set aside a regular time and place to talk, communication will be more comfortable. Do this every couple of weeks as the relationship first becomes serious. Never let more than a couple of months go by without one of these talks—even if all you have to say is that things are going great.

Off Limits!

Ask students why they think the authors take this stand. Ask if they have known people who fished in forbidden waters and what the outcomes were.

Some "fishing grounds" are strictly off limits. Never become romantically involved with your teacher or someone who works over or under you (see Chapter 10). Most of these romantic relationships end in a breakup. But imagine if your ex, who might be hurt or bitter or even want you back, still had power or control over you! If you date a subordinate, when the relationship ends you may find yourself accused of sexual harassment, fired, or sued. Even dating coworkers carries major risks; it will be much harder to heal from a breakup if you must continue to work together.

Becoming Intimate

Chapter 10, which covers sexual decisions, makes this point clearly, but we repeat it here: Although the majority choose to be sexually active, not all students make this choice. (Most students overestimate the number of other students who engage in potentially risky behavior like drinking and sex.) Refer to the critical thinking process, which frees us to make our own choices only after careful consideration of the consequences.

Students may have difficulty believing this statistic, so spend some time on it. Point out that the "actual use" failure rate of condoms (12%) is far higher than the "theoretical" failure rate of 2% (see Chapter 10). And pregnancies are actual, not theoretical. What this means is that for every 100 actual couples who rely on condoms for birth control, each year 12 of them will be facing a pregnancy. If the "failure rate" is 12% each year, then the "success rate" is 88% for each year. Thus they have an 88% chance of getting through the first year okay, but to get through the first 2 years, it is 88% times 88%, the first 3 years it is 88% times 88% times 88%. And to get through all 5 years without a pregnancy the odds are .88 × .88 × .88 × .88 × .88 = .53, or just 53%.

Sexual intimacy inevitably adds a new and powerful dimension to a relationship. We suggest the following:

- Don't hurry into it.
- If sexual activity would violate your morals or values, don't do it. And don't expect others to violate theirs. It is reasonable to explain your values so that your partner will understand and respect your decision. You do not owe anyone repeated justifications, nor should you put up with attempts to argue you into submission.
- If you have to ply your partner with alcohol or other drugs to get the ball rolling, you aren't engaging in sex—you are committing rape. Read Chapter 10 for information on acquaintance rape and on alcohol and other drugs.
- Consult a professional about pregnancy prevention. A pregnancy will drastically curtail your freedom and social life, and finding time for your studies will be much harder. Conception can occur even when couples take precautions. Data based on real-life (as opposed to theoretical) use indicate that students who are sexually active for 5 years of college and use condoms for birth control all 5 years have, on average, about a 50-50 chance of having to deal with a pregnancy during college.

Here are some warning signs that should concern you:

- Having sex when you don't really want to.
- Guilt or anxiety afterward.

- Having sex because your partner expects or demands it.
- Having sex with people to attract or keep them.
- Becoming physically intimate when what you really want is emotional intimacy.

Sex is an unsatisfying substitute for love or friendship. Genuine emotional intimacy is knowing, trusting, loving, and respecting each other at the deepest levels, day in and day out, independent of sex. Establishing emotional intimacy takes time—and, in many ways, more courage. If you build the emotional intimacy first, not only the relationship but even the sex will be better.

Does sex actually add to your overall happiness? A thorough review of the literature on happiness finds no evidence that becoming sexually active increases your general happiness.

If you want sexual activity but don't want the medical risks of sex, consider the practice of "outercourse," mutual and loving stimulation between partners that allows sexual release but involves no exchange of bodily fluids. This will definitely require direct and effective communication, but it is a relatively safe option that can still be satisfying and fun (see Chapter 10).

Getting Serious

You may have a relationship you feel is really working. Should you make it exclusive? Don't do so just because it has become a habit. Ask yourself why you want this relationship to be exclusive. For security? To prevent jealousy? To build depth and trust? As a prelude to a permanent commitment? You may find that you treat each other better and appreciate each other more when you have other opportunities.

Although dating more than one person can help you clarify what you want, multiple sexual relationships can be dangerous. Besides the health risks involved, it's rare to find a good working relationship where the partners have sex with others as well.

If each of you enjoys an exclusive relationship, beware of what might be called "the fundamental marriage error": marrying before both you and your partner are certain of who you are and what you want to do in life. Many 18- to 20-year-olds change their outlooks and life goals drastically. The person who seems just right for you now may be quite wrong for you within 5 or 10 years.

If you want to marry, the person to marry is someone you could call your best friend—the one who knows you inside and out, the one you don't have to play games with, the one who prizes your company without physical rewards, the one who over a period of years has come to know, love, and respect who you are and what you want to be. If you don't have this—don't marry.

Breaking Up

In a national study of 5000 college students, 29 percent admitted they had ended a romantic relationship during their first year in college.

If it is time to break up, do it cleanly and calmly. Don't be impulsive or angry. Explain your feelings and talk them out. If you don't get a mature reaction, take the high road; don't join someone else in the mud. If you decide to reunite after a trial separation, be sure enough time has passed for you to evaluate the situation effectively. If things fail a second time, you may need to forget it.

What about being "just friends"? You may want to remain friends with your partner, especially if you have shared and invested a lot. You can't really be friends, however, until both of you have healed from the hurt and neither of you wants the old relationship back. That usually takes a year or two.

Remind your class that sexual activity among students ebbs and flows. Since the 60s, it has become slightly less prevalent but is a factor in the lives of most college students. Ask what may have caused more college students to choose to have sex, such as explicit scenes in films or suggestive photos and copy in advertisements. Have students furnish samples of magazines and other media that focus on sex and write a brief paper about the impact of such explicitness.

Although we do not recommend multiple, simultaneous sexual relationships, we do suggest that students can date more than one person simultaneously. Not all relationships have to lead to sex. How do your students feel about these seemingly contradictory statements? Or do they feel they are contradictory?

SEE EXERCISE 9.4 BALANCING RELATIONSHIPS AND COLLEGE

Have students form small groups and discuss this: " If you want to get married, the person to marry is someone you could call your best friend." Who agrees? Disagrees? Why? Or conduct a debate in a cooperative learning format known as constructive controversy, in which each pair of students on a four-person team is assigned one side of the issue and marshals the best evidence and arguments while the other pair listens. Then the pairs switch sides and develop further arguments for the opposite position.

A student may avoid counseling centers because "I'm not crazy." Point out that most counseling centers are booked solid, which means it's not unusual to seek help. If you choose, you may want to share your own reasons for seeking counseling at some point in your life and how it helped you.

If you are having trouble getting out of a relationship or dealing with its end, get help. Expect some pain, anger, and depression. Your college counselors have assisted many students through similar difficulties. It is also a good time to get moral support from friends and family. Read a good book on the subject, such as *How to Survive the Loss of a Love.* (See suggestions for further reading at the end of this book.)

Married Life in College

Both marriage and college are challenges. With so many demands, it is critically important that you and your partner share the burdens equally; you cannot expect a harried partner to spoil or pamper you. Academic and financial pressures are likely to put extra strain on any relationship, so you are going to have to work extra hard at attending to each other's needs.

If you are in college but your spouse is not, it's important to bring your partner into your college life. Share what you're learning in your courses. See if your partner can take a course, too—maybe just to audit for the fun of it. Take your partner to cultural events—lectures, plays, concerts—on your campus. If your campus has social organizations for students' spouses, try them out.

Relationships with spouses and children can suffer when you are in college, because you are tempted to take time you would normally spend with your loved ones and use it for your studies instead. You obviously will not profit if you gain your degree but lose your family. It's very important to schedule time for your partner and family just as carefully as you schedule your work and your classes.

If you have married students, or students contemplating marriage, this material may open their eyes about the complex relationships that can occur when students have families of their own.

You and Your Parents

If you are on your own for the first time, home will never be as you left it, and you will not be who you were before. So how can you have a good relationship with your parents during this period of major change? A first step is to be aware of their perceptions. The most common perceptions are:

SEE EXERCISE 9.5
STUDENT-PARENT GRIPES

SEE EXERCISE 9.6
FIVE OVER 30

- Parents fear you'll harm yourself. You may take risks that make older people shudder. You may shudder, too, when you look back on some of your stunts. Sometimes your parents have reason to worry.
- Parents think their daughter is still a young innocent. Yes, the old double standard (differing expectations for men than women, particularly regarding sex) is alive and well.
- Parents know you're 20 but picture you much younger. Somehow, the parental clock always lags behind reality.
- Parents mean well. Most love their children, even if it doesn't come out right; very few are really indifferent or hateful.
- Not every family works. If your family is like the Brady Bunch, you are blessed. But some families are truly dysfunctional. If love, respect, enthusiasm, and encouragement are just not in the cards, other people will give you these things, and you can create the family you need. With your emotional needs satisfied, your reactions to your real family will be much less painful.
- The old have been young, but the young haven't been old. Parental memories of youth may be hazy, but at least they've been there. A younger student has yet to experience their adult perspective.

Turn this into a writing assignment by asking students to choose one or more of these six perceptions and, in a brief essay, justify or refute the perception(s), using critical thinking to defend their decisions.

To paraphrase Mark Twain, when you are beginning college, you may think your parents rather foolish, but you'll be surprised how much they've learned in 4 years! Try setting aside regular times to update your parents on how college and your life in general are going. Ask for and consider their advice. You don't have to take it. Finally, realize that your parents are not here forever. Mend fences while you can.

Finding Diverse Friends

You are who you run with—or soon will be. Studies show that the people who influence you the most are your friends. Choose them carefully.

If you want a friend, be a friend. Learn to be an attentive listener. Give your opinion when people ask for it. Keep your comments polite and positive. Never violate a confidence. Offer an encouraging word and helping hand whenever you can. You'll be amazed how many people will respect your opinions and seek your friendship.

Your friends are usually people whose attitudes, goals, and experiences are similar to your own. But in your personal life, just as in the classroom, you have the most to learn from people who are different from you. To enrich your college experience, try this. Make a conscious effort to make at least one good friend who is someone:

- Of the opposite sex
- Of another race
- Of another nationality
- Of a different sexual orientation
- With a physical disability
- On an athletic scholarship
- Of a very different age
- From a very different religion
- With very different politics
- With very different interests

Have students copy this list and work on making friends until they have filled as many of the items as possible. Ask them to insert the name of the person beside each category, followed by how their friendship with that person has affected their view of the world beyond the safe boundaries of their own kind.

To do this, you will have to learn to get past stereotypes. This requires recognizing stereotypes for what they are. You also need to realize that stereotyping is a two-way street. Social psychologist Chante Cox points out that while people in the majority group may realize that they have stereotyped views of some other groups, they may be surprised to find out that members of minority groups have stereotypes about the majority, too.

For instance, European Americans are often familiar with stereotypes about African Americans but totally clueless about stereotypes that many African Americans have about them. Do you know what "White food" is? Casseroles. Did you know that Whites have head lice, are mean to the elderly, and engage in unusual sex practices, especially the women? If you think these things are ridiculous, that's the point! *All* stereotypes are ridiculous and potentially dangerous. It's just easier to see that fact when you're in the group being stereotyped.

To forge friendships with people very different from you may take more time and effort, but you will have more than just new friends. You will have learned to get past stereotypes and know, appreciate, and get along with a much greater variety of people than before.

Gays and Lesbians

Although many people build intimate relationships with someone of the opposite sex, some people are attracted to, fall in love with, and make a long-term commitment to a person of the same sex. Gay or straight, your sexuality and whom you choose to form intimate relationships with are an important part of who you are.

Of all the topics in this book, sexual orientation may well be the one that students are least comfortable discussing. You could even point this out and ask them why they think it is the case. You may wish to stress that this book is in no way advocating for or against any particular lifestyle. Instead, the authors believe it is important that students who are struggling with their sexual orientation know certain facts and seek appropriate assistance and perspective.

Diversity is about more than racial or ethnic and religious backgrounds. It also encompasses gay, lesbian, bisexual, and transgender individuals who live in a world that is not always tolerant or accepting, much less affirming. All students grow when they learn to find pride in their own communities and to accept the diverse groups around them.

You need to know that professionals do not consider homosexuality a disease or a mental disorder. Most experts believe that sexual orientation is inborn and that no amount of "treatment," prayer, or anything else is going to change it.

If you are a heterosexual, these facts may be puzzling, even troubling, to you. But try putting the shoe on the other foot, as psychologist Robert Feldman suggests. If these and similar questions seem stupid to you—well, they seem just as stupid when heard by gays and lesbians about their sexuality: *What caused your heterosexuality? When and how did you choose it? Why do you flaunt your heterosexuality and try to involve others in this lifestyle? Why do you heterosexuals think about sex so much? Wouldn't a good relationship with a skilled homosexual lover make your heterosexuality go away?*

SEE INTERNET EXERCISE 9.2 QUESTIONS ABOUT HOMOSEXUALITY

To learn to feel comfortable with gay or lesbian students, you must first rid yourself of stereotypical notions. Can you spot a gay or lesbian by appearance? No. Are gays and lesbians attracted to all people of the same sex? Not hardly (are you attracted to all people of the opposite sex?). And just for the record, most child molesters are White heterosexual—or "straight"—males.

Remember that relationships—gay or straight—that involve communication, trust, respect, and love are crucial to *all* people.

Returning Students

Adult students (those 25 and older) are enrolling in college courses in record numbers. Women may make this choice after raising children, to learn skills for a new career. Other adults, men and women, may decide it's time to broaden their horizons or prepare themselves for a better job with a higher starting salary. Many returning students work full-time and attend school part-time. Their persistence is remarkable, given the potential stressors of family and work. One study actually found that older women in college were less stressed than younger students, partly because they had grown accustomed to wearing two or more hats while raising children, working, and living their own lives. Colleges have accommodated the needs of adults with distance education courses, night courses, and other innovations.

Students with Disabilities

Students with learning disabilities cannot master some academic skills, such as listening, thinking, speaking, writing, spelling, or doing math calculations. The number of college students with learning disabilities continues to grow. Even though they lack the ability to learn some skill or skills, these students have normal or above-average intelligence and are motivated to learn coping strategies that aid them in facing different types of academic situations. Most learning disabilities are not readily apparent. If a friend confides to you that he or she is having problems with skills that seem basic to you, you might urge that person to contact the academic skills center.

Unlike learning disabilities, physical disabilities are usually apparent. When you see a student with a physical disability, the most respectful thing to do is to greet him or her just as you would any other person. If the student is in your class, you probably should not go out of your way to offer help unless the person asks for it; overeagerness to help may be seen as an expression of pity. A quadriplegic student once asked his teacher how he could explain to another student that he did not want her to always help him write his papers. He didn't want to hurt her feelings but felt he would learn more by working solo.

Most campuses have a special office to serve students with both types of disabilities.

Finding Meaningful Relationships

Long-Distance Relationships

Relationships change significantly when they turn into long-distance romances. Many students arrive at college still romantically involved with someone back home or at another school. If you restrict yourself to a single, absent partner, you may miss out on a lot, and this often leads to cheating or resentment.

Our advice for long-distance relationships: Keep seeing each other as long as you want to but with the freedom to pursue other relationships, too. If the best person for you turns out to be the person from whom you are separated, this will become evident. Meanwhile, keep your options open.

Ask students what they think about the advice offered concerning long-distance relationships.

Electronic Relationships

Nowadays, through electronic mail, message boards, interest groups, dating sites, and chat groups, it is possible to form relationships with people you have never met. This can be fun and educational.

For instance, imagine having regular email correspondence with the following group, as one student does, who all met online: an aspiring screenwriter in New Jersey, an undercover narcotics agent in Michigan, a professional animator in Georgia, a college teacher in Connecticut, a high school student in Arizona, a librarian in California, a strip club bartender in Tennessee, a mother in Pennsylvania, a police officer in Australia, a flight attendant in Illinois, an entrepreneur in Louisiana, a psychologist in Colorado, a physician in training in Texas, a schoolteacher in Canada, and college students in five states and three countries.

The downside? People may not be what they seem. Meeting them in real life may be delightful—or disastrous. Some people assume false electronic identities. You could literally be corresponding with a state prisoner! Be very cautious about

SEE INTERNET
EXERCISE 9.3
LOOKING FOR LOVE

Be alert for students who may be engaging in electronic relationships "instead of" rather than "in addition to" real-world involvements. There is ample evidence that on-campus connections aid student survival, but none that electronic connections do. Go over with students sensible precautions that they should take with electronic strangers. But emphasize the plus side, too.

Examining Values

Relationships are a major part of your life. So, too, are the values you exercise as you choose and participate in those relationships. For each of the following, make a list of six characteristics that you would value in a person in that role: lover, friend, spouse or partner, parent, teacher, employer. (For instance, you might value a lover who is "sexy" or a friend who is "loyal" or a teacher who has "a sense of humor.") Next, for each person, rank-order the values you have written down, with the most important values at the top of the lists. Are the lists the same? If they are significantly different, why are they so different for the different categories of relationships? If your lists are essentially the same, why is that? What does this exercise tell you about how you approach your relationships?

letting strangers know your name, address, telephone number, or other personal information, and about considering face-to-face meetings.

Don't let electronic relationships substitute for real ones in your life. Your college counselors have experience dealing with students suffering from "computer addiction."

SEE EXERCISE 9.7 COMMON ROOMMATE GRIPES

SEE EXERCISE 9.8 ROOMMATE ROULETTE

Problem roommates are one of the big threats to success, especially for new students. Use some regular form of written feedback (a weekly journal entry to you, an end-of-class note, etc.) in which the student reflects on "how I'm doing." If roommate problems surface, ask the student if he or she needs help in solving the problem. Contact the residence hall advisor or the counseling center for assistance if the student grants you permission to do so.

Roommates

A roommate doesn't have to be a best friend—just someone with whom you can share your living space comfortably. Your best friend may not make the best roommate. Many students have lost friends by rooming together.

With any roommate, establish your mutual rights and responsibilities in writing. Many colleges provide contract forms that you and your roommate can use. If things go wrong later, you will have something to point to.

If you have problems, talk them out promptly. Talk directly—politely but plainly. If problems persist, or if you don't know how to talk them out, ask your residence hall counselor for help; he or she is trained to do this.

Normally, you can tolerate (and learn from) a less than ideal situation; but if things get really bad and do not improve, insist on a change. If you are on campus, your residence counselor will have ways of helping you.

On-Campus Involvement

Almost every college has numerous organizations you may join. Usually, you can check them out through activity fairs, printed guides, open houses, Web pages, and so on. Organizations help you find friends with similar interests. And new students who join at least one organization are more likely to survive their first year.

To Greek or not to Greek? Greek organizations are not all alike, nor are their members. Fraternities and sororities can be a rich source of friends and support. Some students love them. But other students may find them philosophically distasteful, too demanding of time and finances, and/or too constricting. Fraternities and sororities are powerful social influences, so you'll probably want to take a good look at the upper-class students in them. If what you see is what you want to be, consider joining. If not, steer clear.

New students tend to flock to Greek rush on campuses where it is available. Make it clear that although the Greek system may be right for some students, the majority find other ways to stay in touch on campus through other organizations. Tell students that if they feel pressured to join a Greek organization, it may not be the right choice for them.

If Greek life is not for you, a residence hall is one of the easiest places to make new friends. Many campuses have residence halls or special floors for students with common interests or situations, such as first-year students, honors students, students in particular majors, students with strong ethnic or religious affiliations, and so on. Check these out; often they provide very satisfying experiences.

SEE EXERCISE 9.9
CONNECTING WITH
CAMPUS ORGANIZATIONS

Off-Campus Involvement

Co-op Programs

Many schools have co-op programs in which you spend some semesters or quarters in regular classes and other terms in temporary job settings in your field. Although they usually prolong your education somewhat, these programs have many advantages. They offer an excellent preview of what work in your chosen field is actually like, thus helping you know if you have made the right choice. They give you valuable experience and contacts that help you get a job when you finish school; in fact, many firms offer successful co-op students permanent jobs when they graduate.

Alternating work and school semesters may be a more agreeable schedule for you than eight or ten straight semesters of classes would be, and it may help you keep your ultimate goal in mind. Co-op programs can help you pay for school, too; some co-op students, especially in technical fields, make almost as much, or even more, during their co-op semesters as do their professors with PhD's!

SEE EXERCISE 9.10
OFF-CAMPUS
INVOLVEMENT
Have students investigate co-op programs on your campus. Have someone from your career center come to class and discuss the advantages of co-op programs. Share some "success stories" of former students. Most beginning students know little or nothing about co-op programs and do not realize how educational, helpful, and remunerative they can be.

Service Learning Opportunities

Service learning integrates community service with academic study. Instructors design projects in partnership with representatives of community organizations, planning activities that will meet genuine needs in the community and advance the students' understanding of course content. Students work as volunteers, then reflect on their experiences, considering the relationship to their reading and research as well as the impact on their personal values and professional goals.

Service learning might include tutoring children or adults, helping in medical establishments and psychological services, building or repairing housing for disadvantaged citizens, or helping out in soup kitchens and homeless shelters. Such service is usually mandatory and counts in the computation of your course grade. If you prefer to volunteer on your own, by all means do so. You could spend a year or two in VISTA (Volunteers in Service to America) or the Peace Corps. Many students serve a few hours a week in the local community.

If your college has a service learning office, head for it to learn about opportunities. Or check with your school's career center, your local United Way, and various religious organizations. Or search the Web for thousands of choices.

Seriously consider having some kind of service learning experience be an assigned part of your course. Again, share the experiences of some of your former students, and as the term progresses, have your students share their experiences with one another. Once begun, this is often the most rewarding learning that students will have. Also emphasize that service learning is not charity: In doing good, students benefit themselves, as well.

Discrimination and Prejudice on College Campuses

Unfortunately, acts of discrimination and incidents of prejudice are rising on college campuses. Although some schools may not be experiencing overt racial conflict, tension still exists; many students report having little contact with students from different racial or ethnic groups. A national survey, "Taking America's Pulse," conducted for the National Conference of Christians and Jews, indicated that Blacks, Whites,

SEE EXERCISE 9.11
COMBATING
DISCRIMINATION AND
PREJUDICE ON CAMPUS
Confusion can arise over the definition of racism because many students use prejudice and racism interchangeably. Racism is prejudice operationalized, which happens through power. Ask students if they understand this difference and why power can often be misdirected.

Speaking of Careers

Some twenty-odd years ago, the White dean of a prominent college was so overjoyed about his first minority hire that he couldn't wait to tell the rest of the faculty. Meeting with the group, he introduced the new teacher, looked her straight in the eye, and said, "Now you're Black!" The room fell into silence except for the nervous shuffling of chairs. "But," the dean smiled proudly, "I don't think of you as Black!" This true anecdote may give some insight into the awkward transition many organizations—let alone their new minority hires—must have gone through during this time of great change in American society. Even before then, however, the federal Equal Employment Opportunity Commission was enforcing laws prohibiting employment discrimination. Among those laws:

- Title VII of the Civil Rights Act of 1964 prohibits employment discrimination based on race, color, religion, sex, or national origin.
- The Equal Pay Act (EPA) of 1963 protects men and women who perform substantially equal work in the same establishment from sex-based wage discrimination.
- The Age Discrimination in Employment Act (ADEA) of 1967 protects individuals who are 40 years of age or older.
- Title I and Title V of the Americans with Disabilities Act (ADA) of 1990 prohibit employment discrimination against qualified individuals with disabilities in the private sector and in state and local governments.
- Sections 501 and 505 of the Rehabilitation Act of 1973 prohibit discrimination against qualified individuals with disabilities who work in the federal government.
- The Civil Rights Act of 1991, among other things, provides monetary damages in cases of intentional employment discrimination.

For more information, check the following Web site: http://www.eeoc.gov/facts/qanda.html

SEE EXERCISE 9.12 CHECKING YOUR UNDERSTANDING

SEE EXERCISE 9.13 IS HATE SPEECH PERMITTED ON YOUR CAMPUS?

SEE INTERNET EXERCISE 9.4 RESEARCHING RELATIONSHIPS AND DIVERSITY

SEE "WHAT DOES THE FUTURE HOLD FOR YOU, FOR ME, FOR US?"

Hispanics, and Asians hold many negative stereotypes about one another. The good news is that "nine out of 10 Americans nationwide claim they are willing to work with people of all races—even those they felt they had the least in common with—to advance race relations."[2]

In addition to being morally and personally repugnant, you should know that discrimination is illegal. Most colleges and universities have established policies against all forms of racism, anti-Semitism, and ethnic and cultural intolerance. These policies prohibit racist actions, including verbal harassment or abuse, that might deny anyone his/her rights to equity, dignity, culture, or religion. Anyone found in violation of such policies faces corrective action, including appropriate disciplinary action.

Whether you're a traditional-age new student or a returning student with family responsibilities, be sure to approach your relationships with the same effort and planning as you would approach your coursework. Long after you have forgotten whole courses you took, you will remember relationships that began or grew in college.

[2]"Survey Finds Minorities Resent Whites and Each Other," *Jet*, 28 March 1994.

Search Online!

Internet Exercise 9.1 Diversity in the Population and on Campus

Estimate (guess) the percentage of each group listed both in the total U.S. population and in the U.S. undergraduate student population.

GENERAL POPULATION		UNDERGRADUATE POPULATION
American Indian	_____	_____
Asian	_____	_____
Black	_____	_____
Hispanic	_____	_____
White	_____	_____

Compare your general population estimates with the U.S. Census national population projections (http://www.census.gov/population/projections/nation/nsrh/nprh9600.txt) and your undergraduate population estimates with Table 207 in the 1997 edition of the *Digest of Education Statistics 1997* (http://nces.ed.gov/pubs/digest97/d97t207.html). (Go to http://success. wadsworth.com for the most up-to-date URLs.)

- How far off were you in estimating the general population statistics?
- What conclusions can you draw about your perception of society?
- How far off were you in estimating the student population statistics?
- What conclusions can you draw about your perception of the student population?
- Locate statistics for your own institution on your institution's home page.

Internet Exercise 9.2 Questions about Homosexuality

First, write your own responses to the following questions:

- Is sexual orientation a choice?
- Is homosexuality a mental illness, an emotional problem, or simply an alternative lifestyle?
- Can lesbians and gay men be good parents?
- Can therapy change sexual orientation?

Now, compare your answers with those provided by the American Psychological Association's "Answers to Your Questions About Sexual Orientation and Homosexuality": http://www.apa.org/pubinfo/orient.html. (Go to http://success.wadsworth.com for the most up-to-date URLs.)

Internet Exercise 9.3 Looking for Love

Go to http://www.yahoo.com.

A Find a message board that relates to relationships. (Look under "Community" for message boards.)

Name of message board: _____

Address of message board: _____

What questions/issues/themes do people seem to be writing about most? What does it tell you about people's needs in relationships?

B Find a chat room that relates to relationships. (Look under "Chat" for chat rooms.)

Name of chat room: _____

Address of chat room: _____

What questions/issues/themes do people seem to be talking about most? What does this tell you about people's needs in relationships?

(continued)

Search Online! 《●》

C Go to "Personals" and enter a search for the gender, age, and other characteristics that you would be interested in if you were looking for a romantic/dating/marriage partner. Read the first two dozen ads. What seem to be the most important things prospective partners are looking for as they advertise for dates and mates? What does this tell you about your best approach to prospective partners?

Internet Exercise 9.4 Researching Relationships and Diversity

Using InfoTrac College Edition, try these phrases and others for key-word and subject-guide searches: "diversity and campus," "ethnicity and campus," "hate crimes and campus," "disabilities and campus," "gays and campus." Take notes and develop a short research paper, citing sources accurately. Time permitting, also check other sources such as books, periodicals, and databases at your campus library. Remember, the Internet doesn't have everything!

Additional Exercises

These exercises at the end of each chapter will help you sharpen what we believe are the critical skills for college success: writing, critical thinking, learning in groups, planning, reflecting, and taking action. Also check out the CD-ROM that came with your book—you will find more exercises as well as resources for this chapter.

Exercise 9.1 Sharing Your Background

Write a two-part essay. In the first part, describe the racial or ethnic groups to which you belong. Can you belong to more than one? Absolutely. Be sure to include some of the beliefs, values, and norms in your cultural background. How do you celebrate your background? If you don't feel a strong attachment to any group, write what you know about your family history and speculate on why your ethnic identity isn't very strong.

In the second part of your essay, discuss a time when you realized that your racial or ethnic background was not the same as someone else's. For example, young children imagine that their experiences are mirrored in the lives of others. If they are Jewish, everyone else must be too. If their family eats okra for breakfast, then all families do the same. Yet at some point they begin to realize differences. Share your essays with other members of the class. In what ways are your stories similar? In what ways are they different?

Exercise 9.2 Creating Common Ground

Examine the items in the following chart. For each item, decide whether you would describe your preferences, habits, and customs as reflecting the mainstream (macroculture) or a specific ethnic microculture. Enter specific examples of your own preferences in the appropriate column (two examples are given). For a given item, you may enter examples under both macroculture and microculture, or you may leave one or the other blank. In filling out the chart, you may want to look back at the essay you wrote in Exercise 9.1.

CATEGORY	MACROCULTURE	MICROCULTURE
Language		
Food	*hamburgers*	*sushi*
Music (for your peer group)		
Style of dress (for your peer group)		
Religion		
Holidays celebrated		
Heroes/role models		
Key values		
Lifestyle		
Personal goals		

Compare answers in a small group. Do most people in the group agree on what should be considered an example of the macroculture? What do you and others in your class regard as significant differences among you? In what areas do you share common ground?

Exercise 9.3 Diversity on Your Campus

How diverse is your campus? In what specific ways does your school encourage all students to feel welcome? Ask your instructor where to locate materials or appropriate people to interview on these two questions: (1) How easy is it for students to express their culture and to learn about their backgrounds or the backgrounds of others on this campus? (2) In what ways does our school try to make all students feel welcome? Groups should report their findings to the class.

Exercise 9.4 Balancing Relationships and College

A For personal writing and group discussion: If you are in a relationship, what are the greatest concerns you have about balancing your educational responsibilities with your responsibilities to your partner? What can you do to improve the situation?

B If you are married and have children, write a letter to your spouse and another to your children explaining why you must often devote time to your studies instead of to them. Don't deliver the letters; read them first and keep revising them until they sound realistic and convincing. If there are other married students in your class, share letters and get reactions. Then decide whether it's prudent to actually share these thoughts with your spouse and children.

Exercise 9.5 Student-Parent Gripes

A Student Gripes In surveys, these are the most frequent student gripes about parents. Check the ones that hit closest to home for you:

_____ Why are parents so overbearing and controlling, telling you everything from what to major in to whom to date?

_____ Why do parents treat you like a child?

_____ Why are they so overprotective?

_____ Why do parents worry so much?

_____ Why do parents complain so much about money?

_____ Parents say they want to know what's going on in your life; but if you told them everything, they'd go ballistic and you'd never hear the end of it!

Reflect on the gripes you checked. Why do you think your parents are like that? How do your thoughts affect your relations with them?

B **Parent Gripes** Looking at things from the other side, students report the following as the most common gripes their parents have about them. Check off those that ring true for your parents:

_____ Why don't you call and visit more?

_____ Why don't you tell us more about what is going on?

_____ When you are home, why do you ignore us and spend all your time with your friends?

_____ Why do you spend so much time with your boyfriend (or girlfriend)?

_____ Why do you need so much money?

_____ Why aren't your grades better, and why don't you appreciate the importance of school?

_____ Why don't you listen to us about getting into the right major and courses? You'll never get a good job if you don't.

_____ What have you done to yourself? Where did you get that (haircut, tattoo, style of clothes, and so on)?

_____ Why don't you listen to us and do what we tell you? You need a better attitude!

How do such statements affect you? What do you think your parents are really trying to tell you?

Your Personal Journal

Here are a number of topics to write about. Choose one or more. Or choose another topic related to this chapter.

1. If a person with whom you had a romantic relationship before coming to college is now far away, how are you handling your feelings, and what is your plan for the relationship?
2. Many people today are "pushing" for diversity. Others say, "Whatever will be will be." What do you think?
3. If you are in, or have been in, a romantic relationship, how can you apply the discussion of passionate and companionate love to that relationship? Which stage is/was associated with a more meaningful relationship, and why?
4. How can you profit from having a diverse set of friends? How can they profit?
5. This chapter advises you to date others before making a commitment to one individual, but not to have more than one sexual relationship at a time. What is your reaction to that?
6. When someone walks into the room and you know that person is gay, what is your normal reaction? Explain.
7. If you are a married student, what do you see as your biggest problems in balancing your family and your education? What is your plan for dealing with those problems?
8. Describe your relationship with your parents. Has it changed now that you are in college? What is your plan for maintaining and improving it?
9. If you have made friends with some people who are very different than you, write about those relationships and what you have learned from them.
10. If you have a roommate, describe the best and worst things about living with that person. What is your plan for dealing with the things that bother you?
11. What experiences and plans do you have for being involved in campus organizations?
12. What co-op program and service learning opportunities might you like to take advantage of? How would you benefit from these experiences?
13. What behaviors are you willing to change after reading this chapter? How might you go about changing them?
14. What else is on your mind this week? If you wish to share it with your instructor, add it to your journal entry.

Resources

Relationships are important throughout life, and the support you get from them can keep you going with confidence and strength, especially during times of transition—moving to a new place, starting college, changing jobs, changing life situations. You probably have more resources than you realize. Use a sheet of paper to create a map of the relationships in your life. (See example below. Add photos if you want, or transfer your map to a larger sheet of paper and make a collage of the important people in your life.) When you are feeling down, or stressed, or alone, take a minute to look at this page and see the connections you have to other people—and where you can look forward to making new ones. Give someone a call, write a letter, drop by to visit, or simply remember the good feelings and times your relationships bring you. Some people to consider:

Example:

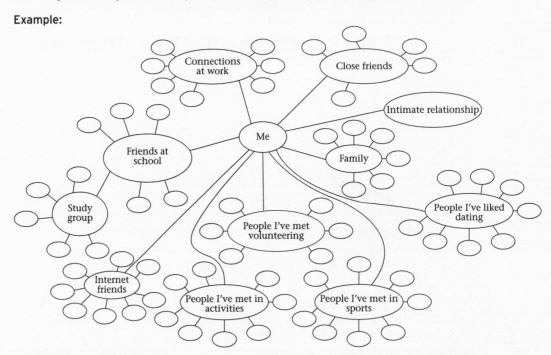

How many connections with diverse communities do you already have in your life? Look at your relationships map and think about the different kinds of diversity and different communities discussed in this chapter. Using different color markers, highlight all the people (including yourself) by gender, racial/ethnic background, sexual orientation, religious background, and so on. Make a key at the bottom of the map to show which color represents which group. (Keep in mind that most people will fall into several groups.) The next step is to educate yourself about communities you don't know as much about.

For example, you may know a great deal about the contributions of Native Americans in U.S. history but know little about the role Asian Americans have played. You may know a lot about African American artists but little about European classical music. Consider some specific activities that would further your knowledge and understanding. (For example, you could plan to attend a lecture that challenges your present thinking, interview a fellow student about his or her experiences on campus, switch the dial on your radio, or make a meal!) List at least three activities that you plan to do this semester to expand your understanding of and appreciation for diversity.

1. ....

2. ....

3. ....

Sex and Alcohol

Making Responsible Choices

Stephen Frisch/Stock, Boston Inc.

**IN THIS CHAPTER,
YOU WILL LEARN**

- Factors in sexual decision making

- Advantages and disadvantages of contraceptive methods

- Ways to prevent sexually transmitted infections

- What to do if your relationship is abusive

- How to avoid sexual assault

- Three reasons college students drink

- "Animal House" versus reality

- Why students overestimate rates of peer drinking

- Heavy drinking and other alcohol-related problems

- Long-term effects of drinking

This chapter was written with the expert assistance of Sara J. Corwin, Bradley H. Smith, Rick L. Gant, and Georgeann Stamper, University of South Carolina.

watch the chemistry

"I'm amazed at what goes on around here! Seems like everyone is always talking or thinking about sex or beer or both! The pressure to drink and to be sexually active is so strong! Maybe it's just me, but I don't want a sexual relationship right now, and I can't keep up with the big drinkers either. I have enough to deal with."

Students may exaggerate the levels of sexual activity and drinking among their peers. Group students into twos or threes and ask them to discuss the accuracy of their perceptions. Do they agree with the student comment? Do they think most first-year students feel the same way?

Approach the subjects of sexuality and drinking with tact, confidence, and a respect for a variety of viewpoints. Above all, don't preach or judge. Remember that you are approaching this material not as an expert, but as an adult mentor. Students may claim "It's all been covered in high school." However, it's unlikely that their prior education included a frank discussion of sexual issues with both genders present or that their lectures on drinking included more than admonitions to abstain rather than data taken from the literature on this subject.

Right off the bat, let's get something straight: We are not about to tell you not to drink alcoholic beverages and not to have sex. What we *are* going to do is put you in a better position to make choices that are sensible for you—not for your friends. You can choose to handle these two powerful urges maturely, or you can allow them to become troublemakers bigtime.

We know from numerous studies that about 75 percent of traditional-age college students have engaged in sexual intercourse at least once. And studies also indicate that students tend to exaggerate how much their peers drink. We will encourage you to know your options and to recognize that you have the right to choose what's comfortable for you. As a result, we hope you'll conclude that (a) choosing to have sex also means choosing to protect yourself against unwanted pregnancy, unwanted sex, and sexually transmitted infections (STIs), and (b) choosing whether to drink also means making your own decision instead of succumbing to the pressures of others.

SELF-ASSESSMENT: EVALUATING YOUR SEXUAL HEALTH AND YOUR USE OF ALCOHOL

Check those statements that are true. Leave the others blank. After reading this chapter, come back to this inventory and place an *X* beside any item you now think differently about.

_____ 1. I appreciate my own body.

_____ 2. I feel comfortable expressing love and intimacy in appropriate ways.

_____ 3. I am able to take responsibility for my own actions.

_____ 4. I can enjoy sexual feelings without necessarily acting upon them.

_____ 5. I fully understand the consequences of sexual activity.

_____ 6. I am able to communicate my desire not to have sex and can accept my partner's refusal to have sex.

_____ 7. I am comfortable asking for help or seeking information about sex and contraception.

_____ 8. The more alcohol you drink, the more fun you will have.

_____ 9. The majority of college students are not heavy or high-risk drinkers.

_____ 10. A drunk person should be left alone to sleep it off.

_____ 11. The legal limit for blood alcohol content is a safe level to aim for when you are drinking.

_____ 12. If you drink heavily and often enough, you will change how your body reacts to alcohol—and those changes actually make alcohol more dangerous.

Sexual Decision Making

Not all first-year students are sexually active. However, college seems to be a time when recent high school graduates begin to think more seriously about sex. Perhaps this has to do with peer pressure or a sense of one's newfound independence or maybe it's just hormones. Regardless of the reasons, it can be helpful to explore your sexual values and to consider whether sex is right for you at this time.

Although the sexual revolutions of the 1960s and 1970s may have made premarital sex more socially acceptable, people have not necessarily become better equipped to deal with sexual freedom. The rate of STIs among college students has increased, and unwanted pregnancies are not uncommon.

Why is it that otherwise intelligent people choose to take sexual risks? If you are in your late teens or early 20s, you may feel you are invincible or immune from danger. There are so many pressures to become sexually active; at the same time, many factors may discourage sexual activity:

Encouragers	**Discouragers**
Hormones	Family values/expectations
Peer pressure	Religious values
Alcohol/other drugs	Sexually transmitted diseases
Curiosity	Fear of pregnancy
The media	Concern for reputation
An intimate relationship	Feeling of unreadiness
Sexual pleasure	Fear of being hurt or used

With such powerful pressures on each side, some people get confused and overwhelmed and fail to make any decisions. Often, sex "just happens" and is not planned.

For your protection, try to clarify your own values and then act in accordance with them. Those who do this usually wind up happier with their decisions.

Birth Control

One issue that heterosexual students need to be concerned about is preventing an unwanted pregnancy.

What is the best method of contraception? It is any method that you use correctly and consistently each time you have intercourse. Table 10.1 compares the major features of some common methods, presented in descending order of effectiveness. Note that the "perfect use effectiveness" numbers represent the percentage of women experiencing an unwanted pregnancy in 1 year per 100 uses of the method, assuming they are using the method correctly and consistently each time.

The "typical use effectiveness" numbers are based on the same data, except that they represent the number of pregnancies with the normal number of human errors, memory lapses, and incomplete or incorrect use. In each case, a low number indicates the method is more effective while a high number signals less effectiveness.

Make sure that, whatever method you choose, you feel comfortable using it. Always discuss birth control with your partner so that you both feel comfortable with the option you have selected. For more information about a particular method, consult a pharmacist, your student health center, a local family planning clinic, the local health department, or your private physician. The important thing is to resolve to protect yourself and your partner *each and every time* you have sexual intercourse.

SEE INTERNET EXERCISE 10.1 GETTING CONFIDENTIAL INFORMATION

Ask students to name and discuss the most powerful encouragers and discouragers until the class reaches some form of consensus. Let them add some of their own. Then ask why these tend to have more far-reaching consequences than others in the list.

For the next class session, ask students to bring two–three magazine or newspaper advertisements that use "sex to sell." (Some students may be given the option to either provide a written summary or a videotape of TV commercials or music videos.) Have students show the ads and explain why they chose them. What types of products tend to contain sexual overtones? Ask the students if they think sex in advertising influences their decisions to purchase products.

SEE EXERCISE 10.1 PERSONAL REFLECTIONS ON SEXUALITY

TABLE 10.1 METHODS OF CONTRACEPTION

It is important that students understand the difference between "typical use" and "perfect use" effectiveness. As explained in Table 10.1, *typical use* is a more practical indication of birth control effectiveness because it takes into account normal use as compared to *perfect*, or without error, use. Methods most often fail because of user error—not because of the method itself.

STERILIZATION

Perfect Use Effectiveness[a]
Female: .05%   Male: .10%

Typical Use Effectiveness[b]
Female: .05%   Male: .15%

What It Is
Tubal ligation in women; vasectomy in men.

Advantages
Provides nearly permanent protection from future pregnancies.

Disadvantages
Not considered reversible; not a good option for anyone wanting children at a later date.

Comments
Although common for people over 30, most traditional-age college students would not choose. Does not protect against STIs.

NORPLANT

Perfect Use Effectiveness[a]
.05%

Typical Use Effectiveness[b]
.05%

What It Is
Six small silicone rubber capsules inserted into a woman's arm, which continually release a low dose of progesterone.

Advantages
Highly effective. Works up to 5 years. Allows sexual spontaneity. Low hormone dose makes this medically safer than other hormonal methods.

Disadvantages
Removal may be difficult. Very expensive to obtain initially.

Insurance may not cover cost. Does not protect against STIs.

Comments
High initial cost. Users may have typical side effects of hormonal methods, causing them to discontinue during the first year. Somewhat risky.

DEPO-PROVERA

Perfect Use Effectiveness[a]
.3%

Typical Use Effectiveness[b]
.3%

What It Is
A progestin-only method, administered to women by injection every 3 months.

Advantages
Highly effective. Allows for sexual spontaneity. Relatively low yearly cost.

Disadvantages
A variety of side effects typical of progestin-type contraceptives may persist up to 6-8 months after termination. Does not protect against STIs.

Comments
Easy and spontaneous, but users must remember to get their shots.

ORAL CONTRACEPTIVES

Perfect Use Effectiveness[a]
.5%

Typical Use Effectiveness[b]
.5%

What It Is
Birth control pills.

Advantages
Highly effective. Allows for sexual spontaneity. Most women have lighter or shorter periods.

Disadvantages
Many minor side effects (nausea, weight gain), which cause a significant percentage of users to discontinue. Provides no protection against STIs.

Comments
Available by prescription only, after a gynecological exam.

INTRAUTERINE DEVICE (IUD)

Perfect Use Effectiveness[a]
1-1.5%[c]

Typical Use Effectiveness[b]
1-2%[c]

What It Is
Device inserted into the uterus by a physician.

Advantages
May be left in for up to 10 years, depending on type. Less expensive than other long-term methods.

Disadvantages
Increased risk of complications such as pelvic inflammatory disease and menstrual problems. Possible increased risk of contracting HIV, if exposed.

Comments
Women who have not had a child may have a difficult time finding a doctor willing to prescribe.

DIAPHRAGM

Perfect Use Effectiveness[a]
6%

Typical Use Effectiveness[b]
20%

What It Is
Dome-shaped rubber cap inserted into the vagina that covers the cervix.

TABLE 10.1 METHODS OF CONTRACEPTION (CONTINUED)

Advantages
Safe method of birth control, virtually no side effects. May be inserted up to 2 hours prior to intercourse. May provide small measure of protection against STIs.

Disadvantages
Wide variation in effectiveness depending on consistent use, the fit of the diaphragm, and frequency of intercourse. Multiple acts of intercourse require use of additional spermicide.

Comments
Must be prescribed by a physician. Must always be used with a spermicidal jelly and left in 6-8 hours after intercourse.

CERVICAL CAP

Perfect Use Effectiveness[a]
9-26%[d]

Typical Use Effectiveness[b]
20-40%[d]

What It Is
Cup-shaped device that fits over the cervix.

Advantages
Similar to diaphragm, but may be worn longer—up to 48 hours. May provide small measure of protection against STIs.

Disadvantages
Not widely available due to lack of practitioners trained in fitting them.

Comments
Longer wearing time increases risk of vaginal infections.

CONDOM

Perfect Use Effectiveness[a]
3%

Typical Use Effectiveness[b]
14%

What It Is
Rubber sheath that fits over penis.

Advantages
Only birth control method that also provides good protection against STIs, including HIV. Actively involves male partner.

Disadvantages
Less spontaneous than some other methods because must be put on right before intercourse. Some men believe it cuts down on pleasurable sensations.

Comments
Experts believe that most condom failure is due to lack of consistent use rather than misuse or breakage.

FEMALE CONDOM

Perfect Use Effectiveness[a]
5%

Typical Use Effectiveness[b]
21%

What It Is
A polyurethane sheath that lines vagina acting as barrier between genitals. Two rings hold it in place, one inside and one outside the vagina.

Advantages
Highly safe medically; does not require spermicide. Theoretically provides excellent protection against STIs—almost perfectly leak proof and better than male condom in this regard.

Disadvantages
Has not gained wide acceptance. Visible outer ring has been displeasing to some potential users.

Comments
Although effectiveness not as high as for male condom, has the advantage of offering good STI protection that is in control of the woman.

SPERMICIDAL FOAMS, CREAMS, JELLIES, FILM, & SUPPOSITORIES

Perfect Use Effectiveness[a]
6%

Typical Use Effectiveness[b]
26%

What It Is
Sperm-killing chemicals inserted into vagina.

Advantages
Easy to purchase and use. Provide some protection against STIs, including HIV.

Disadvantages
Lower effectiveness than many methods. Can be messy. May increase likelihood of birth defects should pregnancy occur.

Comments
As with condoms, it is suspected that failure is due to lack of consistent use. However, work better in combination with other methods, such as the diaphragm.

COITUS INTERRUPTUS

Perfect Use Effectiveness[a]
4%

Typical Use Effectiveness[b]
19%

What It Is
Withdrawal.

Advantages
Requires no devices or chemicals and can be used at any time, at no cost.

Disadvantages
Relies heavily on man having enough control to remove himself from the vagina well in advance of ejaculation. May diminish pleasure for the couple.

Comments
Ejaculation must be far enough away so that no semen can enter the vagina. Provides no protection against STIs.

TABLE 10.1 METHODS OF CONTRACEPTION (CONTINUED)

PERIODIC ABSTINENCE

Perfect Use Effectiveness[a]
1-10%[e]

Typical Use Effectiveness[b]
25%

What It Is
Choosing not to have intercourse when ovulation is predicted; may be called natural family planning, calendar, or rhythm method.

Advantages
Requires no devices or chemicals.

Disadvantages
Requires period of abstinence each month, when ovulation is expected. Requires diligent record keeping.

Comments
For maximum effectiveness, consult a trained practitioner for guidance in using this method.

CHANCE/NO METHOD

Perfect Use Effectiveness[a]
85%

Typical Use Effectiveness[b]
85%

What It Is
Not using any form of contraception.

Advantages
No monetary costs or side effects.

Disadvantages
High risk for pregnancy and STIs.

Comments
Some individuals choose not to use birth control for religious or moral reasons. Others may fear health risks. This decision should be thoroughly discussed with a health care professional.

[a]Perfect Use Effectiveness: the percentage of women experiencing an unintended pregnancy within 1 year per 100 uses of the method without, or with minimal, error (i.e., using the method consistently and correctly each time).

[b]Typical Use Effectiveness: the percentage of women experiencing an unintended pregnancy within 1 year per 100 uses of the method with the normal number of human errors, memory lapses, and incorrect or incomplete uses.

[c]Range depends on type of IUD: Progesterone T, Copper T 380A, or LNg 20.

[d]Range depends on the number of children a woman has had; women who have not given birth may have a lower percentage.

[e]Range depends on the method used: calendar = 9%; ovulation = 3%; symptothermal (mucus + calendar + basal body temperature) = 2%; postovulation = 1%.

SOURCE: Adapted from Rebecca J. Donatelle and Lorraine G. Davis, *Access to Health*, 6th ed., p. 175. Copyright © 2000 Allyn & Bacon.

Almost no one finds it easy to talk about sex with a potential partner. That's no excuse. Express your needs and concerns. Be sure you understand the other person's feelings and concerns as well.

Heather Dutton

Critical Thinking

Contraception

An important distinction in birth control effectiveness is between "perfect use failure rate" and "typical use failure rate."

Which of the contraceptive methods have the lowest *typical use* failure rates? Now, compare and contrast the advantages and disadvantages of each method. Does one method seem to stand out? Before deciding upon, or continuing to use, a particular method, you may want to talk to your doctor, other health-care provider, or counselor for more information or clarification.

Sexually Transmitted Infections (STIs)

Once referred to as venereal disease (VD) or sexually transmitted diseases (STDs), the current term for these conditions is *sexually transmitted infections* (STIs). The problem of STIs on college campuses has received growing attention in recent years as an epidemic number of students have become infected. In general, STIs continue to increase faster than other illnesses on campuses today, and approximately 5 to 10 percent of visits by U.S. college students to college health services are for the diagnosis and treatment of STIs.

The belief that nice young men and women don't catch these sorts of infections is inaccurate and potentially more dangerous than ever before. If you choose to be sexually active, particularly with more than one partner, exposure to an STI is a real possibility.

STIs are usually spread through the following types of sexual contact: vaginal–penile, oral–genital, hand–genital, and anal–genital. Sometimes, however, STIs can be transmitted through mouth-to-mouth contact. There are more than twenty known types of STIs; we will discuss the most common ones on campuses.

SEE "SEXUALLY TRANSMITTED INFECTIONS"

SEE EXERCISE 10.2 WHAT'S YOUR DECISION?

This information is provided to make students aware of the variety and significance of STIs and to help them recognize symptoms so they can seek proper treatment. Like much of the information in this chapter, it may be more appropriate to have students read this information themselves rather than discuss it in class.

Chlamydia

The most common STI in the United States is chlamydia. More than 4 million new cases are diagnosed each year, and college students account for more than 10 percent of these cases. Chlamydia is particularly threatening to women because a large proportion of women who are infected do not show symptoms, allowing the disease to progress to pelvic inflammatory disease (PID), now thought to be the leading cause of infertility in women. When chlamydia does produce symptoms in women, the symptoms may include mild abdominal pain, change in vaginal discharge, and pain and burning with urination.

In men, symptoms are typically pain and burning with urination and sometimes a discharge from the penis. Occasionally, the symptoms will be too mild to notice.

Human Papilloma Virus (HPV)

Although chlamydia may still be the most prevalent STI nationwide, human papilloma virus (HPV) has become the leading STI affecting the health of college students. Some recent studies show that as many as 40 to 50 percent of sexually active college students may be infected.

SEE INTERNET
EXERCISE 10.2
GATHERING ACCURATE
INFORMATION ABOUT STIs

HPV is the cause of venereal warts, which affect both men and women on their outer genitals and in the rectum of those who practice anal-receptive intercourse. They may even grow inside a man's urethra or a woman's vagina.

Because HPV is a virus, there is no cure, but treatment is available in the form of burning, freezing, chemical destruction, and in severe cases, laser surgery. Wart removal often takes multiple treatments, which can be painful.

The major long-term problem associated with HPV concerns women. Certain strains of HPV don't cause visible warts but invade the cervix. The subsequent cervical cell changes produce dysplasia, a precancerous condition that can lead to cervical cancer. In the past few years, the correlation between cervical cancer and HPV has become very strong, and most experts believe HPV is responsible for the large majority of cases of cervical cancer in the United States today. The incubation period for these changes can take many years. Fortunately, if women are screened regularly with Pap smears, precancerous changes can be detected and treated before they lead to cervical cancer.

Gonorrhea

Gonorrhea is a bacterial infection that produces symptoms similar to chlamydia. Although not quite as common as chlamydia, with approximately 2 million new cases nationwide per year, it still has a significant impact on the health of Americans. As with chlamydia, men will usually show symptoms, but women often do not.

Herpes

A recent Centers for Disease Control (CDC) study estimates that 45 million Americans are infected with genital herpes, a 30 percent increase since the late 1970s. The large majority of those testing positive for the virus were asymptomatic (showing no symptoms), and many were not aware they carried the virus. When those infected have symptoms, the most obvious are blisters on the genitals, which are similar to the cold sores and fever blisters people get on their mouths. In fact, oral and genital herpes are caused by different strains of the same virus, and both strains can be transmitted through oral sex.

Although there is no cure, the drugs Valtrex and Zovirax seem to reduce the length and severity of herpes outbreaks. People are most contagious after or right before lesions erupt, so it is important to abstain from any sexual contact at this time. It is difficult to determine exactly how contagious a person is at other times, but people without symptoms can transmit herpes because the virus continues to live in the body indefinitely.

Hepatitis B

Each year there are about 300,000 new cases of hepatitis B nationwide, most of them in adolescents and young adults. Hepatitis B is transmitted through unprotected sex and through contact with infected blood and is 100 times more infectious than HIV.

People who are infected with hepatitis B can have varying symptoms, and it's common to show no symptoms. When present, symptoms may include those similar to a stomach virus, in addition to yellowing of the skin and eyes. Occasionally, people become very ill and are disabled for weeks or months. Most people will recover completely, but some remain carriers for life. A small percentage of infected people will get permanent liver disease.

There is no cure for hepatitis B, and no treatment other than rest and a healthy diet. What is unique about this STI is that a vaccine can prevent it. A series of three shots is recommended by the CDC and the American Academy of Pediatrics for all young adults. The vaccine costs about $100 for the three shots.

Hepatitis C

Like hepatitis B, hepatitis C is a long-term infection caused by a virus (HCV). The CDC has estimated that nearly 4 million Americans have hepatitis C. Most people with HCV have no signs or symptoms and may eventually develop liver disease.

Unlike hepatitis B, there currently is no vaccine to prevent hepatitis C. Transmission of HCV happens when blood or bodily fluids from an infected person enter the body of a person who is not infected. It is also spread through sharing needles when "shooting" drugs, through needle sticks or sharp object sticks on the job (a risk for nurses, EMTs, safety officers, lab technicians, and similar personnel), or from an infected mother to her baby. Although less common, HCV can be spread through tattoos or body piercing if the tools are not cleaned properly. It can be spread through unprotected sex, but this is rare.

Even so, if you are having sex with more than one partner, or don't know your partner's sexual activities—past and present—use condoms correctly every time to prevent the spread of any STIs.

HIV/AIDS

HIV/AIDS is very difficult to discuss briefly. We assume that you have already been exposed to a good deal of information on this STI. The main thing for you to know now is that the number of people with AIDS and the virus that causes it—HIV—continues to increase. As of June 2000, the number of persons living with AIDS in the United States had grown to over 753,000. Although the rate of new cases has slowed, there has been a steady increase in this disease over the years. The CDC estimates that at least 1 to 1.5 million Americans are infected with HIV. The routes of transmission for HIV are through blood, semen, vaginal fluids, and breast milk, or by being born to an HIV-infected mother.

Beginning in the late 1990s and continuing today, the greatest increases in new HIV infections and cases of AIDS were among teens, Hispanic Americans, African Americans (who continue to be disproportionately represented among those with AIDS), and women who have sex with men. Although we're discussing risk groups here, it's important to keep in mind that it's not who you *are* but what you *do* that puts you at risk for becoming infected with HIV.

By the mid-1990s in several United States cities, AIDS had become the number-one killer of men and women ages 25 to 44 years. Considering the long incubation period for HIV, it is likely that those dying in their late 20s and early 30s contracted HIV during their adolescent or college-age years.

Because other STIs are occurring at such a high rate, we know that many students are engaging in behaviors that put them at risk for all STIs, including HIV. In addition, having other STIs may predispose people to contract HIV more readily if they are exposed to the virus.

As with other STIs, abstinence, having only one uninfected partner, and condoms are the best ways to prevent the sexual spread of HIV. Get as much information as you can through your student health service, your local health department, or the National AIDS Hotline at 800-342-AIDS (2437) or www.ashaSTI.org.

Although these infections can be very serious, the news is not all bad. Good methods of protection are available, if used consistently and correctly, and if you can choose what's right for you. The worst thing you can do is nothing.

If you think that students need more information about HIV, call your campus student health center or community public health department for information or a guest speaker. The National AIDS Hotline (800-342-2437) or Web site (www.ashastd.org) is an excellent resource for a quick update on the latest national statistics of reported HIV/AIDS cases.

A misperception among many college students is that if they're not gay, they aren't at risk for AIDS. Knowing how HIV is spread and looking at the groups experiencing the greatest number of new infections will help dispel this myth. Point out that heterosexual women are one of the groups at increased risk.

Options for Safer Sex

SEE EXERCISE 10.3 WHAT'S NORMAL?

Topics such as masturbation, celibacy, monogamy, and condom negotiation are often uncomfortable to discuss and have stigmas and myths attached. Students should know that it is perfectly natural and normal for individuals to have sexual desires, feelings, and urges. The key point of this section is to let students know that there are options to intercourse, including a range of behaviors on a continuum of varying risk.

Celibacy

The first choice you always have is not to have sex with others. Even if 75 percent of college students are having sex, that still leaves 25 percent who are not. Some people choose to be completely celibate (not even engaging in masturbation) or partially celibate (engaging in masturbation or fantasizing) at different points in their lives. You may decide to be sexually inactive for religious or moral reasons, because you have just broken up with someone, lost a partner for other reasons, or because you haven't found the right person. Whatever your reasons, choosing celibacy can be a time for introspection, assessing your values, and personal growth.

Abstinence

Abstinence (with a partner) encompasses a wide variety of behaviors from holding hands to more sexually intimate behaviors short of intercourse. These carry a lower risk of spreading disease, having an unwanted pregnancy, or possibly regretting sex than do vaginal or anal intercourse. Deciding to abstain from sex (either with a partner or without) doesn't have to mean a lack of intimacy, or even of sexual pleasure, for that matter.

Masturbation

Although many people are uncomfortable talking (or even reading!) about masturbation, it is a common sexual practice for people of all ages. As part of healthy growth and development, infants and children may unknowingly explore their bodies.

Self-stimulation (or with a partner) can provide a safe sexual outlet and is one way to learn about our bodies and feelings. Sexual desires are normal, and masturbation is a healthy option.

Monogamy

A safe behavior, in terms of disease prevention, is having sex exclusively with one partner who is uninfected. However, having a long-term monogamous relationship is not always practical because many college students want to date and may not be interested in becoming serious. The love of your life this fall may not be the same love next spring. Also, it is hard to know for sure that your partner was not infected to begin with. Your chances of remaining healthy are better if you limit the number of sexual partners and maintain a relationship disease-free over a reasonably long period.

SEE EXERCISE 10.4 WHICH BIRTH CONTROL METHOD IS BEST?

Although today's college students are more sophisticated and experienced than earlier generations, they are also exposed to a great deal of misinformation. They may have heard about abstinence, and perhaps the importance of condoms, but have they learned how to negotiate for safer sex, how to communicate with potential partners, or how to be assertive about their own bodies and sexuality? If they have, would we be experiencing the high level of unwanted pregnancies and sexually transmitted diseases still prevalent on college campuses?

Condoms

Other than providing very good pregnancy protection, the condom can help prevent the spread of STIs, including HIV. The condom's effectiveness against disease holds true for anal, vaginal, and oral intercourse. The most current research indicates that the rate of protection provided by condoms against STIs is similar to its rate of protection against pregnancy (90–99%). Not only has independent research supported this statistic, but in 1993, the CDC approved condom use as a safe and effective method for STI/HIV prevention, when used correctly and consistently for each and every act of intercourse or oral sex.

Selecting a Condom

1. **Use condoms made of latex rubber.** Latex serves as a barrier to bacteria and viruses, even those as small as HIV. "Lambskin" or "natural membrane" condoms are not as good for disease prevention because of the pores in the material. Look for "latex" on the package. For those allergic to rubber, there is a polyurethane condom. Ask your pharmacist.

2. **Try different condoms until you find one that's comfortable and suits you.** Some men and women believe that condoms don't feel good. Different brands and styles have their own unique feel. If the first condom you select isn't totally desirable, try another brand.

3. **Use a lubricant.** One of the main reasons condoms break is lack of lubrication. Check the list of ingredients on the back of the lubricant package to make sure the lubricant is water based. Do not use petroleum-based jelly, cold cream, baby oil, or cooking shortening. These can weaken the condom and cause it to break.

SOURCE: Adapted from *Understanding AIDS: A Message from the Surgeon General*, HHA Publication No. (CDC) HHS-88-8404, Washington, DC: Government Printing Office.

To some degree, however, using a condom is easier said than done. The condom has long had a reputation of being a less spontaneous method for sex and of diminishing pleasurable sensations. Couples who learn to put the condom on together are generally more successful with this method. It may take some discussion to convince your partner that using condoms is the right thing to do. If he or she responds negatively to the suggestion, here are some comments that may help.

Your partner: Condoms aren't spontaneous. They ruin the moment.

You: If you think they're not spontaneous, maybe we're not being creative enough. If you let me put it on you, I bet you won't think it's interrupting anything!

Your partner: Condoms aren't natural.

You: What's not natural is to be uptight during sex. If we know we're protected, we'll both be more relaxed.

Your partner: I won't have sex with a condom on.

You: Well, we can't have sex without one. There are other things we can do without having intercourse. Why don't we stick to "outercourse" until we can agree on using condoms for intercourse?

Unhealthy Relationships

Intimate Partner Violence

Some individuals express their love in strange and improper ways—ways that should be reported to the authorities. It's called relationship, or intimate partner, violence: emotional, abusive, and violent acts occurring between two people who presumably care very much for each other. First-year students are at particular risk because they are in a new and unfamiliar environment, may not realize the risks, may want to fit in, and may appear to be easy targets.

Approximately one-third of all college-age students will experience a violent intimate relationship. Almost every 15 seconds, a woman in the United States is battered by her boyfriend, husband, or live-in partner. And nearly half a million women report being stalked by a partner in the previous year.

How concerned are your students about sexual assault and relationship violence on your campus? A number of professional videos are available to help you broach this topic; ask your student health center, local rape crisis network, sexual assault organizations, or local or campus police. They may also be willing to provide a guest speaker.

SEE EXERCISE 10.5
RELATIONSHIP CHECKUP

Women ages 16–24, according to the July 2000 National Institute of Justice *Findings from the National Violence Against Women Survey,* experience the highest per capita rates of intimate relationship violence. Though statistics indicate that the majority of abusers involved in intimate partner violence are male, females can also be physically, emotionally, and verbally abusive to their partners.

It's important to recognize the warning signs and know what to do if you find yourself (or know a friend) in an abusive relationship.

- An abuser typically has low self-esteem, blames the victim and others for what is actually his or her own behavior, can be pathologically jealous of others who approach the partner, may use alcohol or drugs to manage stress, and views the partner as a possession.
- A battered person typically has low self-esteem, accepts responsibility for the abuser's actions, is passive but has tremendous strength, believes no one can help, and thinks no one else is experiencing such violence.

How to Tell If Your Relationship Is Abusive

- You're frightened by your partner's temper and afraid to disagree.
- You apologize to others for your partner's abusive behavior
- You avoid family and friends because of your partner's jealousy.
- You're afraid to say no to sex, even if you don't want it.
- You're forced to justify everything you do, every place you go, and every person you see.
- You're the object of ongoing verbal insults.
- You've been hit, kicked, shoved, or had things thrown at you.

Ask students, in groups of 4–5, to make a list of what they would do if a partner were abusing them. Have them prioritize their lists into a group list. Then ask each group to share its list with the rest of the class.

What to Do If Your Relationship Is Abusive Tell your abuser the violence must stop. If you don't want sex, say no firmly. Have a safety plan handy: Call the police at 911, consult campus resources (women's student services, the sexual assault office, and so forth), call a community domestic violence center or rape crisis center, or call someone else on campus you can trust. Find a counselor or support group on campus or in the community. You can even obtain a restraining order through your local magistrate or county court. If the abuser is a student at the same institution, schedule an appointment with your campus judicial officer to explore campus disciplinary action.

Evidence indicates that violence tends to escalate once a person decides to make a break. Should you reach that point, it's wise to remove yourself from the other person's physical presence. This may include changing your daily patterns.

For further advice, contact your counselor to find out about restraining orders, listing the abuser's name at the front desk, changing your locks, securing windows, and other precautions.

To support a friend whose relationship is abusive, be there. Listen. Help your friend recognize the abuse. Be nonjudgmental. Help your friend contact campus and community resources for help. If you become frustrated or frightened, seek help for yourself as well.

SEE "EXAMINING VALUES: SEXUALITY"

SEE EXERCISE 10.6
SEX AND THE MEDIA

SEE "AVOIDING SEXUAL ASSAULT"

Sexual assault and intimate partner violence are sensitive topics that can stir up emotions. Many people are uncomfortable and unqualified to counsel those who have experienced such abuse and violence. Inviting a guest speaker to talk to the class about local (both campus and community-based) support services for victims and their families and friends is a good idea. Consult campus resources and community agencies for recommended speakers and referral materials.

Sexual Assault

Anyone is at risk for being raped, but the majority of victims are women. By the time they graduate, an estimated one out of four college women will be the victim of attempted rape, and one out of six will be raped. Most women will be raped by someone they know, a date or acquaintance, and most will not report the crime. Alcohol is a factor in nearly three-quarters of the incidents. Whether raped by a date or a stranger, a victim can suffer long-term traumatic effects.

Tricia Phaup of the University of South Carolina offers this advice on avoiding sexual assault:

- **Know what you want and do not want sexually.**
- **Go to parties or social gatherings with friends, and leave with them.**
- **Avoid being alone with people you don't know very well.**
- **Trust your gut.**
- **Be alert to unconscious messages you may be sending.**
- **Be conscious of how much alcohol you drink, if any.**

If you are ever tempted to force another person to have sex:

- **Realize that it is *never* okay to force yourself sexually on someone.**
- **Don't assume you know what your date wants.**
- **If you're getting mixed messages, ask.**
- **Be aware of the effects of alcohol.**
- **Remember that rape is legally and morally wrong.**

Regardless of whether a victim chooses to report the rape to the police or get a medical exam, it is very helpful to seek some type of counseling to begin working through this traumatic event.

The following people or offices may be available on or near your campus to deal with a sexual assault: campus sexual assault coordinator, local rape crisis center, campus police department, counseling center, student health services, student affairs professionals, women's student services office, residence life staff, local hospital emergency rooms, and campus chaplains. Use them wisely.

Relationships with Teachers

Entering into a romantic relationship with one of your teachers can result in major problems. On most campuses, faculty and staff are prohibited from having such relationships with students. It is tempting fate to enter into a personal, romantic relationship with someone who has power or authority over you—as you may learn if the relationship goes bad and you receive a low grade in the course. This is one reason it's important to avoid such relationships and to report sexual harassment to the proper campus authorities immediately.

Sexual harassment can include unwelcome sexual advances, requests for sexual favors, improper touching, inappropriate comments or sexual humor, and inappropriate uses of power. Even a compliment about a coworker's appearance ("That color looks great on your body!") may be interpreted as sexual harassment.

When sex happens in ignorance, in haste, or without regard for the other party involved, it may leave emotional scars that are difficult to erase. When individuals who have genuine feelings for each other can agree on the degree of intimacy and involvement, be honest and candid with each other, take proper precautions, and show respect for each other's needs and feelings, that's a different matter entirely.

Using Alcohol and Other Drugs

Even if you don't drink, this information could be very important because 50 percent of college students reported helping a drunken peer (friend, classmate, study partner) in the past year. What you learn here could improve, or even save, your life or the life of someone you care about.

In the final analysis, it's your decision to drink or not to drink alcoholic beverages; to drink moderately or to drink heavily; to know when to stop or to be labeled as a drunk who isn't fun to be around. Every day, thousands of college students

Research shows that alcohol often is involved in unplanned, unintended sexual activity—whether consensual or not. Ask your students if they believe that alcohol often plays a role in forced or unplanned consensual sex. As a class, discuss scenarios where this may be true and brainstorm ideas for preventing and/or managing the situation.

A teacher has power over a student's future. There is never an excuse for a teacher—married or not—to become romantically involved with a student. Be certain your students understand this and remind them that a teacher who engages in such a relationship and is found out may be fired. Give students relevant contact information on campus to report instances of sexual harassment.

Ask students to form small groups (2–3 people) to brainstorm the pros and cons of becoming romantically involved with someone at work. Also ask them to prepare a rationale for workplace policies for such relationships. How can someone be sure sexual advances are unwanted? As each small group reports back to the class, the discussion may become heated and emotional. The point of the activity is to increase awareness and to get your students thinking!

make such decisions, and between 10 and 20 percent of people in the United States become addicted to alcohol at some point in their lives. Alcohol can turn people into victims even though they don't drink: people killed by drunk drivers or family members who suffer from the behavior of an alcoholic.

Thankfully, very few college students are alcoholics, but you do not have to be an alcoholic to experience problems with alcohol. According to most college presidents, alcohol abuse is the greatest single threat to your health, safety, and academic performance. Over the course of 1 year, about 20 to 30 percent of students report serious problems related to excessive alcohol use. You may have heard news reports about college students who died from acute alcohol poisoning or were fatally, seriously, or permanently injured as a result of excessive drinking. Although habitual heavy drinkers suffer the highest rate of negative consequences from drinking, just one occasion of heavy or high-risk drinking also can lead to problems.

Yet it is important to understand that not every college student drinks frequently or excessively. In fact, statistics indicate that a majority of college students do not drink excessively on a regular basis.

Although the decision to drink is up to you, decisions about drinking are strongly influenced by your environment. As a college student, you are bombarded with conflicting messages about drinking. On the one hand, you learn in health class or orientation that drinking is potentially dangerous and that underage drinking can have serious legal consequences. Yet each year students see thousands of commercials that portray drinking as fun and glamorous. Movies and TV shows sometimes depict problems with drinking, but the majority of shows portray drunkenness as fun and alcohol-related problems as silly. Parents may scold children for underage drinking, yet drink in front of their children.

SEE EXERCISE 10.7
SURVEY OF ALCOHOL
USAGE

Why College Students Drink

Students drink alcoholic beverages for many reasons, but those reasons can be divided into three major categories: (1) social learning, (2) to feel good, and (3) not to feel bad.

Social Learning

SEE EXERCISE 10.8
A SAFE STRESS
ANTIDOTE

Social learning simply means learning by watching others. A teenager may view alcohol as pleasurable after watching a friend or adult who enjoys drinking. The major sources of social learning for drinking are parents, mass media, and peers.

Parents Although parents and teenagers often disagree on superficial things such as clothes and music, when it comes to values about major life issues—such as educational or career goals, religious or political beliefs, and attitudes toward alcohol or other drug use—parent and teen values in one family tend to be very similar. A parent who comes home from a hard day at work and says "I need a drink" may be conditioning his or her children to use alcohol as a stress-relief drug.

Mass Media Commercial marketers have learned that associating sex appeal, the outdoors, and healthy-looking young people with their products catches your attention and encourages you to think favorably about their product. Although some new drinkers try alcohol out of curiosity, it is more likely that they try alcohol because they expect something positive from it. Commercials and beverage company "swag" (free gifts covered with logos and slogans) help to encourage positive feelings or expectations about alcoholic beverages.

Peers The best social predictor of your drinking behavior is the behavior of the people you hang out with, especially friends and close associates. Students tend to seek out individuals with similar values and behavior. Certain peer behaviors can encourage or discourage heavy drinking. For example, a drinking game may drive a group of friends to drink more than usual. Also, the overall campus culture or the behaviors of members of clubs or Greek societies can have a big influence on your decisions about drinking. You may feel you need to change your drinking habits to be accepted by certain groups.

Ask students to talk about individuals who have affected their decision to drink or not to drink.

Drinking to Feel Good or Not to Feel Bad

At low to moderate doses, alcohol is a drug that can produce feelings of relaxation or pleasure. When people do something that is pleasurable, they are likely to do it again. This process is called positive reinforcement. So if one drink makes you feel good, it may encourage you to drink more frequently.

Related to the concept of drinking to feel good is the phenomenon of drinking not to feel bad. Some people may experience temporary relief of unpleasant feelings when drinking, such as feeling less tense or less sad. Alcoholics may drink to avoid symptoms of alcohol withdrawal, such as "the shakes" (a tremor in the hands). In extreme cases, a person may drink to forget. When people do something that stops them from feeling bad, they are likely to do it again. This process—called negative reinforcement because it takes away something bad or undesirable—may encourage someone coping with stress, alcohol withdrawal, or painful memories to drink more often. But such a risky and temporary checking out from reality is a solution that may create more problems over the long run.

Myths Versus Realities of Student Drinking

Although peer behavior is one of the best predictors of college student drinking, *perceived* student behavior is a better predictor. In numerous studies, students tended to exaggerate how much their peers drank. For example, when heavy drinking was defined by researchers as five or more drinks in one day, several national

Students often strongly argue that the data must be wrong. Be prepared for such disbelief and resistance. Remind them that even if they did a survey, many students would feel pressured to claim they drink more than they actually do.

Not all college students drink frequently and in excess or even at all. There are many enjoyable activities and events that do not need alcohol to make them fun.

© Matthew McVay/Allstock/PictureQuest

surveys found that a minority of students (about 40 percent) were classified as heavy drinkers. However, the same studies found that students *thought* that the majority of their peers were heavy drinkers. Thus, the perceived rate of heavy drinking was nearly twice the actual rate.

In a survey of about 1100 students, first-year students estimated that their peers drank once or twice a week, when in reality their peers drank only one to three times a month. As shown in Figure 10.1, a similar discrepancy between perceived and self-reported drinking was found for the number of drinks consumed per drinking day.

Why Students Overestimate Peer Drinking

One reason students overestimate rates of drinking among peers is that drunken students are more easily noticed than sober students. For example, at a party with 100 students, 10 drunk students might do some stupid things like get loud and dance on a table, throw up in the corner, start a fight, or run around naked.

Naturally, these drunk students tend to get noticed and talked about. But the 60 students who drank but did not get intoxicated, the 30 students who had nothing to drink at the party, and the hundreds of students who were studying that night are forgotten. Furthermore, when students talk about the party, they may exaggerate the number of drunken students who were doing "those stupid things."

Ironically, programs intended to prevent or reduce heavy drinking may actually contribute to misperceptions of drinking norms. Many programs dwell on negative behavior or tragic incidents in an effort to motivate students through fear or shame to avoid heavy drinking. By doing so, some of these programs may inadvertently create the impression that "everybody's doing it." This can make the majority of students who drink responsibly or don't drink at all believe they are in the minority when, in truth, responsible behavior tends to be the norm and heavy drinkers are a deviant subgroup.

Consequences of Overestimating Peer Drinking

The effects of overestimating drinking norms depend on your own level of drinking. If you are not a heavy drinker, overestimating the rate of heavy drinking may encourage you to drink more in order to fit in with your peer group. If you are a heavy drinker already, overestimating the rate of heavy drinking may lead to a false sense of being normal and thereby discourage any attempt to drink in a less risky manner.

Ask students to write anonymously whether they believe they drink more or less than their peers. Now ask them to estimate the number of drinks they consume in a week. Tell them to be as accurate as possible. Collect the unsigned papers and determine the average number of drinks per week per student. Reflect on the answer.

Have students describe in writing a person they remember clearly from a recent occasion where alcohol was served. Was this person drunk or sober? What made it easy to remember this person? What feelings did the observer have about this person?

Students may be surprised and very interested in the chemistry of alcohol and its toxic, solvent, and flammable properties in high concentration. Further interest can be generated by discussing the uses of alcohol as a cleaning solvent, an antiseptic, as a fuel. A warning not to drink straight alcohol may also be in order. (See "What Is Alcohol?" on CD-ROM.)

FIGURE 10.1
Number of Drinks Consumed per Drinking Occasion

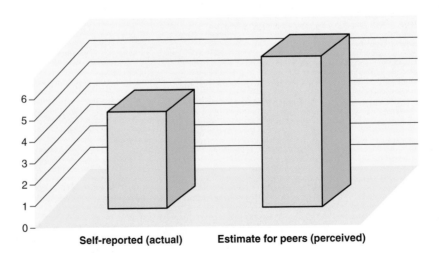

SOURCE: Smith, B., Stamper, G., and Grant, R. (2001). *A peer-led, small-groups approach to changing perceptions of drinking norms among college students.* Manuscript submitted for publication. Used by permission.

Examining Values: Alcohol and Other Drugs

You may agree with some of the values about drinking expressed by peers, parents, or the media. You may disagree with others. Think about your values regarding drinking. Would you consider it okay to drink and drive, engage in underage drinking, get drunk on weekends, or drink to drown your sorrows? What are your friends' and your parents' values about drinking?

How do your values compare with theirs? How do you deal with the differences between your values and those of the important people in your life? How might some of the values you have in common lead to safer decisions about drinking? How might some values you hold in common lead to riskier decisions about drinking?

Several recent studies suggest that simply knowing actual rates of alcohol consumption leads to better decisions about drinking. Many colleges and universities have programs designed to teach students the real rates of alcohol consumption on campus. On several campuses, more accurate perceptions of drinking have been associated with fewer alcohol-related problems. However, some students react to data on actual drinking norms with disbelief and denial, especially heavy drinkers who must then admit that they are extreme drinkers and not the norm. A greater understanding of how mass media and highly visible drunken behavior distort drinking norms may help overcome resistance to the truth.

SEE "WHAT IS ALCOHOL?"

Drinking and Blood Alcohol Content

How alcohol affects behavior depends on the dose of alcohol, which is best measured by blood alcohol content, or BAC. The effects of alcohol in various dosages are summarized in Table 10.2. We want to emphasize that most of the pleasurable effects of alcoholic beverages, such as feeling energized and sociable, are experienced at lower BAC levels, when alcohol acts as a behavioral stimulant. For most people, the stimulant level is around one drink per hour, but this depends on many variables.

TABLE 10.2 CORRELATION OF BLOOD ALCOHOL CONTENT (BAC) WITH BEHAVIOR

BAC RANGE	COMMON EFFECTS ON BEHAVIOR	MAJOR DANGERS
0.00 to 0.04	Increased energy, animation	No impairment
.05 to .08	Feeling a "buzz" Slowed reflexes	4 times the risk of accident*
.09 to .20	Impaired walking, poor social judgment, slurred speech, nausea, fighting, vandalism, sexual aggression, blackouts	25 times the risk of an accident* Risk of indiscriminate sex (and consequences such as AIDS or pregnancy)
.20 to .30	Vomiting, stupor, passing out	Death from suffocation or choking on vomit
.31 to .45	Coma, shock from alcohol poisoning	Brain damage Death
.45 or higher	.45 is the fatal level for 50% of people	As the BAC rises higher than .45, death becomes more and more certain

*Compared to a driver with a BAC less than .01.
SOURCE: Robert Julien, *A Primer of Drug Action*, 9th ed., New York: Worth, 2001.

Ask students to identify as many physiological effects of alcohol on the body as they can. What are some of the early effects? What are the later effects? Some research might be of interest here.

Usually, problems begin to emerge at doses higher than .05, when alcohol acts as a sedative and begins to slow down areas of the brain. Most people who have more than four or five drinks at one occasion feel "buzzed," show signs of impairment, and are likely to be higher risks for alcohol-related problems. However, significant impairment at lower doses can occur when someone is physically ill, stressed out, or tired from lack of sleep or heavy exercise. Women may be more strongly affected by alcohol during their menstrual cycle. The point to remember is that what you consume safely on some days may lead to problems on other days.

Many variables affect BAC levels. Your physical size affects the concentration of alcohol in your system, with smaller people registering higher BACs with smaller amounts of alcohol. Since men tend to be bigger than women, women tend to be more susceptible to the effects of alcohol. Even if a man and a woman of the same weight consume the same amount of alcohol, the woman still will tend to have a higher BAC because muscles can absorb alcohol easily, and men tend to be relatively more muscular than women. Thus, athletes may experience different BACs than people who are less physically fit.

Ask students to make a collective list of times or situations when it would be unwise to drink alcohol.

Diet also makes a difference. A dehydrated athlete who drinks alcohol on an empty stomach may experience much higher BACs than someone who is properly hydrated and well fed. Other factors that affect BAC are experience with alcohol, physical health, and genetic background.

How fast you drink makes a difference, too. Your body gets rid of alcohol at a rate of about one drink an hour. If you finish one drink every 2 hours, your body can eliminate the alcohol and your BAC will stay low. Drinking more than one drink an hour may cause a rise in BAC because the body is absorbing alcohol faster than it can eliminate it.

Because so many variables affect BAC levels, commonly available BAC charts can contain errors. To get an accurate BAC, you should take a breath test, or even better, a blood test. The measure of BAC most commonly used is milliliters of alcohol per deciliter of fluid. For example, the legal limit for driving while intoxicated in most states is a BAC of .08.

Trained professionals can estimate BAC from your behavior. When someone is stopped for drunk driving, police may videotape the person completing a series of tasks such as walking on a line and tipping his or her head back, or touching the nose with eyes closed. The degree of impairment shown in these tests can be presented as evidence in court because many studies have closely correlated behavioral impairment on such tasks with BAC levels.

Alcohol and Behavior

The biphasic effect of alcohol is something students should keep in mind. Ask them to discuss how they feel after that initial buzz, and why so many people keep drinking even after they feel as good as they're going to feel from alcohol.

At low doses, alcohol has a stimulating effect on the human brain. At BAC levels of .025 to .05, a drinker tends to feel animated and energized. At a BAC level of around .05, a drinker may feel rowdy or boisterous. This is where most people report feeling a buzz from alcohol. At a BAC level between .05 and .08, alcohol starts to act as a depressant. When the brain starts to slow down, your coordination, thinking, and judgment may be impaired. So as soon as you feel that buzz from alcohol, remember that you are on the brink of losing coordination, clear thinking, and judgment!

Driving, riding a bicycle, and similar activities are measurably impaired at BAC levels *lower* than the legal limit of .08, meaning the legal BAC limit is hardly safe for driving. In fact, an accurate safe level for most people may be half the legal limit (.04). As BAC levels climb past .08, you will become progressively less coordinated and less able to make good decisions. Most people become severely uncoordinated with BAC levels higher than .08 and may begin falling asleep, falling down, or slurring their speech. At BAC levels higher than .15, people tend to suffer memory loss or blackouts. Although they may be awake and doing things, they will not recall what they did or whom they were with. For most people, poison receptors in the brain are activated at BACs between .08 and .15. This may lead to nausea and vomiting. Commonly associated with nausea is a feeling of dizziness or a sensation that the room is spinning, a result of the disruption of the brain's balancing system.

Warning Signs, Saving Lives

Most people pass out or fall asleep when the BAC is above .25. Unfortunately, even after you pass out and stop drinking, your BAC can continue to rise as alcohol in your stomach is released to the intestine and absorbed into the bloodstream. Your body may try to get rid of alcohol by vomiting, but you can choke if you are unconscious, semiconscious, or severely uncoordinated.

Worse yet, high BAC levels depress the activity of brain areas that support life functions. At BAC levels higher than .30, most people will show signs of severe alcohol poisoning such as an inability to wake up, slowed breathing, fast but weak pulse, cool or damp skin, and pale or bluish skin. People exhibiting these symptoms need medical assistance *immediately*. If you ever find someone in such a state, remember to keep the person on his or her side with the head lower than the rest of the body. Check to see that the airway is clear, especially if the person is vomiting. Even if the person is not vomiting, a severely drunk person lying on his or her back can be so relaxed that the airway can close if the tongue is blocking the back of the throat.

If a drinker passes out but does not have these severe symptoms, he or she should be watched carefully and checked frequently until awake. Even when the person is awake, you may need to protect him or her from doing something dangerous, such as falling down a flight of stairs or starting a fire. When in doubt, call for help. Most colleges and universities have staff on call 24 hours a day who are trained to deal with alcohol-related emergencies.

To emphasize the seriousness of alcohol-related emergencies and to prepare students for the likely event that they will be confronted with such an emergency, have one or two students role-play helping an "intoxicated" student. Ask others in the class to offer suggestions to those helping out. Do this once with the "intoxicated" person reacting to the treatment and another time when the person doesn't respond. Discuss the difference in the role play.

Death by Alcohol

Alcohol is fatal for most people when their BAC reaches .45; many people die at lower BACs from accidents. To be on the safe side, you should avoid strong drinks made with high-alcohol-content distilled spirits (such as 151-proof rum) or multiple shots of distilled spirits. Chugging a fifth of alcohol in 1 hour is enough to get your BAC to .50. Although chugging distilled spirits is particularly lethal, you can also overdose on beer or wine. In fact, any form of chugging alcoholic beverages is dangerous.

Be aware that one or more students in class knows someone who has died or has come close to dying from acute alcohol poisoning. Be prepared for emotional reactions to this topic.

Heavy Drinking: The Danger Zone

SEE EXERCISE 10.9
HELPING A FRIEND

Research suggests that light to moderate drinking has some risks, but heavy drinking is associated with a substantially elevated risk of alcohol-related problems.

Heavy drinking is typically defined as drinking more than five or six drinks on one social occasion. Some studies make a distinction between males and females, using lower cutoffs for females, whose body composition and lower body weight make them more susceptible to the effects of alcohol. Thus, heavy drinking, sometimes called binge drinking, is commonly defined as five or more drinks for males and four or more drinks for females on a single occasion.

Even though this standard does not consider (a) the size of the person or (b) how long the person has been drinking at one occasion, it tends to be a good rule for all drinkers to follow. Presumably, for a very large person who drinks slowly over a long period of time (several hours), four or five drinks may not lead to a BAC associated with impairment. However, based on research that finds that heavy drinkers

Ask students to discuss how they define heavy drinking. Under what conditions might four or five drinks be problematic? Under what conditions would the same amount be less likely to be problematic? If the statistics in Table 10.2 are accurate, why do so many people abuse alcohol?

SEE EXERCISE 10.10
QUALITY OF LIFE

SEE INTERNET
EXERCISE 10.3
THE CORE ALCOHOL AND
DRUG SURVEY

suffer a high rate of alcohol-related problems, it appears that in many cases the BAC of heavy drinkers exceeds the legal limit for impairment (+.08). At this level, there is no legal or scientific doubt that the person is impaired.

The academic, medical, and social consequences of heavy drinking can seriously endanger quality of life. Research based on surveys conducted by the Core Institute at Southern Illinois University (http://www.siuc.edu/~coreinst) provides substantial evidence that heavy drinkers have significantly greater risk of adverse outcomes, as shown in Table 10.3.

Among other problems, the Core data identify heavy drinking with increased risk of poor test performance, missed classes, unlawful behavior, violence, memory loss, drunk driving, regretful behavior, and vandalism, compared with all drinkers and all students. At the same time, college health centers nationwide are reporting increasing occurrences of these serious medical conditions resulting from excessive alcohol use:

- Alcohol poisoning causing coma and shock
- Respiratory depression, choking, and respiratory arrest
- Head trauma and brain injury
- Lacerations
- Fractures
- Unwanted or unsafe sexual activity causing STDs and pregnancies
- Bleeding intestines
- Anxiety attacks and other psychological crises
- Worsening of underlying psychiatric conditions such as depression or anxiety

Don't let students be lulled into a false sense of security after reading that frequent heavy drinkers are worse off than those who infrequently drink heavily. Where do they think infrequent heavy drinking will lead?

Researchers at the Harvard School of Public Health have found that increased *frequency* of heavy drinking affects the risk of problems associated with drinking.

TABLE 10.3 ANNUAL CONSEQUENCES OF ALCOHOL AND OTHER DRUG USE AMONG ALL STUDENTS, ALL DRINKERS, AND HEAVY DRINKERS

CONSEQUENCES	PERCENT EXPERIENCING CONSEQUENCE		
	All Students	All Drinkers	Heavy Drinkers
Had a hangover	59.7	81.1	89.5
Performed poorly on a test	21.8	31.4	40.8
Trouble with police, etc.	11.7	17.4	23.7
Property damage, fire alarm	7.8	11.8	16.5
Argument or fight	29.5	42.0	52.2
Nauseated or vomited	47.1	63.9	73.5
Driven while intoxicated	32.6	47.0	57.3
Missed a class	27.9	40.9	52.9
Been criticized	27.1	37.2	45.3
Thought I had a problem	12.3	16.4	21.6
Had a memory loss	25.8	37.3	48.0
Later regretted action	35.7	49.8	60.4
Arrested for DWI, DUI	1.7	2.4	3.3
Tried, failed to stop	5.8	8.1	10.6
Been hurt, injured	12.9	18.8	25.2
Taken advantage of sexually	11.4	15.9	19.9
Took sexual advantage of someone	6.1	9.0	11.9
Tried to commit suicide	1.6	1.9	2.6
Thought about suicide	5.1	6.7	8.2

SOURCE: Adapted from C. A. Presley, P. W. Meilman, J. R. Cashin, and R. Lyerla, *Alcohol and Drugs on American College Campuses: Use, Consequences, and Perceptions of the Campus Environment*, Volume IV: 1992–94, Carbondale: The Core Institute, Southern Illinois University.

TABLE 10.4 COMPARISON OF PERCENTAGE OF STUDENTS REPORTING ALCOHOL-RELATED PROBLEMS
EXPERIENCED BY LIGHT TO MODERATE DRINKERS, HEAVY DRINKERS, AND FREQUENT HEAVY DRINKERS

Problem	Light to Moderate Drinkers	Heavy Drinkers	Frequent Heavy Drinkers
Got behind on schoolwork	9	25	48
Missed a class due to drinking	10	33	65
Argued with friends while drinking	10	24	47
Got hurt or injured	3	11	27
Damaged property	3	10	25
Got in trouble with campus police	2	5	15
Had 5 or more alcohol-related problems since the beginning of the school year	4	17	52

SOURCE: Data from Henry Weschler et al., "Changes in Binge Drinking and Related Problems Among American College Students Between 1993 and 1997: Results of the Harvard School of Public Health College Alcohol Study," *Journal of American College Health, 47,* (1998), 57–68.

As shown in Table 10.4, frequent heavy drinkers suffered a higher rate of problems than heavy drinkers, while heavy drinkers suffered more problems than light to moderate drinkers.

Consequences for All

All Core Institute surveys conducted since the early 1990s have consistently shown a negative correlation between grades and the number of drinks per week—and not just for heavy drinkers. Findings are similar for both two-year and four-year institutions, as shown in Figure 10.2.

Students who are heavy drinkers harm not only themselves but also others around them. Four out of five students who were not heavy drinkers and who lived on campus experienced at least one secondhand effect of heavy drinking, such as being the victim of an assault or an unwanted sexual advance, having property vandalized, or having sleep or study interrupted. The Core Institute reports the

SEE EXERCISE 10.11
LOWER THE DRINKING
AGE?

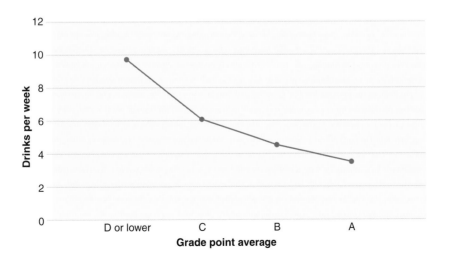

FIGURE 10.2
Negative Correlation Between Drinks per Week and Grade Point Average

SOURCE: Adapted from C. A. Presley, P. W. Meilman, J. R. Cashin, and R. Lyerla, *Alcohol and Drugs on American College Campuses: Use, Consequences, and Perceptions of the Campus Environment,* Volume IV: 1992–94, Carbondale: The Core Institute, Southern Illinois University.

Although this "grades versus drinking" graph may seem simplistic, underscore that the data from which it was taken is very real, and the reasons grades go down as drinking goes up are very obvious.

following percentages of students who have experienced adverse effects as a result of others' drinking:

Ask students to compile a list of all the times they have been affected by someone else's drinking. Then have the class brainstorm ways to reduce such annoyances.

Study interrupted	29%
Space messed up	25%
Felt unsafe	22%
Unable to enjoy events	19%
Interfered with in other ways	32%

Thus, the majority of students—who are not heavy drinkers—are frequently affected by behaviors caused by the few out-of-control students who are heavy or high-risk drinkers.

Long-Term Effects of Drinking

Ask students to read the labels of any over-the-counter drugs they take to see if there is a warning about combining the drug with alcohol. What symptoms might the combination cause? Have them report on their findings.

As Table 10.5 shows, drinking is never without risk. Even light to moderate drinkers—defined as those who consume fewer than two drinks a day—who generally don't suffer major physical problems may experience a multitude of social

TABLE 10.5 FOUR PHASES OF DRINKING AND RELATED PROBLEMS

	INTERPERSONAL	VOCATIONAL	PHYSICAL	LEGAL
No drinking, no altered tolerance, no risk of drinking related problems	None	None	None	None
Phase 1: Low risk, no altered tolerance	Parents, friends may disapprove of drinking	Unlikely unless on the job or if caught for underage drinking	· Allergic reactions · Dangerous interactions with other drugs	· Underage drinking · Alcohol as a gateway drug for other drugs
Phase 2: High-risk drinking, low to moderate increase in tolerance	All of above, plus · Fighting · Risky sex · Sexual assault · Poor judgment · Impaired sexual performance	All of above, plus · Missed work or class from hangovers (impairment after drinking) · Legal consequences impact vocational (e.g., expelled from school)	All of above, plus · Disrupted sleep · Irritation of stomach · Vomiting · Hangovers · Alcohol poisoning · Blackouts · Injuries from accidents	· Arrest for drunk and disorderly · Arrest for DUI · Arrest for behavior related to impaired judgment
Phase 3: High-risk drinking, substantially increased tolerance	All of above, plus · Relationship with alcohol affects choice of friends · Increasingly deviant peer group	All of above, plus · Missed work/school due to health problems from heavy drinking · Pattern of poor performance limits new opportunities	All of above, plus · Chronic irritation of stomach (gastritis, ulcers) · Pancreatitis · Signs of dependence (e.g., shakes in the morning)	All of above, plus · As quantity and frequency of drinking increases, so does the likelihood of legal consequences · Increasingly deviant peer group increases exposure to legal problems
Phase 4: High-risk drinking and tolerance beyond the trigger point (alcoholism)	All of above, but worse	All of above, but worse, plus · Cognitive deficits from alcohol abuse limit academic or work skills	All of above, but worse, plus · Liver damage · Cancer · Heart disease	All of above, but worse

consequences. Some people are actually allergic to alcohol or may suffer dangerous interactions between alcohol and commonly used drugs, including over-the-counter cold medicines. Even a couple of drinks in combination with certain prescription drugs can slowly destroy the liver or cause death in other ways. Thus, any level of drinking is potentially dangerous. Protect yourself: Never take alcohol in combination with another drug without asking a physician.

In large amounts, alcohol can cause serious changes in your body. For one thing, the more you drink, the more alcohol your body can tolerate. As you consume more alcohol, your body tries to protect itself against alcohol's toxic effects by speeding up its elimination from your system. As a result, it takes increasingly larger amounts of alcohol to get the same buzz as before. So, heavy drinkers who drink to get drunk feel the need to drink even more. The only way to break this tolerance cycle is to stop drinking, or at least begin drinking in moderation. If you engage in heavy drinking so long that your body can tolerate large amounts, you may become dependent on alcohol. According to the medical definition, someone is alcohol-dependent or alcoholic if he or she exhibits three of the following symptoms:

1. A significant tolerance for alcohol
2. Withdrawal symptoms such as the shakes
3. Overuse of alcohol
4. Attempts to control or cut down on use
5. Preoccupation with drinking or becoming anxious when you do not have a "stash"
6. Making new friends who drink and staying away from friends who do not drink or who do not drink to get drunk
7. Continued heavy drinking despite experiencing alcohol-related social, academic, legal, or health problems

SEE "CRITICAL THINKING: STUDENT DRINKING"

Fortunately, most college students do not become alcoholics. However, if you or someone you know is progressing toward alcoholism, you should contact a source on campus that can help. Student health centers are almost always a good place to start, but many other sources are typically available. Your course instructor, residence hall advisor, or academic advisor should be able to help you decide where to seek help for yourself or someone you care about.

Speaking of Careers

If you think drinking is an important part of your personal life, imagine what effect it can have on your career. The biggest cause of lost time and underachievement at work in this country is heavy drinking and its consequences. Performance on most jobs, especially highly skilled jobs, is measurably impaired for 1 to 3 days after a bout of heavy drinking. Making good decisions about drinking can help both your health and earning power.

You may be interested in a career that offers counseling and treatments for the prevention of heavy drinking. To earn a license to provide treat-

ment services for people having problems with alcohol and other drugs, you should explore a master's degree in social work (MSW) or a PhD in psychology. Some people receive specialty training to work with those who have substance abuse problems without getting advanced graduate training. Such workers typically are college graduates who have been trained to become certified alcohol counselors (CAC). Also, people who work in college or university student affairs programs typically have at least a master's degree in counseling or education and may be called upon to counsel students with alcohol problems.

Many college students do not drink at all. Many who choose to drink do so responsibly and are best described as light to moderate drinkers. Yet a visible minority of college students drinks heavily, experiences a high rate of alcohol-related problems, and may cause a great deal of discomfort to the lives of the majority who have made sensible choices about alcohol. Few people realize that most of the fun associated with drinking is at lower doses. Unfortunately, many believe that more alcohol means more fun. Ironically, high doses of alcohol may cause people to become aggressive, accident-prone, drowsy, or sick.

A good formula for controlling drinking is to keep your BAC below half the legal criterion for intoxication. You can accomplish this by

- Not drinking at all
- Drinking slowly enough to avoid a rising BAC—for example, a nonalcoholic drink after every alcoholic drink
- Eating a good meal before drinking
- Avoiding high-alcohol-content drinks such as shots of whisky, vodka, or other distilled spirits
- Avoiding drinking games or groups of peers that engage in heavy or high-risk drinking
- Paying attention to your drinking and what others say about your drinking

Making Decisions, Finding Help

SEE "OTHER DRUGS"

SEE INTERNET
EXERCISE 10.4
RESEARCHING SEX
AND ALCOHOL AND
OTHER DRUGS

If you are a responsible drinker, we hope you won't be goaded into becoming a problem drinker. If you don't drink at all, we hope we have assured you that it's okay.

But if you do have an alcohol or drug problem, seek appropriate professional care before things get worse. College is a time for growing up, for discovering your talents, for preparing to succeed in life. Why let something as potentially damaging as alcohol—or tobacco, cocaine, marijuana, or other drugs—put a kink in those plans?

You need to know if your drinking behavior is consistent with the healthy majority of college students or if it puts you in the unhealthy minority of high-risk heavy drinkers. If you or someone you care about is in the high-risk minority, seek help before things go from bad to worse.

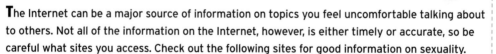

Search Online!   《 ● 》

Internet Exercise 10.1 Getting Confidential Information

The Internet can be a major source of information on topics you feel uncomfortable talking about to others. Not all of the information on the Internet, however, is either timely or accurate, so be careful what sites you access. Check out the following sites for good information on sexuality.

A Healthy Devil Online This Duke University Web site offers information on such topics as sex, abstinence, rape and sexual assault, sexual orientation, and sexual dysfunction. Take a look at "101 Ways to Please Your Lover Without Doing It." See also the resources on pregnancy testing, options, and suggested resources (**http://dmi-www.mc.duke.edu/h-devil/**).

Go Ask Alice The Columbia University Health Services Web site allows users to type in their questions about sex and provides immediate answers to the questions. "Alice" also answers questions about other health topics, including relationships, nutrition, physical activity, weight loss, drugs and alcohol, and stress (**http://www.goaskalice.columbia.edu**).

(continued)

Search Online!

Internet Exercise 10.2
Gathering Accurate Information about STIs

Go to the Centers for Disease Control and Prevention (CDC) Web site http://www.cdc.gov. On the home page, click on the navigation bar "Data & Statistics." Next, under the heading "Scientific Data," double-click the link "Sexually Transmitted Diseases." You will be taken to the "CDC Wonder" home page, where you can log on as an "Anonymous User." Then you can request specific, custom information about STIs in various locations in the United States. For example, you may want to know the number of reported gonorrhea cases for the state in which you attend school. To do so, after logging on as an "Anonymous User," click the "Get Information" button and link to the "Select STI Morbidity" box. Then select (1) Location & Years, (2) Disease Type(s) (from the drop-down list), and (3) Output (by gender and region, for example). Then click the "Send" button to generate your custom report.

It may take a few tries to get the data you are interested in. Be patient, and spend some time requesting the information in different formats. Were you successful in navigating the CDC Web site and retrieving the statistics you wanted? If not, why? You may want to ask someone from your class, or a friend, to walk through the exercise with you. If you were successful in getting the data, were you surprised about the rates of STIs in your area? Are the rates higher or lower than you thought they would be? Suggest some strategies for reducing the STI rates in the areas you selected.

Internet Exercise 10.3 The Core Alcohol and Drug Survey

Estimate the percentage of students who reported using each of the following drugs during the year prior to the Core survey.

Tobacco_____ Alcohol_____ Marijuana_____ Cocaine_____ Amphetamines_____

Now go to http://www.siu.edu/departments/coreinst/public_html/recent.html and compare your estimates to the results in the most recent Core Survey. What seems to be the trend in use of alcohol and other drugs over the years? (Go to http://success.wadsworth.com for the most up-to-date URLs.) Also check the following Web sites:

BACCHUS/GAMMA, http://www.bacchusgamma.org
The College Experience: Alcohol and Student Life, http://www.factsontap.org
The National Clearing House for Alcohol and Drug Information, http://www.health.org
Higher Education Center for Alcohol and Drug Prevention, http://www.edc.org/hec
College Alcohol Study–Harvard School of Public Health,
http://www.hsph.harvard.edu/cas

Some students may have difficulty retrieving data from the CDC Web site. You may want to suggest an alternative activity. Ask students to go to the site (www.cdc.gov) and click on "Health Topics A-Z" from the main navigation bar. Have them select one or more sexuality related topic(s) and summarize the data and statistics reported. Some of the topics have a "Hoaxes & Rumors" link that students may find interesting.

Additional Exercises

These exercises at the end of each chapter will help you sharpen what we believe are the critical skills for college success: writing, critical thinking, learning in groups, planning, reflecting, and taking action. Also check out the CD-ROM that came with your book—you will find more exercises as well as resources for this chapter.

Exercise 10.1 **Personal Reflections on Sexuality**

Ask yourself the following questions:

A Have you taken time to sort out your own values about sexual activity? If you aren't willing to commit to a particular plan of action at this time, what keeps you from doing so? If you are sexually active, do your values take into account your own and your partner's health? If that's not a priority for you, what would it take to get you to a point where safer sex took priority over unsafe sex?

B Write down some of your thoughts and intentions about sexuality. This should be for you alone to read. The act of writing may help you organize your thoughts. Committing your values to paper may also help you live by them when faced with tough decisions.

Exercise 10.2 **What's Your Decision?**

Although you might know about the strategies to keep yourself from contracting an STI, knowledge doesn't always translate into behavior. Use the following chart to brainstorm all the reasons you can think of that people wouldn't practice each of the prevention strategies: abstinence, monogamy, or condom use. In other words, think about the barriers to safer sex (p. 171). Then go back over your list and consider whether the barrier would apply to you (yes, no, or maybe). In this way, you can better evaluate where you stand on the issue of safer sex and determine what areas you may need to work on to ensure that you protect yourself—always!

BARRIERS   **DOES THIS APPLY TO YOU?**

_____   _____

_____   _____

_____   _____

_____   _____

_____   _____

Exercise 10.3 **What's "Normal"?**

Often when we read or talk about sex, we hear or use the words *natural, normal, moral, good/bad,* or *abnormal.* Take a few minutes to think about what you view as "normal." Review the sexual behaviors listed in the table below and check whether you feel each is natural or unnatural, normal or abnormal, and moral or immoral.

	Natural/Unnatural	Normal/Abnormal	Moral/Immoral
Sexual Intercourse			
Oral Sex			
Anal Sex			
Gay/Lesbian Sex			
Masturbation			
Sex Before Marriage			
Extramarital Sex			
Sex with Multiple Partners			

Next, write out the answers to these questions:

1. What factors went into your decision to classify a behavior as moral or immoral?
2. Do you use similar or different factors when deciding if sexual behaviors are natural, normal, or moral? Why or why not?
3. Are there situations that could change how you view the behaviors? What would they be?
4. Are there some people who may be more open to trying different sexual behaviors than others? Describe such people. On what do your base your answer?

SEE EXERCISES 10.4, 10.5, AND 10.6 ON CD-ROM

Note: Exercises 10.4, 10.5, and 10.6 are on your CD-ROM.

Exercise 10.7 Survey of Alcohol Usage

Using data from the Core and Harvard studies in this chapter, as well as any other information you can find, interview three to five students about their beliefs regarding alcohol and other drugs. Here are some questions you might ask:

1. How can students have a social life without drinking?
2. What influence do advertising, movies, and television have on your desire to drink and/or use other drugs? Explain your answer.
3. Is there any situation in which it is safe to drive when you're drunk? Describe the situation(s).
4. How many drinks does the average college student consume at a party? How do you feel about that? (You can then give them the official results.)
5. Can you give me a definition of heavy drinking? (Tell them it's drinking five drinks very quickly for men or four for women.)
6. Why do you think college students drink heavily?
7. What are the consequences of heavy drinking or use of other drugs in college? Is it worth the risk? Why or why not? (Share information from this chapter after they answer.)

Discuss your findings with others in the class. Use the critical thinking process to arrive at a comprehensive portrait of attitudes toward alcohol/drug use on your campus. Then brainstorm to find ways to change that attitude if it needs changing.

Exercise 10.8 A Safe Stress Antidote

In groups of three to five, make a list of activities that can be used by students at your institution as an antidote for stress. In other words, brainstorm activities that can be extremely pleasurable and can relieve the stress of daily living. The only caveat is that these activities should be safe and fun. Share your list with other groups in the class. Try one out.

Your Personal Journal

Here are a number of things to write about. Choose one or more, or choose another topic related to this chapter.

1. Do you feel comfortable discussing sexuality? Are there areas you wish you knew more about or were more comfortable discussing with others?

2. Do you consider homophobia a problem in our society? What should be done about hate crimes against persons who have sex with persons of the same sex?

3. Is it okay for people to use alcohol or other drugs to put themselves in a sexy mood? Or, after drinking or using drugs, might people indulge in sexual behaviors that they really didn't intend to? If so, how might they feel about it afterward?

4. What are the qualities of "healthy" intimate relationships? Think of your own intimate (not necessarily sexual) relationships, past or present. How would you characterize them? Healthy, unhealthy, or a combination?

5. Before reading this chapter, what were your attitudes about using alcohol and other drugs? How has this chapter affected those attitudes?

6. If you know someone who drinks heavily on a regular basis, write how you feel about that person. If you don't know anyone like that, write how you feel about heavy drinking.

7. How does your campus culture encourage drinking behavior? How does your campus culture discourage drinking behavior?

8. Which of the issues presented in this chapter concerns you the most? Why? Which angers you the most? Why?

9. What behaviors are you willing to change after reading this chapter? How might you go about changing them?

10. What else is on your mind this week? If you wish to share something with your instructor, add it to this journal entry.

Resources

SEXUAL DECISIONS

List some of the resources that will help you make sensible decisions about sex by filling in the names, addresses, and phone numbers for any of the following people or places you might use:

Personal doctor ....

Student health center ....

    Name of physician to see ....

Planned Parenthood chapter ....

Local AIDS foundation or project ....

Local gay/lesbian resource center ....

Counseling center ....

Spiritual advisor/pastor/rabbi ....

Friends or relatives ....

Campus sexual assault coordinator ....

Local rape crisis or sexual assault center ....

Campus police ....

Women's student services office ....

If a friend or acquaintance tells you that he or she has been involved in relationship violence or sexual assault, be prepared. List steps you can take to provide assistance.

1. Let the person talk as much as she/he needs to.

2. Try to find out what actually happened.

3. ....

   ....

4. ....

   ....

5. ....

   ....

6. ....

   ....

Note: If you are not sure of what steps to take, ask your instructor to find a speaker from the sexual assault office, student health center, or another related group to help you complete this exercise.

ALCOHOL AND OTHER DRUGS

Whether or not to drink, smoke, or use drugs are decisions you must make for yourself. It's wise to know the consequences. Here are some ways to gather such information.

Visit your campus alcohol and drug office. If you don't know where to find it, ask your instructor or call the student services division. Chat with someone in the office about what tactics he or she uses to educate students on the use of these substances. Mention that research indicates that anti-drinking campaigns may actually tempt students to drink. Summarize what you learned.

Find copies of current or recent magazines that are targeted to a young audience (18–25). Go through them and note the ads for alcohol products and cigarettes. Explain what you believe are the tactics the advertiser is using to make the reader buy the product and why they work (or don't work).

Beginning College in Uncertain Times

Perspectives on Terrorism, Prejudice, and Patriotism

Some people might say that America's concern with terrorism began with the destruction of the World Trade Center towers. Yet terrorism, in one form or another, is something we have lived with and ultimately conquered for as long as we can remember. In this special section, the editors of *Your College Experience* bring together divergent points of view about terrorism and its effect on Americans in general and college students in particular.

When we were about your age, we feared our world would fall apart as a result of a series of events that began in 1961, when communists erected the Berlin Wall, virtually separating East Berlin from the rest of the democratic world and resulting in massive call-ups of Army reservists to participate in the struggle for freedom. The very next year, our government learned that the Russians were building missile sites in Cuba, less than 200 miles from Key West and aimed at the United States mainland. And in 1963, the world was stunned by the assassination of President John F. Kennedy. Civil rights leader Martin Luther King and presidential candidate Robert F. Kennedy were both gunned down in 1968, and on college campuses across the United States, students were protesting the Viet Nam war, some crossing the border to Canada to escape the draft.

The history of this country and the world are punctuated by times marked by uncertainty or instability. We could go back further and recount the atrocities of World War II. Or ask you to imagine yourself in the throes of the stock market crash of 1929, which initiated the Great Depression of the 1930s and left millions of families destitute and fearful for their futures.

One of the most powerful weapons against fear is understanding, and understanding comes from knowledge. As you begin college, one of the most important lessons we hope you'll learn is to embrace the process of critical thinking. For one thing, being able to think critically will help you through crises such as we have mentioned because it will help you see an issue from all sides and work toward a logical conclusion. Critical thinking—as this textbook explains—begins with abstracting larger ideas from details, using those larger ideas to creatively brainstorm other ideas, organizing your thoughts by retaining only those ideas that seem purposeful, and being able to back up your ideas logically. The ability to gather knowledge on your own is not only power; it can also serve as a comfort in trying times.

Critical thinking depends on your ability to evaluate different perspectives and challenge assumptions made by you or others. To challenge how you think, a college teacher may insist that how you solve a problem is as important as the solution.

Far from telling you how to think about terrorism, prejudice, and such, our goal is to encourage you to use your inherent critical thinking skills to draw conclusions only after you've studied everything you can about this topic—including, but not limited to, the articles that follow. Don't be surprised if you discover that several of these articles take opposing sides on a particular issue. Without listening carefully to all sides, you're not thinking as a college student should.

Introduction

The collapse of the World Trade Center on 9/11/01 triggered a symbolic collapse in the way Americans felt about their futures.

Certainty became uncertainty. Tomorrow became a question mark. Travel plans were cancelled. From Maine to California, few felt as safe as they had the day before.

And whether or not you realize it, you also were changed. Some of you who had eagerly awaited the day when you could begin college were left wondering, "What's the point now?" Some of you may have found that your families were no longer able to afford tuition hikes because of the effects of terrorism on investments coupled with tuition hikes averaging 10 percent in public colleges and 6 percent at private colleges.

Concerned about the safety of urban areas, your parents may have advised you to attend a college closer to home, which may account—in part—for dramatic gains at flagship public universities such as the University of Georgia, the University of South Carolina, and the University of Maryland.

Another result of the times is that, following a long hiatus, student activism has returned to college campuses. Students are thinking more about how to settle disputes with the people with whom they live, learn, and work—without resorting to violent speech or acts.

Other relatively recent events—the bombing of a Federal building in Oklahoma City, the uncertainty in the stock market and economy, and the sniper attacks in the Washington, D.C., area—have caused us all to feel more vulnerable in a number of ways. College students in particular are asking things such as: "With the faltering economy, will I be able to get a good job? If I can't, what's the point of college?" "If my roommate or friend asks me to join a protest march, what should my answer be?"

The events of 9/11 have even affected the career goals of many college students. Enrollments are up in criminal justice departments as students are moved by the gallantry of firefighters and police. Public service careers, to many, seem the only way to help improve the quality of American life and a certain way to enjoy a guaranteed pension plan upon retirement.

The Impact of Terrorism on Your Generation of College Students

Flying Off to College, Defying Terrorism

By Mark Clayton, Staff writer of *The Christian Science Monitor*

Clayton writes about the decisions made by a number of students and their parents about where it's safe to attend college. As you read the article, jot down a few thoughts about its central theme. After you've read the article, write in your own words what it is saying to you and how you feel about what these families have done. How does this relate to any decisions you or your parents have had to make about where you attend college?

After September 11, reports of thousands of unexpected applications to state and regional schools had some admissions officials wondering: Were students, goaded by parents, shifting en masse toward colleges closer to home, away from cities terrorists might target?

As it turns out, many high school seniors, though initially shaken, were determined to pursue their top-choice schools, even if they were far flung or in large cities.

Matthew Nelson of Denver was heading to the University of San Diego, his first choice, even though the presence of a naval base nearby worries his mother.

Sharon Lefkowitz of Dartmouth, Mass., planned to study at the University of Pennsylvania in Philadelphia, not concerned that it's a big population center and the birthplace of American independence.

And Kristen Moffitt was headed to East Carolina University in Greenville, N.C.— several hours by plane from her home in Andover, Mass.

All three students had the attacks in mind last fall as they filled out applications for nearby universities. Yet their decisions to go away to school indicate a tough-minded "terrorists aren't going to derail my life" attitude.

"Obviously it's a huge tragedy," says Ms. Moffitt. "But I try not to let it affect decisions I make. I wouldn't have changed, and didn't think about changing."

Her determination seems to run in the family. Her sister Susie, a senior at the University of Maryland, College Park, which is inside the Washington beltway not far from the Pentagon, has bounced back since being initially disturbed by the attacks, and has no thoughts now of transferring to another school. "I'm staying put," she says.

"We just weren't going to give in to terrorism," agrees their mother, Patricia.

Such attitudes may have played a part in buoying freshman classes at key universities in Washington and New York. Numbers of applications tipped slightly down in a few cases in these cities, but the all-important "yield"—the percentage of students deciding to attend the school once admitted—remained steady.

At George Washington University in the nation's capital, for instance, the yield was similar to the previous year's, with about 34 percent of admitted students deciding it was their final pick. Applications hit 17,000—an all-time high, but admissions officers say the yield is more indicative of student and parent attitudes.

At New York University, the yield rose to 40.7 percent from 38.4 percent a year ago, despite applications dipping 3 percent.

"It really would be a surprise if there were not some people who chose not to apply here . . . because of 9/11," says NYU spokesman John Beckman. He sees the slight decline in applications as more linked to the economy, though, and is relieved to see the school holding its own.

In fact, several observers who thought the terrorist attacks would sweep students toward in-state and regional schools now say the softer economy has had a much bigger impact.

David Hawsey, vice president of enrollment management at Albion College, a private school in Albion, Mich., thought more top local students might enroll there, instead of heading to the coasts.

Albion's yield rose slightly, but he's found a "softer market" generally among competitive schools in the Midwest region.

"When I talked to parents alone, they were very concerned. But they also wanted to honor what their son or daughter wanted to do," Mr. Hawsey says.

A survey by the National Association for College Admission Counseling reports that among 80 four-year colleges and universities that responded, there was a drop in applications by international students. Many of the schools saw more in-state applications this year, which suggested that some students wanted to stay close to home—but perhaps for economic as much or more than for safety reasons.

But it's not just the economy that accounts for the fact that "people are thinking more regionally—tending not to travel cross-country," says Michael London, president of College Coach, a Newton, Mass., company that helps high school students get into college.

He says applications to a number of New York City's colleges and universities—those with a less powerful draw than prestigious schools such as NYU—dipped as much as 10 percent. In Boston and Washington, some application pools shrank about 5 percent.

Some parents are clearly still on edge. Mrs. Lefkowitz, for one, has made it clear to daughter Sharon that Philadelphia is as far as she is going—even though Sharon at one time argued for a California school. "We told her, 'If you want to do graduate school in California, be my guest'," she says. "'But for undergraduate we want you on this side of the Continental Divide'."

SOURCE: From the June 11, 2002, edition—http://www.csmonitor.com/2002/0611/p13s02-lehl.html (Christian Science Monitor). Email claytonm@csps.com. Copyright 2002 *The Christian Science Monitor.* All rights reserved.

Parents Want to Know

One thing this next article indicates is that you often need to go beyond the numbers to capture the whole picture. What would cause respondents to answer a questionnaire one way and then make anecdotal comments which put their responses in some doubt? What should the researcher do with this information? How much of the findings below relate to discussions you had with your parents about where to go to college?

Although a study in November 2001 by Stamats, a higher-education marketing company, discovered that 9/11 has not affected students' decisions about college, anecdotal data collected as part of the study suggests that a number of students are very sensitive about issues related to safety, study abroad, and distance they are willing to travel to attend school. Some highlights of the study:

While students indicated 9/11 has not affected their college choice, they also said that should another incident occur, they will likely reevaluate where they will attend school.

Parents want to know where their children are at all times and they want to be able to communicate with them instantaneously.

While students are interested in study abroad, they are less interested in studying in the Middle East. Their preferences at this time are for study-abroad programs in Asia, Europe, and South America.

Finally, students are very concerned about going to a college that will require a plane trip and seem to prefer distances that are more manageable by car.

Based on comments from students and admissions officers, the role of parents has changed. While parents have never really told their sons and daughters to attend a specific school, they are increasingly likely to tell them not to attend a specific institution. At this point, parents are slightly more concerned about their children studying in large cities than the students are themselves.

SOURCE: 2002 National Online Survey of Recruiting and Marketing Trends and Practices, © 1995–2002 Stamats. Email info@stamats.com. Phone 1.800.553.8878

The College Crunch

By Daniel Kadlec, with reporting by Sean Gregory in New York, Jeffrey Ressner in Los Angeles, and Leslie Whitaker in Chicago

Although many families have saved for college, a foundering stock market, a drop in interest rates, layoffs, or declines in income due to the sluggish economy may have caused their savings to plummet. Your parents may well have been in this plight. What steps did they take to assure that you would be able to start college? Did your choice of college change as a result of financial insecurities?

What advice would you give to other students who have suddenly discovered that their parents' savings will no longer cover the cost of college?

Funding college is an urgent problem that many families with college-age children now face: while retirement is still some years away, college, which they thought they had prepared for, is suddenly a crisis. Some parents are postponing their children's education; others are bypassing private schools in favor of good old State U.

For Robert and Kyuja Kafka, it's a mad scramble. Their son, Gene, agreed to early acceptance at Colby College in Maine, and half his $37,000 first-year tuition, room and board was due Aug. 1. But the Kafkas' savings had fallen more than 50 percent, to just $16,000.

Jack Girvan, a college-funding adviser in Hyannis, Mass., recounts how a couple burst into tears in his office after telling their daughter that she would have to transfer from St. Mary's, a private college in Maryland, to the University of Massachusetts at Amherst (not to be confused with private Amherst College). "She was devastated," Girvan says. But the family had few alternatives after its savings in stocks designated for her remaining education and that of two siblings dropped from $121,000 to $37,000.

Universities across the United States have reported a sharp increase in requests for financial aid. At Arizona State, students qualifying for need-based loans were up 30 percent over the past two years. Mark Evans, director of financial aid at Kent State, reports that requests for additional aid because of "special circumstances" have risen 65 percent.

State schools, meanwhile, are being deluged. At Kennesaw State University in Kennesaw, Ga., freshman applications doubled. "That's just stunning for us," says Joe Head, dean of enrollment services. He attributes the increase to heightened job insecurity, layoffs, a post-9/11 desire among parents to keep the kids close to home, and the meltdown in stock savings.

The much-touted 529 college savings plans aren't providing much shelter. The plans, whose earnings are exempt from federal and some state tax, came into wide acceptance just as the market was peaking. They now have $11 billion in assets, much of it stuffed into aggressive-growth portfolios—the ones that have fallen hardest. For one Arizona Family College Savings 529 plan, nearly a quarter of the assets are in funds that have fallen 30 percent to 60 percent since its inception in 2000.

How best to cope? If you've taken a big hit or lost your job, go back to the financial-aid office. That's what Esther Park, 49, of Allentown, Penn., did after her husband was laid off. Now daughter Michelle can stay at Northwestern University in suburban Chicago. Originally, Esther and her husband were responsible for $23,000 of the $40,000 annual bill for tuition, room, and board. The school agreed to reduce the Parks' contribution to $7,000. Another option is borrowing and giving your stocks a chance to rebound. If you stay with stocks, diversify. Look for low-fee 529 plans like the ones run by TIAA-CREF, and for safety's sake, select funds that automatically shift into conservative investments as college age approaches.

SOURCE: *Time*, July 29, 2002 v160 i5 p30. Full Text: COPYRIGHT 2002 Time, Inc. Reprinted by permission.

A Dangerous Time

In the following article, one thought stands out: We need to be multicultural and antiracist. . . . The only way we can make sense of this moment in history is through a multicultural lens. How would you apply this imperative to the current world situation and to your situation on campus? What is your reaction to the author's criticism of U.S. military aid to Israel as well as to the revelation that the United States once considered Osama bin Laden a "freedom fighter"? Can you discuss these matters impartially and not let racism get in the way of logical thinking?

Crisis will always be used to further agendas of racial privilege. In multiple ways this is a dangerous time: immigrants are made to feel more fearful; as military budgets swell, programs that could ameliorate racial inequality suffer; the "war against terrorism" emboldens defenders of the status quo who have new tools to stifle activism aimed at racial justice.

We need to be multicultural and antiracist. This stems both from a commitment to the kind of world we want to live in—one where the lives of people of all races and cultures are equally valued—as well as from a methodological imperative: The only way we can make sense of this moment in history is through a multicultural lens.

We need to ask the deep "Why?" questions. Nothing can justify the heinous attacks of Sept. 11. But to unequivocally condemn these attacks does not relieve us of the responsibility to *explain* them. Some U.S. policies that have led to antipathy, especially in the Middle East: U.S. support for antidemocratic regimes, and the overthrow of more democratic ones, like Iran's Mossedegh in 1953; the tenacity of U.S. support for sanctions against Iraq that have killed hundreds of thousands of children; U.S. arming of Israel and its support of Israeli occupation of the West Bank and Gaza; and the global economic system's relentless emphasis on profit that continues to dislocate cultural patterns and impoverishes millions around the world.

Terms like *terrorism, freedom, liberty, patriotism,* and *unity* evoke powerful images, and consequently must be critically examined. When Osama bin Laden was fighting Soviet troops in Afghanistan, President Reagan called him a "freedom fighter." Now he's a terrorist. In the 1980s the U.S. government considered Nelson Mandela a terrorist. Now he's a statesman. Language is marshaled for political ends, and we need to remember this.

Too often, students are denied knowledge about individuals and social movements that have made the world a better place. They learn that obedience is a synonym for patriotism and that citizenship gives you the right to vote and do as you're told. We urge students to question basic premises about terrorism and war, to gain permission to think independently from the Official Story.

Clearly, these principles remind us that if a better world is possible, we're the ones who have to build it.

Source: © 2002 Rethinking Schools, 1001 E. Keefe Avenue, Milwaukee, WI 53212. Phone (414) 964-9646 or (800) 669-4192; FAX: (414) 964-7220; Email: webrs@execpc.com

College Students Choose Conservatism

By Liz Marlantes, Staff Writer of *The Christian Science Monitor*

What might have been your reaction to a speech on the importance of protecting civil liberties (see the article below)? Why do you suppose the speaker was booed off the stage, and what does this suggest about the attitudes of present-day college students? As you read about the issues cited in this piece, think which side you would be most likely to take, and why.

When *Sacramento Bee* publisher Janis Heaphy delivered a commencement address at California State University, she chose a topic that might be expected to resonate among a young, idealistic student audience: the importance of protecting civil liberties.

Instead, Ms. Heaphy was booed off the stage.

The students' reaction to what they perceived as criticism of the government may just reflect the nearness of the terrorist attacks. But it might also be a sign of what some analysts see as an emerging shift toward more conservative politics.

Just as Pearl Harbor and Vietnam ushered in new cultural and political eras, Sept. 11 has shaped the outlook of the nation—and particularly the generation now coming of age—for years to come. Desire that government "do more" to solve the nation's problems is way up, for example, an approach that doesn't square with conservative politics. But attitudes on a variety of other issues—from support for the military and the use of American force abroad, to approval of President Bush and his administration's actions on civil liberties—seem to indicate a rightward tilt, which could translate into electoral gains for Republicans, and perhaps the start of a new chapter in politics.

"All this can be summed up as a shift in favor of more conservative and traditional politics," says David King, a political scientist at Harvard University in Cambridge, Mass. "The shift is not simply one along a policy dimension, but it's a generational shift."

The new mood has been most striking on college campuses, where conservatives note a falling off of certain liberal attitudes that have held sway there since the 1960s.

Consider this: At Ivy League schools, some of the longest lines at recruiting fairs are not for banks or consulting firms but for the FBI and CIA. A recent poll by Harvard's Institute of Politics found that 75 percent of college students trust the military to "do the right thing" all or most of the time, while 92 percent consider themselves patriotic.

"We're so used to thinking in terms of the '60s generation, that it's just stunning to see college students who like their country," says Shelby Steele, a fellow at the Hoover Institute at Stanford University in California. "It's sort of a reverse split from the '60s. In the '60s, the faculty was conservative and the students were liberal. Now, the students are more pro-American and the faculty is liberal."

A Trend Already in Progress

Some of these shifts in attitude were taking place well before Sept. 11—so the attacks have merely compounded the trend, analysts say. Support for certain government institutions, such as the military, has been rising for some time.

"It is remarkable in my lifetime to see the CIA go from revered in the '50s, to despised in the '60s, '70s, and '80s, to rehabilitated in the '90s—and now we're going back toward domestic surveillance," says Bruce 'Cain, a political scientist at the University of California at Berkeley. Likewise, he says, there's "absolutely" been a pro-military shift nationwide, "as the link between the military and personal safety became tighter"—though that support could diminish, he cautions, if the link becomes less clear.

A Boon to Republicans?

In the short term, all this could create a political climate more friendly to Republicans. Significantly, a new Ipsos-Reid/Cook Political Report poll shows that while Democrats had a nine-point lead in party identification—meaning more people identified themselves as Democrats—last August, Republicans have made gains since Sept. 11. One reason for this shift may simply be that President Bush has proved to be an extremely popular wartime president. During the boom years of the Clinton administration, analysts say, the public began to view the office of the president as almost irrelevant. But now, the events of Sept. 11 have "reestablished the president," says Floyd Ciruli, a Denver-based pollster. "And he happens to be a Republican."

Ciruli points out that President Bush's approval ratings remain extremely high even as the public's concern about the threat of terrorism is diminishing. "Bush has gained a level of public support for a length of time that indicates it's more than just doing a good job—that people may have bonded here," he says.

Still, some observers say that, whatever shift might be under way, it's likely to be short-lived. Even FDR saw his party lose seats in Congress as soon as the war ended.

"These kinds of events and challenges do have an impact, but it's interesting how we get back to fundamental domestic issues pretty quickly," says former

Massachusetts Gov. Michael Dukakis. Indeed, some analysts see the effects of Sept. 11 as transcending, rather than shaping, ideology. "Sept. 11 is likely to make an overall impression on all Americans, without changing the distribution of party or ideology," says political commentator Bill Schneider. "Ideology comes out of divisiveness, like the '60s or Clinton," he says. "The one thing about this entire conflict is, it is not divisive."

While Sept. 11 may not immediately change Americans' views on domestic issues like how to provide healthcare or help the economy, it has altered the nation's priorities—and may, in the long run, shape domestic politics in more subtle ways.

Professor King agrees that, whereas Vietnam and Watergate tended to have a polarizing effect on past generations, Sept. 11 is an event around which the entire country has essentially united. But this, too, can have a political impact: "Instead of polarizing or dividing a generation, this will give them a common vision or a common set of issues that we need to pay attention to," he says.

How Prejudice Distorts

Learning to Think Logically

The following article by education writer Alfie Kohn was rejected by several leading education publications that have often published his writings. "No one challenged the accuracy of anything in the piece," according to Kohn. "Rather, it was argued that there are times when it's not appropriate to say things even if they are true." Kohn was also disinvited as keynote speaker for the March meeting of the California League of Middle Schools (CLMS) conference. Apparently, someone on the CLMS board saw a copy of this essay (which had appeared only on Kohn's Web site) and convinced the executive director to break the contract with Kohn, even though his planned talk had nothing to do with Sept. 11. Why do you think the article was rejected? What do you make of Kohn's arguments? Are there "times when it's not appropriate to say things even if they are true?" Justify your answer.

Some events seem momentous when they occur but gradually fade from consciousness, overtaken by fresh headlines and the distractions of daily life. Only once in a great while does something happen that will be taught by future historians. Just such an incident occurred on Sept. 11, 2001. The deadly attacks on New York and Washington left us groping for support, for words, for a way to make meaning and recover our balance.

We have all suffered an attack that has stolen from us, individually and collectively, our sense of invincibility. Our airplanes can be turned into missiles. Our skyline can be altered. We can't be sure that our children are safe.

It is unimaginable that people could patiently plan such carnage, could wake up each morning, eat breakfast, and spend the day preparing to destroy thousands of innocent lives along with their own. But while the particulars seem unfathomable, the attack itself had a context and perhaps a motive that are perfectly comprehensible—and especially important for us to grasp.

The historical record suggests that the United States has no problem with terrorism as long as its victims don't live here or look like most of us. In the last couple of decades alone, we have bombed Libya, invaded Grenada, attacked Panama, and shelled Lebanon—killing civilians in each instance. We created and funded an army of terrorists to overthrow the elected government of Nicaragua and, when the World Court ruled that we must stop, we simply rejected the court's authority. We engineered coups in Iran, Zaire, Guatemala, and Chile (the last of which coincidentally also took place on Sept. 11).

In 1991, we killed more than 100,000 men, women, and children in Iraq, deliberately wiping out electricity and water supplies with the result that tens of thousands of civilians died from malnutrition and disease. We continue to vigorously defend (and subsidize) Israel's treatment of Palestinians, which has been condemned by human rights organizations and virtually every other nation on the planet. We have aided vile tyrants, including some who later turned against us: Manuel Noriega, Saddam Hussein, and, yes, Osama bin Laden (when his opposition to the Soviets served our purposes). We are not the only nation that has done such things, but we are the most powerful and, therefore, arguably the most dangerous.

Does any of this justify an act of terrorism against us? No. Our history may help to explain, but decidedly does not excuse, the taking of innocent lives. Nothing could. By the same token, though, the September attack does not justify a retaliatory war launched by our government that takes innocent lives abroad. Early polls showed overwhelming American support for revenge, even for killing civilians in Muslim countries. If this seems understandable given what has just happened, then the same must be said about the animosity of our attackers, some of whom may have suffered personally from U.S.-sponsored violence. Understandable in both cases—and excusable in neither.

But our broader obligation is to address what writer Martin Amis recently described as Americans' chronic "deficit of empathy for the sufferings of people far away." Schools should help children locate themselves in widening circles of care that extend beyond self, beyond country, to all humanity.

Likewise, education must be about developing the skills and disposition to question the official story, to view with skepticism the stark us-against-them (or us good, them bad) portrait of the world and the accompanying dehumanization of others that helps to explain that empathy deficit. Students should also be able to recognize dark historical parallels in the President's rhetoric, and to notice what is not being said or shown on the news.

One detail of the tragedy carries a striking pedagogical relevance. Official announcements in the south tower of the World Trade Center repeatedly instructed everyone in the building to stay put, which posed an agonizing choice: follow the official directive or disobey and evacuate.

Here we find a fresh reason to ask whether we are learning to think for ourselves or simply to do what we are told.

Ultimately, though, the standard by which to measure our schools is the extent to which the next generation comes to understand—and fully embrace—this simple truth: The life of someone who lives in Kabul or Baghdad is worth no less than the life of someone in New York or from our neighborhood.

SOURCE: © 2002 Rethinking Schools. 1001 E. Keefe Avenue, Milwaukee, WI 53212. Phone (414) 964-9646 or (800) 669-4192; FAX (414) 964-7220; Email webrs@execpc.com

Alfie Kohn (www.alfiekohn.org) is the author of eight books on education and human behavior, including *The Schools Our Children Deserve* and *What to Look for in a Classroom.* © 2001 by Alfie Kohn. Winter 2001/2002. This issue and many others are available for order online.

Where Does Prejudice Come From?

Where does racial–ethnic prejudice come from? How do moderately or highly prejudiced people end up that way? People are not born with stereotypes and prejudices. Research shows that they are learned and internalized through the socialization process, including both primary socialization (family, peers, and teachers) and secondary socialization (such as the media). Children imitate the attitudes of their parents, peers, and teachers. If the parent complains about "Japs taking away jobs" from Americans, then the child grows up thinking negatively about the Japanese, including Japanese Americans.

Attitudes about race are formed early in childhood, at about age three or four (Allport, 1954; Van Ausdale and Feagin, 1996). There is a very close correlation between the racial and ethnic attitudes of parents and those of their children (Ashmore and DelBoca, 1976). The more ethnically or racially prejudiced the parent, the more ethnically or racially prejudiced on average will be the child. Later in life, peers will reinforce these negative feelings, for example, by jeering at Japanese American children on their way to school in the morning.

A major vehicle for the communication of racial–ethnic attitudes to both young and old is the media, especially television, magazines, newspapers, and books. For many decades, African Americans, Hispanics, Native Americans, and Asians were rarely presented in the media, and then only in negatively stereotyped roles. The Chinese were shown in movies, magazines, and early television in the 1950s as buck-toothed buffoons who ran shirt laundries. Japanese Americans were depicted as sneaky and untrustworthy. Hispanics were shown as either ruthless banditos or playful, happy-go-lucky "Pedros" who took long siestas. American Indians were presented as either villains or subservient characters such as the Lone Ranger's famed sidekick, Tonto. Finally, there is the drearily familiar image of the black person as subservient, lazy, clowning, and bug-eyed, a stereotypical image that persisted from the late nineteenth century all the way through the 1950s and early 1960s (Thibodeau, 1989).

The late 1960s, which included the Black Power movement and greatly increased civil rights activity in the country, saw some improvements in media stereotypes, which continued into the 1970s and 1980s. During this time, the media became somewhat less culpable in fostering racial and ethnic prejudice. TV programs such as The Cosby Show, featuring an African American doctor (played by Bill Cosby), his lawyer wife (played by Phylicia Rashaad), their well-educated children, and their positive interactions with whites and Asians, may have contributed to blunting anti-black prejudice. The Huxtables were a well-to-do family headed by black professionals and thus could serve as positive role models for black youth, but they also underscore what African Americans and other minorities in society have not attained. As one critic wryly noted from observing other black sitcoms, black people seem to be doing better on TV than in real life (Gates, 1992).

Despite the Huxtables, careful content analyses have shown that improvements in the portrayal of minorities on television have been minimal. For example, positive crossrace interactions have always been infrequent, even into the 1990s. During this period, positive interactions between blacks and whites (those in which blacks and whites interact as professional equals or friends) have been a mere 5 percent or less of total interactions, including dramas, comedies, and other types of television shows (Wei et al., 1990).

SOURCE: This excerpt is taken from Margaret L. Andersen and Howard F. Taylor, *Sociology: Understanding a Diverse Society,* Second Edition (Wadsworth Publishing, 2001).

Arab Americans: Confronting Prejudice

Whenever violent confrontations in the Middle East reach one of their periodic surges, Marvin Wingfield braces for the worst: ethnic taunts, stereotypes in the mass media, and violence against Arab Americans.

"The pattern seems to be that whenever there is a crisis in the Mideast, the incidence of hate crimes against Arab Americans increases," says Wingfield, coordinator of conflict resolution for the American-Arab Anti-Discrimination Committee (ADC) in Washington, D.C. "It becomes even more pronounced when the United States is involved directly."

The backlash, Wingfield notes, is simply one manifestation of centuries-old misperceptions in the West about the nature of Arab culture. Colonial arrogance, he says, fostered stereotypes of Arabs as camel-riding hedonists and devious traders.

The more modern stereotype of the "Muslim terrorist" led initially to false assumptions about the Oklahoma City bombing.

Another offshoot of this arrogance, Wingfield points out, is the tendency of many white Americans to view other broad segments of the population as homogeneous. References to "the black community," for example, ignore the diversity among African Americans and their interests. Similarly, "the Arab World" is vast and varied. Most Arabs speak Arabic, and most are Islamic, but neither attribute is a prerequisite for "Arab-ness."

Part of the ADC's mission is to help combat stereotypes and reduce anti-Arab hate crimes through educational and political programs. A large part of this effort involves encouraging Arab Americans to play higher profile roles in their communities.

The ADC has prepared guidelines for community activists to follow in trying to increase the presence and awareness of Arab culture in school districts. Called "Working with School Systems," it describes various scenarios for involvement, ranging from volunteering at the classroom level to lobbying for districtwide curriculum development. One notable success occurred in Portland, Oregon, where Arab American activists persuaded the local newspaper, *The Oregonian,* to include a special Mideast page in its annual "Newspapers in Education" issue.

In metro Detroit, several programs through public schools and nonprofit organizations work to bridge differences between Arab Americans and the broader community. An organization called Arab-Jewish Friends runs an annual contest in which Arab and Jewish high school students cowrite essays. It helps the students break down their own stereotypes by working with students from cultures with whom they have historically been at odds.

"We have them write about issues that are important to Arabs and Jews," says Jeannie Weiner, one of the contest's founders. "It's good for them to put these thoughts down in writing. And it's good for us because we can use the essays as tools to show what the kids are thinking."

Another project, directed by Wayne State University's Center for Peace and Conflict Studies, brought together students from high schools in suburban Dearborn, where metro Detroit's Arab-Muslim population is concentrated, to negotiate a contract for behavior among Arab and non-Arab students. They quickly found common ground in their dissatisfaction with the district's multicultural programs and petitioned school officials for classes in such topics as world religions.

Little came of the demands, but the students learned that they have more in common than they thought, says Mickey Petera, assistant director of the Peace and Conflict Studies Department. "We need to start at the elementary and preschool levels," she says, "and raise a generation of students that can get along."

SOURCE: *Teaching Tolerance* (Spring 1997): 49. This article is reprinted by permission of *Teaching Tolerance,* a publication of the Southern Poverty Law Center.

Two Views of Islam and Terrorism

In the following article, the writer blames the media for creating the impression that all followers of Islam are, in effect, terrorists who are at war with the United States and other democracies. The article also underscores the fact that Islam, Judaism, and Christianity are closely related to one another. It might be revealing to do some research on your own about Islam. If what the writer says is true, are the media—especially television—to be blamed for fostering the view that Islam = Terrorism?

The American view of Islam has been influenced by various presentations of Islamic extremism in the electronic media, and it has been influenced by popular misconceptions and stereotypes. An analysis of Western attitudes towards Islam shows that many are incorrect. Islam is a religion more closely related to traditional Judaism than Christianity, even though all three religions worship the same God.

Islam is no more a religion of violent fanatics than Judaism or Christianity. Yet, many Americans have little knowledge of Islam. Today most Americans subscribe to one of two positions about Islam and terrorism. One view states that Islamic fundamentalism is related to political violence in the Middle East. In this view, Islam sees itself in a global war with the West. Since Muslims in general see themselves in a struggle—not in a war—with the West for social and political reasons, some have concluded that popular support of militant Islam indicates an "Islamic terrorism" exists.

Others are not so quick to accept such logic. Radical groups of Islamics in Egypt, Saudi Arabia, Iran, and other areas appear to have declared war on the United States and its allies. Yet many believe such fears are unfounded and explain that, while there are pockets of Islamic extremism in the Middle East that sustain terrorism, these segments are isolated and divided. There is a broad spectrum of religious and political beliefs in Islam that rejects violence. Therefore, some urge caution in labeling Middle Eastern violence as "Islamic terrorism."

Others add that American fears and misunderstandings of Islam make it appear as if fundamentalists were united and threatening to gather the Middle East in a war against the West. This is not the case. Fundamentalists are a divided lot, just as religious fundamentalists in the United States are divided. The history of the West and the Middle East involves centuries of religious wars. More can be gained by examining the religious similarities between the two regions than by using such terms as "Islamic terrorism."

SOURCE: The excerpt is taken from Jonathan R. White, *Terrorism: An Introduction,* Third Edition (Wadsworth Publishing, 2002).

Osama's Private War Against the United States

Are bin Laden's terrorist actions done in the name of a country, a political party, a religion? Or does this man from a wealthy family possess the wherewithal, as this article claims, to take action on his own? Is wealth by itself a destructive force, or does that depend on the way it is used? Name some incidents in which money was used for evil purposes and some others in which money was used for good deeds.

Osama bin Laden redefined the meaning of terrorism in the modern world. With the wealth of his construction empire as backing, bin Laden transcended the state and operated on his own. Such entrepreneurial efforts gave him the freedom to finance and command his own terror network. His connections with his Afghans and his reputation as a warrior give him legitimacy. Bin Laden did not need a government to support his operations. He had the money, personnel, material, and infrastructure necessary to maintain a campaign of terrorism. He only needed a place to hide.

In 1996, Osama bin Laden officially "declared war" on the United States. He followed this by two religious rulings, called *fatwas,* in 1998, which called for the killing of any American anywhere in the world.

In August 1998, bin Laden's terrorists were behind two horrendous attacks in Africa, bombing the American embassies in Nairobi, Kenya, and Dar es Salaam, Tanzania. The Nairobi bomb killed 213 people and injured 4,500. The Dar es Salaam explosion killed 12 and wounded 85.

SOURCE: The excerpt is taken from Jonathan R. White, *Terrorism: An Introduction,* Third Edition (Wadsworth Publishing, 2002).

Discussion Questions

1. Describe as honestly as you can how much of an influence terrorism has had on your life. Are you more careful, for example, about where you go after dark? What else? Do you feel you are more watchful than your friends or less watchful? Explain.
2. As a result of the increase in the volume of news about terrorism, do you think America is more or less vulnerable now? Explain.
3. How should we educate students in the public schools about terrorism? Would it be better to ignore it, or better to offer some logical commentary? What would that commentary include?
4. How have movies and TV programs been affected by terrorism? Do you think movies and TV programs should emphasize more patriotic themes? Explain.
5. How best can Americans commemorate September 11? Should September 11 be a national holiday? Why or why not?

Writing a Letter

Imagine you are writing a letter to your grandchildren. Describe how terrorism and threats of terrorism affected your generation.

Suggestions for Further Reading

Chapter 1

Strategies for Success

Gordon, Virginia. *Foundations: A Reader for New College Students.* Belmont, CA: Wadsworth, 1995.

Newman, Richard. *The Complete Guide to College Success: What Every Student Needs to Know.* New York: New York University Press, 1995.

Pathways to Success. Washington, DC: Howard University Press, 1997.

Siebert, Al, & Bernadine Gilpin. *The Adult Student's Guide to Survival and Success.* Portland, OR: Practical Psychology Press, 1997.

Tufariello, Ann Hunt. *Up Your Grades: Proven Strategies for Academic Success.* Lincolnwood, IL: VGM Career Horizons, 1997.

Time Management

Campbell, William E. *The Power to Learn: Helping Yourself to College Success,* "Managing Your Time" (Chapter 2). Belmont, CA: Wadsworth, 1997.

Smith, Laurence N., & Timothy Walter. *The Adult Learner's Guide to College Success,* rev. ed., "Five Strategies for Time Management" (Chapter 3). Belmont,CA: Wadsworth, 1995.

Sotiriou, Peter Elias. *Integrating College Study Skills: Reasoning in Reading, Listening, and Writing,* 4th ed., "Your Learning Inventory: Your Learning Style, Study Time, and Study Area" (Chapter 2). Belmont, CA: Wadsworth, 1996.

Wahlstrom, Carl, & Brian K. Williams. *Learning Success: Being Your Best at College and Life,* "Time" (Chapter 4). Belmont, CA: Wadsworth, 1996.

Chapter 2

Learning Styles

Lawrence, Gordon. *People Types and Tiger Stripes.* Gainesville, FL: Center for the Application of Psychological Types, 1982.

Malone, John C., Jr. *Theories of Learning: A Historical Approach.* Belmont, CA: Wadsworth, 1991.

Perry, William. *Forms of Intellectual and Ethical Development in the College Years: A Scheme.* New York: Holt, Rinehart & Winston, 1970.

Chapter 3

Critical Thinking

Browne, M. Neil. *Asking the Right Questions: A Guide to Critical Thinking.* Englewood Cliffs, NJ: Prentice-Hall, 1997.

Daly, William. "Thinking As an Unnatural Act." *Journal of Developmental Education,* 18(2) Winter 1994.

Daly, William. *Teaching Independent Thinking.* Columbia, SC: National Resource Center for the First Year Experience and Students in Transition, 1995.

Smith, Donald E. P., Glenn M. Knudsvig, & Tim Walter. *Critical Thinking: Building the Basics.* Belmont, CA: Wadsworth Publishing Company, 1997.

Whitehead, Alfred North. *The Aims of Education.* New York: Mentor, 1949 (Originally published 1929).

Chapter 4

Listening, Note Taking, and Participating

Allen, Sheila. *Making Connections.* "The Student's Role as Learner," Unit 4. Fort Worth, TX: Harcourt Brace College Publishers, 1998.

Chaffee, John. *The Thinker's Guide to College Success,* "Reading Critically" (Chapter 6). Boston: Houghton Mifflin, 1995.

Laskey, Marcia L., & Paula W. Gibson. *College Study Strategies: Thinking and Learning,* "Questioning Strategies That Lead to Critical Thinking" (Chapter 11). Boston: Allyn & Bacon, 1997.

Pauk, Walter. *How to Study in College,* 6th ed., "Learning from Your Textbook" (Chapter 11), "Noting What Is Important" (Chapter 12), "Thinking Visually" (Chapter 13). Boston: Houghton Mifflin, 1997.

Seyler, Dorothy U. *Steps to College Reading,* "Developing a Reading Strategy" (Chapter 2). Needham Heights, MA: Allyn & Bacon, 1998.

Chapter 5

Reading to Remember

Allen, Sheila. *Making Connections.* "The Student's Role As Learner," Unit 4. Fort Worth, TX: Harcourt Brace College Publishers, 1998.

Chaffee, John. *The Thinker's Guide to College Success,* "Reading Critically" (Chapter 6). Boston: Houghton Mifflin, 1995.

Laskey, Marcia L., & Paula W. Gibson. *College Study Strategies: Thinking and Learning,* "Questioning Strategies That Lead to Critical Thinking" (Chapter 11). Boston: Allyn & Bacon, 1997.

Pauk, Walter. *How to Study in College,* 6th ed., "Learning from Your Textbook" (Chapter 11), "Noting What Is Important" (Chapter 12), "Thinking Visually" (Chapter 13). Boston: Houghton Mifflin, 1997.

Seyler, Dorothy U. *Steps to College Reading,* "Developing a Reading Strategy" (Chapter 2). Needham Heights, MA: Allyn & Bacon, 1998.

Van Blerkom, Dianna L. *College Study Skills: Becoming a Strategic Learner,* 2nd ed., "Reading Your Textbook" (Chapter 6), and "Marking Your Textbook" (Chapter 7). Belmont, CA: Wadsworth, 1997.

Chapter 6

Exams and Quizzes

Campbell, William E. *The Power to Learn: Helping Yourself to College Success,* "Remembering and Reproducing What You Learn" (Chapter 6). Belmont, CA: Wadsworth, 1997.

Galica, Gregory S. *The Blue Book: A Student's Guide to Essay Exams.* Troy, MO: Harcourt Brace Jovanovich, 1991.

Longman, Debbie Guice, & Rhonda Holt Atkinson. *College Learning and Study Skills,* 3rd ed., "Tests: Preparing for and Taking Them" (Chapter 7). Minneapolis/St. Paul: West, 1993.

McKowen, Clark. *Get Your "A" Out of College: Mastering the Hidden Rules of the Game,* rev. ed., "The Art of Remembering" (Chapter 2) and "Raising Test Scores" (Chapter 3). Menlo Park, CA: Crisp Publications, 1996.

Pauk, Walter. *How to Study in College,* 8th ed., "Mastering Objective Tests" (Chapter 15). Boston: Houghton Mifflin, 1997.

Chapter 7

Developing Values

Bok, D. C. (1996). *The State of the Nation: Government and the Quest for a Better Society.* Cambridge, MA: Harvard University Press.

Braithwaite, V. A., & W. A. Scott. (1991). "Values." In Robinson, J. P., P. R. Shaver, & L. S. Wrightsman. (Eds.), *Measures of Personality and Social Psychological Attitudes,* San Diego, CA: Academic Press, Inc., pp. 661–753.

Gerson, K. (1991). "Coping with Commitment: Dilemmas and Conflicts of Family Life". In Alan Wolfe (Ed.), *America at Century's End.* Berkeley, CA: University of California Press, pp. 35–57.

Hodgkinson, V., & M. Weitzman. (1984). *Dimensions of the Independent Sector: A Statistical Profile.* Washington, DC: Independent Sector.

Index of Social Health. (1994). Monitoring the Social Well-Being of the Nation, Fordham Institute for Innovation in Social Policy, New York.

Jowell, R., S. Witherspoon, & L. Brook. (Eds.). (1989) *British Social Attitudes: Special International Report,* pp. 46 and 55.

Lynd, R. S. (1939). *Knowledge for What?* Princeton, NJ: Princeton University Press.

Putman, R. (1995). "Bowling Alone: America's Declining Social Capital," *Journal of Democracy,* 65.

Rokeach, M. (1973). *The Nature of Human Values.* New York: Free Press.

Rokeach, M. (1979). *Understanding Human Values: Individual and Societal.* New York: Free Press.

Shaver, J. P., & W. Strong. (1982). *Facing Value Decisions: Rationale-Building for Teachers,* New York: Teacher College Press, 17–34.

Stacey, J. (1991). "Backward toward the Postmodern Family: Reflections on Gender, Kinship, and Class in the Silicon Valley." In Alan Wolfe (Ed.), *America at Century's End.* University of California Press: Berkeley, CA.

Trudeau, G. B. (1972). *Doonesbury.* New York: Universal Press Syndicate.

Wolfe, A. (Ed.). (1991). *America at Century's End.* Berkeley, CA: University of California Press.

Chapter 8

Careers and Courses; New Economy

Burton-Jones, Alan. *Knowledge Capitalism: Business, Work and Learning in the New Economy.* Oxford University Press, 1999.

Cortada, James. *21st Century Business: Managing and Working in the New Digital Economy.* New York: Prentice-Hall, 2000.

Herzenberg, Stephen, et al. *New Rules for a New Economy: Employment and Opportunity in Postindustrial America.* Cornell University Press, 2000.

Jones, Candace, & R. J. DeFillippi. "Back to the Future in Films." *Academy of Management Executives.* 1996, Vol 10(4), 89–103.

Jones, Laurie Both. *The Path.* New York, NY: Hyperion, 1996.

Kelly, Kevin. *New Rules for the New Economy: 10 Radical Strategies for a Connected World.* Penguin, 1999.

Reich, Robert. *The Work of Nations: Preparing for 21st Century Capitalism.* Vintage Books, 1992.

Skill Development

Evers, Frederick T., et al. *The Bases of Competence: Skills for Lifelong Learning and Employability.* San Francisco, CA: Jossey-Bass, 1998.

Holland, John. *The Self-Directed Search Professional Manual.* Gainesville, FL: Psychological Assessment Resources, 1985.

Keirsey, David. *Please Understand Me II: Temperament, Character, Intelligence.* Del Mar, CA: Prometheus, Nemesis Book Co., 1998.

Scheeze, Adele M. *Jumpstart Your Career in College: Build the Skills to Build Your Future.* Kaplan, 2000.

Tulgan, Bruce. *Career Skills for the New Economy.* Human Resource Development Press, 2000.

Young, Stephen. *Straight Talk on College: An Employer's Perspective: 100 Tips for Success in College and Beyond.* Paragon Press, 1998.

Career Guides

Berg, A. *Finding the Work You Love: A Woman's Career Guide.* San Jose, CA: Resource Publications, 1993.

Bolles, Richard. *What Color Is Your Parachute? 2001: A Practical Manual for Job Hunters and Career Changers.* Berkeley, CA: Ten Speed Press, 2000.

Coombs, Patrick. *Majoring in Success: Make College Easier, Fire Up Your Dreams and Get a Very Cool Job.* Berkeley, CA: Ten Speed Press, 2000.

Field, S. *100 Best Careers for the 21st Century.* New York: Macmillan, 1996.

Web Sites

www.act.org

www.dbm.com/jobguide/index.html (the Riley Guide to Employment Opportunities and Job Resources)

www.fastcompany.com/homepage (magazine dealing with dynamics of new economy)

www.jobweb.com/catapult (springboard to career- and job-related sites)

www.review.com (the Princeton Review has a great career assessment center)

www.stats.bls.gov/ocohome.html (source of career information)

Chapter 9

Creating Diverse Relationships

Bass, Ellen, & Kate Kaufman. *Free Your Mind: The Book for Gay, Lesbian, and Bisexual Youth—And Their Allies.* New York: HarperCollins, 1996.

Bellah, Robert, et al. *Habits of the Heart: Individualism and Commitment in American Life.* New York: Harper & Row, 1985.

Bowden, Randall, & Richard Merritt, Jr. "The Adult Learner Challenge: Instructionally and Administratively." *Education,* Spring 1995 v115 n3 p426(7).

Cosgrove, Melba, Harold Bloomfield, & Peter McWilliams. *How to Survive the Loss of a Love.* New York: Bantam, 1976.

Daloz, Laurent, A. Parks, et al. *Common Fire: Lives of Commitment in a Complex World.* Boston: Beacon, 1996.

Gaines, Stanley O. *Culture, Ethnicity, and Personal Relationship Processes.* New York: Routledge, 1997.

Hendricks, Gay, & Kathlyn Hendricks. *Conscious Loving: The Journey to Co-Commitment—A Way to Be Fully Together Without Giving Up Yourself.* New York: Bantam, 1990.

Heuberger, Barbara, Diane Gerber, & Reed Anderson. "Strength Through Cultural Diversity," *College Teaching,* Summer 1999 v47 i3 p107.

Hirsh, Sandra, & Jean Kummerow. *LifeTypes.* New York: Warner, 1989.

Lapchick, Richard. "Still a White Man's World (report on gender and race diversity of college athletic departments.)" Brief Article. *The Sporting News,* August 23, 1999 v223 i34 p12.

Myers, David G. *The Pursuit of Happiness: Who Is Happy and Why.* New York: Morrow, 1992.

Seligman, Martin P. *What You Can Change . . . and What You Can't.* New York: Fawcett Books, 1995.

Service in Higher Education. Providence, RI: Campus Compact, 1996.

Simplicio, Joseph. "Teaching a simple lesson in fostering tolerance regarding personal choices." *Education,* Fall 1995 v116 n1 p148(5).

Taylor, Ula. "Proposition 209 and the affirmative action debate on the University of California campuses." *Feminist Studies,* Spring 1999 v25 i1 p95(1).

Chapter 10

Sex

Elliott, L., C. Brantley, & C. Johnson. (1997). *Sex on Campus: The Naked Truth About the Real Sex Lives of College Students.* New York: Random House.

Gray, J. (1993). *Men Are from Mars, Women Are from Venus: A Practical Guide for Improving Communication and Getting What You Want in Your Relationships.* New York: Harper-Collins.

Hoffamn, A., J. Schuh, & R. Fenske. (1998). *Violence on Campus.* Gaithersburg, MD: Aspen.

Koman, A. (1997). *How to Mend a Broken Heart: Letting Go and Moving On.* Chicago, IL: Contemporary Books.

Lear, D. (1997). *Sex and Sexuality: Risk and Relationship in the Age of AIDS.* Newbury Park, CA: Sage.

Nevid, J. S. (1995). *Choices: Sex in the Age of STDs.* Boston: Allyn & Bacon.

Powell, E. (1996). *Sex on Your Terms.* Boston: Allyn & Bacon.

Sanday, P. R. (1992). *Fraternity Gang Rape: Sex, Brotherhood, and Privilege on Campus.* New York: New York University Press.

Tannen, Deborah. *You Just Don't Understand: Women and Men in Conversation.* New York: Ballantine, 1990.

Alcohol

Berkowitz, A. D. (2000). The social norms approach: Theory and research. Internet article at *http://www.edc.org/hec/socialnorms/theory.html*

Berkowitz, A. D., & H. W. Perkins. (1986). Problem Drinking Among College Students: A Review of Recent Research. *Journal of American College Health, 35,* 21–28.

Haines, M., & S. F. Spear. (1996). Changing the perception of the norm: A strategy to decrease binge drinking among college students. *Journal of American College Health, 45*(3), 134–140.

Keeling, R. P. (2000). Social norms research in college health. *Journal of American College Health, 49,* 53–56.

Marlatt, G. A., J. S. Baer, D. R. Kivlahan, L. A. Dimeff, M. E. Larimer, L. A. Quigley, J. M. Somers, & E. Williams. (1998). Screening and brief intervention for high-risk college student drinkers: Results from a 2-year follow-up assessment. *Journal of Consulting and Clinical Psychology, 66*(4), 604–615.

Meilman, P. W., J. R. Cashin, J. McKillip, & C. A Presley. (1998). Understanding the three national databases on collegiate alcohol and drug use. *Journal of American College Health, 46,* 159–162.

Nye, E. C., G. Agostinelli, & J. E. Smith. (1999). Enhancing alcohol problem recognition: A self-regulation model for the effects of self-focusing and normative information. *Journal of Studies on Alcohol, 60,* 685–693.

Perkins, H. W., & A. D. Berkowitz. (1986). Perceiving the community norms of alcohol use among students: Some research implications for campus alcohol education programming. *International Journal of the Addictions, 21,* 961–976.

Perkins, H. W., & H. Wechsler. (1996). Variation in perceived college drinking norms and its impact on alcohol abuse: A nationwide study. *Journal of Drug Issues, 26*(4), 961–974.

Werch, C. E., D. M. Pappas, J. M. Carlson, C. C. DiClemente, P. S. Chally, & J. A. Sinder. (2000). Results of a social norm intervention to prevent binge drinking among first-year residential college students. *Journal of American College Health, 49,* 85–92.

Index/Glossary

A

Abstinence, sexual, 174, 178
Abstract thinking, 48
Abusive relationships, 179–180
Academic advising   counseling by a college faculty or staff member whose duties include advising students on their choice of courses and majors, fulfillment of various academic requirements, and other matters.
and career planning, 141, 142–143
as success strategy, 7
Academic freedom   the ability of faculty and students to pursue whatever inquiry they wish without undue external influence and to speak about it in classrooms without fear of censorship; it can also be described as the open search for truth, honesty, collegiality, and civility, as well as a tolerance for dissenting views. 54–55
Academic honesty, 95–97, 106, 110
Acquaintance rape   rape by an individual who has some prior acquaintance and presumed friendship with the victim. 154, 180
Active learning, 49–55
and academic freedom, 54–55
benefits of, 6, 50
and collaboration, 52
exercises, 57–58
Internet exercises, 56
journal, 59
and learning teams, 52–53
one-minute paper technique, 51–52, 54
personal resources, 61–62
self-assessment exercise, 44
and teachers, 6, 50, 51, 53–54
See also Classroom learning
Activities. *See* Campus activities
Adult students. *See* **Returning students**
Advising. *See* **Academic advising**
Aesthetic values, 118
African American students, 152
AIDS, 177
Alcoholism, 183

Alcohol use, 181–192
and behavior, 186–187
and blood alcohol content, 185–186
consequences of, 189–190
exercises, 196
heavy drinking, 187–189
Internet exercises, 193
journal, 197
long-term effects of, 190–192
myths about, 183–185
personal resources, 199
reasons for, 182–183
and sexual assault, 154
America at Century's End (Wolfe), 120
Artistic personality type, 136, 137
Assertiveness   behavior that is clear, direct, respectful, and responsible; behavior that permits a person to stand up for his or her rights without denying others their rights. 8
Attendance. *See* Class participation
Auditory (aural) learning style, 29, 66, 70

B

BAC (blood alcohol content), 185–186
Battering, 179–180
Bigotry. *See* **Prejudice**
Binge drinking, 187–189
Birth control, 171–175
Black students, 152
Block scheduling, 19. *See also* Time management
Blood alcohol content (BAC), 185–186
Blume, Steven, 32–33
Bok, Derek, 122–124
Breaking up, 155–156
Bulletin. *See* **Catalog**

C

Campus activities, 7, 132, 160–161
Campus culture, 152–153, 183
Career counseling   a variety of career-related services such as self-assessment and interest tests, job search workshops, decision-making workshops, and résumé workshops, usually offered by counseling, student affairs, or career centers. 7
See also Career planning
Career planning, 130–148
and academic advising, 141, 142–143
and college catalog, 144
and economic changes, 131, 132–134
exercises, 146
experience, 138–139
factors affecting, 134–136
Holland model, 136–138
Internet exercises, 145
journal, 147
and majors, 131–132
personal resources, 148
and quality of life, 11
résumés/cover letters, 139–142
support services, 7, 132
See also Career planning exercises; Employment
Career planning exercises
alcohol use, 191
classroom learning, 75
critical thinking, 49
diversity, 162
learning styles, 34
reading, 87
summer jobs, 138
test preparation, 98
Catalog   the official publication of the institution, containing information about its regulations, requirements, and procedures, as well as opportunities for growth as a college student. It includes general information, admissions information, general academic regulations, general nonacademic information, financial aid and scholarship information, and academic programs. Catalogs usually include an academic calendar. In Canada, the catalog is called a calendar. 144
Celibacy, 178
Cervical cancer, 176

Cervical cap, 173

Cheating. *See* Academic honesty

Chlamydia, 175

Chugging, 187

Chunking, 81–82

Class participation, 68–69, 74–75
and active learning, 50, 51, 54
and listening, 6, 65, 68
as success strategy, 5, 6
See also Note taking

Classroom learning, 64–78
and class participation, 68–69, 74–75
and critical thinking, 67
exercises, 76
journal, 77
and learning styles, 65–66
listening, 6, 65, 68, 76
and note taking, 64–65, 69–73
personal resources, 78
preparation, 67–68, 73
and reviewing, 72–74
See also Class participation; Note taking

Clubs. *See* Campus activities

Coitus interruptus, 173

Collaborative learning, 34, 52. *See also* Study groups

College catalog, 144

Combs, Patrick, 131

Commuter students students who live off campus and have to commute, or travel, to campus each day. Includes about 80 percent of all U.S. college students today. 19

Companionate love, 154

Competition, positive, 52

Computers, 7, 72. *See also* **Internet**

Condoms, 173, 178, 179

Contraception, 171–175

Conventional personality type, 136–137

Cooperative (co-op) education programs that provide an opportunity to work in academic major-related settings off campus in public and private agencies, as well as in business and industry, either by parallel scheduling (going to school part-time and working part-time) or by alternate scheduling (staying out of school for an academic term and working full-time). 138, 161

Cornell format for note taking, 69, 70, 72–73

Counseling a wide variety of services to which students are entitled based on their payment of tuition. Most campuses provide confidential professional counseling and referral services in numerous different offices, including admissions, financial aid, residence halls, career planning,

placement, veterans' affairs, study skills, academic advising, and counseling. *See* Academic advising; Support services

Courses. *See* Class participation; Classroom learning; **Majors**

Cover letters, 141–142

Creative thinking, 48

Critical thinking careful observation of a problem or phenomenon followed by thoughtful, organized analysis resulting in a logical, reasoned response. 45–49
and classroom learning, 67
exercises, 57–58
Internet exercises, 56
journal, 59
personal resources, 60–61
self-assessment exercise, 44
as success strategy, 6
and test preparation, 94

Critical thinking exercises
active learning, 54
career planning, 133
classroom learning, 74
diversity, 151
learning styles, 30
reading, 83
sexuality, 175
success strategies, 9
test preparation, 103
values, 123

Criticism, 6

Crowe, Russell, 116

Cultural pluralism a concept of the integration of various cultures into a larger society that envisions continuing individual adherence to and general respect for separate cultural traditions. *See* **Diversity**

Culture, defined, 152

Cuseo, Joseph, 52

D

Daily plans. *See* Planners

Daly, William T., 47

Databases computer application programs for categorizing, storing, and manipulating large amounts of data. 7

Date (acquaintance) rape, 154, 180

Depo-Provera, 172

Diaphragm, 172–173

Diet. *See* Nutrition

Digest of Education Statistics, 20

Disabilities, students with, 159

Discrimination, 151, 161–162

Discussion classes, 70–71

Distractions, 19–20

Diversity a reference to the growing variety of college students and faculty bodies, which include men, women, minorities, foreign students, and other groups that have been underrepresented on college campuses in the past. 150–153
and discrimination, 161–162
exercises, 164–165
and friendship, 157
gay/lesbian/bisexual students, 157–158, 163
increase in, 9
Internet exercises, 163
journal, 167
personal resources, 168
returning students, 158
students with disabilities, 159
and study groups, 32, 52
See also Learning styles

Dropping a course most colleges allow students to drop (or quit) a course without penalty during specified periods of time. When dropping a course, you must follow the proper procedures, which include completing certain forms and obtaining official signatures. If you're receiving financial aid, your status may change if you drop a course. 19, 97

Drug use, 177, 193. *See also* Alcohol use

E

Email electronic mail. Various systems by which computers are linked so that personal computers can be used to send and receive messages and information. 159–160. *See also* **Internet**

Employment
and critical thinking, 46
during college, 6, 138
effects of college education on later, 9–10
and time management, 19
See also Career planning

Enterprising personality type, 136, 137

Essay tests, 102–103

Ethnicity, defined, 152

Examinations. *See* Test preparation

Exercise, 98

Exercises
active learning, 57–58
alcohol use, 196
career planning, 146
classroom learning, 76
critical thinking, 57–58

diversity, 164–165
learning styles, 35–38
note taking, 76
reading, 90
relationships, 165–166
sexuality, 194–195
success strategies, 21–22
test preparation, 107–108
time management, 4
values, 126
See also Career planning exercises;
Critical thinking exercises; Internet
exercises; Self-assessment exercises;
Values exercises
Expectations, 7
Extracurricular activities. *See* Campus
activities
Extroverted personality preference,
29, 31

F

Family
and alcohol use, 182
relationships with, 7, 156–157,
165–166
and values, 116, 121, 122
Feeling learning style, 30
Feldman, Robert, 158
Female condoms, 173
Financial aid, 19
Financial aid package   the total
amount of aid awarded to you.
Financial aid   student scholarships,
grants, and loans. Some forms of
financial aid are gifts, but others are
loans that must be repaid with interest. Some aid is offered only to new
college students, while other sources
of financial aid are available to all students. To determine your eligibility
for any aid, see your financial aid
counselor. The application process
for financial aid for a fall semester
usually begins during the preceding
January.
Financial need   the eligibility for
financial aid you are determined to
have based on need; mostcommonly
determined through the federal
needs analysis system (the congres-
sional methodology).
Flaming   highly emotional, highly
critical messages via email.
Flash cards, 101
Fraternities/sororities, 160
Freedom, 8–9
Free time, 13, 14
Friendship, 157–160
and alcohol use, 183

and breaking up, 155
and values, 115, 126
See also Relationships
Fussman, Cal, 105

G

Gay/lesbian/bisexual students, 157–158,
163
Gerson, Kathleen, 121
Gift assistance   any type of financial
aid that does not have to be repaid.
Goal-setting
and academic honesty, 97
and career planning, 146
and reading, 83
as success strategy, 12
and time management, 14, 20
Gonorrhea, 176
Grades, 55, 96
Grades   most schools use the A–F
system. A is the highest grade, and
F means failure. A–D are passing
grades for which you will earn
points and credits. If you transfer
colleges, however, the D grades
may not transfer. Most colleges
require a minimum 2.0 GPA, or C
average, for graduation; in addition,
you might lose financial aid, housing, and other benefits when your
GPA falls below a certain level. Bad
grades and low GPAs also may lead
to dismissal or suspension. Some
schools have pass/fail grades (P/F
or S/U) and an incomplete grade (I),
the latter representing work not
completed during the term it was
taken.
Grants   a type of financial assistance
that does not have to be repaid.
Greek organizations (fraternities/
sororities), 160
Groups. *See* Campus activities; Study
groups

H

Health, 7, 98. *See also* Alcohol use; Drug
use; Sexuality; Stress
Helping resources. *See* Support services
Hepatitis B, 176–177
Hepatitis C, 177
Herpes, 176
High school–college contrasts
active learning, 53–54
critical thinking, 45
personal freedom, 8–9
HIV/AIDS   acquired immune deficiency
syndrome; a sexually transmitted

disease for which there is currently
no known cure. As the disease progresses, it gradually breaks down
the body's immune system and
thus lowers its defense mechanisms,
making it impossible for the body to
function normally or properly. 177
Holland, John, 136–138
Homework, 5, 71–72. *See also* Time
management
Homosexual students. *See* Gay/lesbian/
bisexual students
Honor codes. *See* Academic honesty
Human papillomavirus (HPV), 175–176

I

Income, 9–10
InfoTrac, 19. *See also* Internet
exercises
Institutional aid   Financial aid
awarded from the college or university's budget and not from federal or
state aid programs.
Instrumental values, 118
Interactive learning style, 66, 70, 72, 82,
97
Internet   a worldwide system of
telecommunication connections and
procedures that lets computer users
exchange messages and information
via computer.
addiction, 21
and relationships, 159–160
skills, 7
See also Internet exercises
Internet exercises
academic honesty, 106
active learning, 56
alcohol/drug use, 193
career planning, 145
classroom learning, 75
college statistics, 20
critical thinking, 56
diversity, 163
learning styles, 35
reading, 89
relationships, 163–164
sexuality, 192–193
test preparation, 107
time management, 21
values, 125
Internships, 138
Intimacy. *See* Sexuality
Intrauterine device (IUD), 172
Intrinsic values, 118
Introverted personality preference, 29,
31, 34
Intuitive personality preference, 29–30,
31, 32–34

Investigative personality type, 136, 137
IUD (intrauterine device), 172

J

Jobs. *See* Career planning; Employment
Journal
    active learning, 59
    alcohol/drug use, 197
    career planning, 147
    classroom learning, 77
    critical thinking, 59
    diversity, 167
    learning styles, 39
    reading, 91
    relationships, 167
    sexuality, 197
    success strategies, 23
    test preparation, 109
    time management, 23
    values, 127
Judging personality preference, 30, 31
Jung, Carl, 29, 153

K

Kinesthetic learning style, 66
Kipling, Rudyard, 133

L

Learning disabilities, 159
Learning styles, 28–40
    and classroom learning, 65–66
    exercises, 35–38
    journal, 39
    and note taking, 72
    and personality, 29–32, 35–38
    personal resources, 40
    as success strategy, 6
    and teaching styles, 32–34
    and time management, 12
Learning teams, 52–53. *See also* Study
    groups
Lectures. *See* Classroom learning; Note
    taking
Leisure time, 13
Liberal education, 11–12
**Library of Congress Subject
    Headings (LCSH)** a set of refer-
    ence volumes in the library that
    defines standard headings used in
    classifying books and articles by
    subject.
Listening, 6, 65, 68, 76
Listservs telecommunication systems
    in which messages from one com-
    puter are automatically distributed
    to other computers.
Long-distance relationships, 159

M

Mailing lists. *See* Listservs
Major in Success (Combs), 131
Majors undergraduate students' fields
    of specialization in college. 131–132
Mapping. *See* **Mind mapping**
Marking (textbooks), 83–86
Marriage, 156
Masturbation, 178
Matching test questions, 105
Means vs. ends values, 118
Media, 182
Memory, 66
    aids, 105–107
    and listening, 6, 65, 76
Mind mapping using a personal study
    device consisting of words and
    drawings on a single page that sum-
    marizes information about a topic.
    81, 90, 100
Minority students, 7, 9. *See also* **Diversity**
Misconduct. *See* Academic honesty
Mnemonic devices techniques of
    using acronyms, rhymes, or other
    bits of language to help remember
    lists or phrases. 105–107
Monitoring, 83
Monogamy, 178
Moral values, 117
Multiple-choice test questions, 104
Myers–Briggs Type Indicator, 29–32, 40

N

Nontraditional students. *See* **Returning
    students**
Norplant, 172
Note taking
    and classroom learning, 64–65,
        69–73
    exercises, 76
    skills, 6
Nutrition, 18, 98, 186

O

Occupations. *See* Career planning
Off-campus activities, 161
Office hours. *See* Teachers, out-of-class
    interaction with
Olfactory learning style, 66
One-minute paper technique, 51–52, 54
Online. *See* **Internet;** Internet exercises
Oral contraceptives, 172
Organization, 67–68. *See also* Time
    management
Outercourse, 179
Outlining, 81, 101, 102
Overextension. *See* Stress

P

Parents. *See* Family
Part-time enrollment, 6, 19
Passionate love, 154
Pelvic inflammatory disease (PID), 175
Perceiving personality preference, 30, 31
Perceptual modes, 65–66
Performance values, 118
Personality, 29–32, 35–38, 136
Personal resources
    active learning, 61–62
    alcohol/drug use, 199
    career planning, 148
    classroom learning, 78
    critical thinking, 60–61
    diversity, 168
    learning styles, 40
    reading, 92
    relationships, 168
    sexuality, 198
    support services, 24–26
    test preparation, 110
    values, 128
Personal responsibility, 123–124
Personal values. *See* Values
Phaup, Tricia, 181
PID (pelvic inflammatory disease), 175
Plagiarism a form of academic mis-
    conduct that involves presenting
    another's ideas, words, or opinions
    as one's own. 95–96
Planners, 14, 18
Positive competition, 52
Positive self-talk, 98, 101
Pregnancy, 154. *See also* Birth control
Prejudice a preconceived judgment or
    opinion; for example, prejudgment
    of a person based solely on his or
    her ethnic or racial background. 8,
    161–162
Presentation skills, 6
Previewing, 80–82
Priorities, 13
Procrastination, 20
Professors. *See* Teachers

Q

Quality of life, 11–12
Questions. *See* Class participation

R

Race, 151–152, 151–153. *See also*
    Diversity; Minority students
Racism discriminatory or differential
    treatment of individuals based on
    race.
Rape, 154, 180–181

Reading, 80–92
  and classroom learning, 67, 68
  exercises, 90
  Internet exercises, 89
  journal, 91
  marking, 83–86
  personal resources, 92
  previewing, 80–82
  reviewing, 86–87
  skills, 6
  and vocabulary, 88
Realistic personality type, 136, 137
Recall columns, 69, 70, 72–73, 76, 101
References, 141
Relationships, 153–161
  and campus activities, 160–161
  electronic, 159–160
  exercises, 165–166
  family, 7, 156–157, 165–166
  friendship, 115, 126, 155, 157–160, 183
  Internet exercises, 163–164
  journal, 167
  marriage, 156
  and off-campus activities, 161
  personal resources, 168
  romantic, 153–156, 159
  roommates, 160
  self-assessment exercise, 150
  violence in, 179–181
  See also Sexuality
Relaxation, 98
Research, 7, 139
Residence halls, 161
Résumés, 139–140

Returning students students for whom several or many years have elapsed between their previous education and the start or continuation of a college program. Also called nontraditional students or adult students. 8, 158

Reviewing, 18, 72–74, 86–87
Review sheets, 100
Rokeach, Milton, 116–117, 118
Romantic relationships, 153–156, 159
Roommates, 160

S

Safer sex, 178–179
Scheduling. *See* Time management

Scholarships financial awards made for academic achievement.

Self-assessment exercises
  active learning, 44
  alcohol use, 170
  career planning, 130
  classroom learning, 64
  critical thinking, 44
  diversity, 150
  learning styles, 28
  reading, 80
  relationships, 150
  sexuality, 170
  test preparation, 94
  time management, 4
  values, 114

Self-help assistance any type of financial aid for which you must do something in return—usually work or repayment.

Sensing personality preference, 29, 31, 32–33
Service learning, 138, 161

Sexism discriminatory or differential treatment of individuals based on sex. 55

Sexual assault, 154, 180–181

Sexual harassment behaviors such as unwelcome sexual advances, requests for sexual favors, or demeaning sexist remarks that affect or become a condition of an indi-vidual's employment or educational status or that create an atmosphere interfering with an individual's academic or work performance. 55, 181

Sexuality, 170–181
  and birth control, 171–175
  decision making, 171
  exercises, 194–195
  Internet exercises, 192–193
  journal, 197
  personal resources, 198
  and relationships, 154–155
  and relationship violence, 180
  safer sex, 178–179
  sexual assault, 154, 180–181
  and STIs, 175–177, 193
  and teachers, 154, 181
Sexually transmitted infections (STIs), 175–179, 193
Sexual orientation, 158. *See also* Gay/lesbian/bisexual students
Shaver, J. P., 116
SI (supplemental instruction), 70–71
Sleep, 98
Social personality type, 136, 137
Sororities/fraternities, 160
Spermicidal contraceptives, 173

Spreadsheets computer application program used mainly for budgeting, financial planning, and other tasks requiring calculations based on lists of numerical information.

The State of the Nation (Bok), 122
Stereotyping, 157, 158
Sterilization, 172
STIs (sexually transmitted infections), 175–177, 193

Stress, 6, 19, 196
Strong, W., 116
Student competitions, 139
Student development, 51
Student organizations. *See* Campus activities
Study abroad, 138
Study groups
  and active learning, 50, 52–53
  and learning styles, 32
  and note taking, 71
  personal resources, 78
  as success strategy, 6
  and test preparation, 99
Study skills
  Internet exercises, 75
  and learning styles, 32
  as success strategy, 6–7
  and time management, 18
  See also Classroom learning; Note taking; Reading; Study groups; Test preparation
Styles. *See* Learning styles
Success strategies, 4–9
  exercises, 21–22
  goal-setting, 12
  journal, 23
Summer jobs, 138. *See also* Employment
Supplemental Instruction (SI), 70–71
Support services
  career counseling, 7, 132
  and learning styles, 34
  personal resources, 24–26
  and relationships, 156, 180
  as success strategy, 7
  tutoring, 99
  See also **Academic advising**

Syllabus one or more pages of class requirements that an instructor gives out on the first day of a course. The syllabus acts as a course outline, telling when you must complete assignments, readings, and so on.

Systematic thinking, 48

T

Tactile learning style, 29, 66, 71, 72
Task words, 102–103
Teachers
  and academic freedom, 54–55
  and active learning, 6, 53–54
  choice of, 6
  problems with, 55
  responsibilities of, 56
  teaching styles, 32–34
  See also Teachers, out-of-class interaction with

Teachers, out-of-class interaction with
    and active learning, 50, 51, 54
    and career planning, 132
    and email, 56
    personal resources, 61–62
    sexual relationships, 154, 181
    as success strategy, 7
Teaching styles, 32–34
Term assignment preview, 14, 15–16
Test preparation, 94–95, 97–110
    emotional, 98
    exercises, 107–108
    and health, 98
    journal, 109
    and learning styles, 32–33
    memory aids, 105–107
    personal resources, 110
    question types, 102–105
    study groups, 99
    test-taking process, 101
    tools for, 99–101
Textbooks. *See* Reading
Thinking personality preference, 30, 31
Time management, 12–21
    and academic honesty, 96
    distractions, 19–20
    exercises, 4
    Internet exercises, 21

    journal, 23
    planners, 14, 18
    and priorities, 13
    procrastination, 20
    self-assessment exercise, 4
    as success strategy, 6
    term assignment preview, 14, 15–16
    and test preparation, 97
    "to do" lists, 14, 20
    weekly plans, 14, 17
"To do" lists, 14, 20
Trudeau, Garry, 124–125
True-false test questions, 104
Tutoring, 99

V

Values, 114–128
    and career planning, 136, 145
    challenges to, 10, 115
    changes in, 120–122
    definitions, 115–116
    dualisms, 118–120
    exercises, 126
    Internet exercises, 125
    journal, 127
    personal resources, 128
    societal, 122–124

    types of, 117–118
    See also Values exercises
Values exercises
    academic advising, 144
    academic honesty, 97
    alcohol use, 185
    challenges, 10
    classroom learning, 69
    critical thinking, 47
    learning styles, 32
    reading, 86
    relationships, 160
Venereal warts, 176
Vision statements, 145
Visual learning style, 28, 66, 70, 97
Vocabulary, 88, 102–103
Volunteer/service learning, 138, 161

W

Walster, Elaine, 154
Weekly plans, 14, 17. *See also* Planners
Wolfe, Alan, 120
Women, 121–122. *See also* **Sexism**
Work. *See* Employment
World Wide Web. *See* **Internet;** Internet
    exercises
Writing, 6

Photo Credits

This page constitutes an extension of the copyright page. We have made every effort to trace the ownership of all copyrighted material and to secure permission from copyright holders. In the event of any question arising as to the use of any material, we will be pleased to make the necessary corrections in future printings. Thanks are due to the following authors, publishers, and agents for permission to use the material indicated.

Chapter 1. 3: PhotoDisc **5:** Less Todd/Photo Courtesy of Duke University **13:** CORBIS

Chapter 2. 27: © Tony Freeman/ PhotoEdit **33:** PhotoDisc **33:** Richard Howard/Black Star Publishing/ PictureQuest

Chapter 3. 43: Stephen Frink/Index Stock Imagery/PictureQuest **48:** ©1992 Chuck Savage/photo courtesy of Beloit College **53:** © Mark Richards/PhotoEdit

Chapter 4. 63: Alvis Upitis/Getty Images/The Image Bank **67:** David Gonzales

Chapter 5 79: CORBIS **87:** Tom Jorgenson/Photo courtesy of University of Iowa

Chapter 6. 93: William Saliaz/CORBIS **101:** © Seth Resnick/Stock, Boston Inc./PictureQuest **104:** © Matthew McVay/Stock, Boston Inc./PictureQuest

Chapter 7. 113: Lisette Le Bon/ SuperStock **117:** Photo by Angela Mann **121:** © Michael Newman/PhotoEdit

Chapter 8. 129: Richard Cummins/ CORBIS **135:** © Bill Bachman/Stock, Boston Inc./PictureQuest **143:** © Syracuse Newspapers/The Image Works

Chapter 9. 149: Mark Harwood/Getty Images/Stone **153:** Courtesy of Earlham College **153:** © David Young-Wolff/ PhotoEdit **158:** © Jonathan Nourok/ PhotoEdit

Chapter 10. 169: Stephen Frisch/ Stock, Boston Inc. **174:** Heather Dutton **183:** Matthew McVay/Allstock/ PictureQuest

We'd Like to Hear from You

Thank you for using *Your College Experience,* Concise Media Edition, Fifth Edition. We care a lot about how you liked this book and how useful you found it. Please let us know how we can improve the next edition by returning this page with your comments, using the postage-free label on the other side. Or send us an e-mail message to *csuccess@wadsworth.com.* Either way, we'd like to hear your thoughts.

Overall, how valuable was the book as part of the course? Why? _____

_____

_____

_____

Which parts or exercises were particularly helpful? Why? _____

_____

_____

_____

Which parts or exercises should be changed? Why? _____

_____

_____

_____

Are there any topics not covered in the book that you think should be added? _____

_____

_____

_____

How else can we improve the next edition of *Your College Experience,* Concise Media Edition? _____

_____

_____

_____

Thanks and good luck!

John N. Gardner   A. Jerome Jewler

Your name _____ School _____

Your address _____

City/State _____ Zip _____

Your email address _____

Your instructor's name _____

May Wadsworth quote you, either in promotion for *Your College Experience* or in future publishing ventures?

Yes _____ No _____

FOLD HERE

TEAR PAGE OUT

FOLD HERE

BUSINESS REPLY MAIL
FIRST CLASS   PERMIT NO. 34   BELMONT, CA

POSTAGE WILL BE PAID BY ADDRESSEE

John N. Gardner / A. Jerome Jewler
Your College Experience, Concise Media Edition, Fifth Edition
c/o College Success Editor
Wadsworth/Thomson Learning
10 Davis Drive
Belmont, CA 94002-9801